The Agile Developer's Handbook

Get more value from your software development: get the best out of the Agile methodology

Paul Flewelling

BIRMINGHAM - MUMBAI

The Agile Developer's Handbook

Commissioning Editor: Amarabha Banerjee
Acquisition Editor: Namrata Patil
Content Development Editor: Deepti Thore
Technical Editor: Sneha Hanchate
Copy Editor: Safis Editing, Laxmi Subramanian
Project Coordinator: Shweta Birwatkar
Proofreader: Safis Editing
Indexer: Aishwarya Gangawane
Graphics: Tania Dutta
Production Coordinator: Melywn Dsa

First published: February 2018

Production reference: 2090518

Published by Packt Publishing Ltd.
Livery Place
35 Livery Street
Birmingham
B3 2PB, UK.

ISBN 978-1-78728-020-5

www.packtpub.com

`mapt.io`

Mapt is an online digital library that gives you full access to over 5,000 books and videos, as well as industry leading tools to help you plan your personal development and advance your career. For more information, please visit our website.

Why subscribe?

- Spend less time learning and more time coding with practical eBooks and Videos from over 4,000 industry professionals

- Improve your learning with Skill Plans built especially for you

- Get a free eBook or video every month

- Mapt is fully searchable

- Copy and paste, print, and bookmark content

PacktPub.com

Did you know that Packt offers eBook versions of every book published, with PDF and ePub files available? You can upgrade to the eBook version at `www.PacktPub.com` and as a print book customer, you are entitled to a discount on the eBook copy. Get in touch with us at `service@packtpub.com` for more details.

At `www.PacktPub.com`, you can also read a collection of free technical articles, sign up for a range of free newsletters, and receive exclusive discounts and offers on Packt books and eBooks.

Contributors

About the author

Paul Flewelling began looking for a better way to build software after one fateful project that ticked all the boxes, yet failed to deliver what the customer needed. That search led him to help grow one of NZ's first Agile software teams. As word of the team's success spread, he also began training others. He currently coaches the product teams who are transforming NZ's largest newspaper company for the digital economy. He speaks nationally and internationally on all things Agile, shares coaching insights on his blog, co-hosts monthly meet-ups, and is often seen wisely stroking his beard.

I want to thank all the teams I've coached for coming on the journey with me. Your willingness to try out many of our crazy ideas and make them work inspires me to be a better coach.

Thank you to the many coaches I've worked and shared ideas with. You've always stretched me to think beyond my horizons; I'm humbled to work with such great humans.

Finally, I want to express my gratitude to my wife; I wouldn't be on this journey if it weren't for her.

About the reviewer

Kamal Prasad Bansod has around 15 yrs of experience in IT. He has spent around 8 years exploring and experimenting with Agile/Scrum. He has worked with different team dynamics and transformation of Agile teams. He strongly believes in the Agile principles and engineering practices. If they are followed properly then value-based delivery can be done to the market with expected quality. He loves to share his knowledge and ideas with companies that adopt and improve their use of Agile processes and techniques to build high-performing teams.

Packt is searching for authors like you

If you're interested in becoming an author for Packt, please visit `authors.packtpub.com` and apply today. We have worked with thousands of developers and tech professionals, just like you, to help them share their insight with the global tech community. You can make a general application, apply for a specific hot topic that we are recruiting an author for, or submit your own idea.

Table of Contents

Preface

Agile thinking has caused a fundamental shift in how we deliver software. The aim of this book is to offer the reader a pragmatic, easy-to-follow approach to mastering this transformative way of working. It's roughly divided into three sections to reflect the three stages of adoption—beginner, intermediate, and master.

In the first few chapters, we'll look at the origins of the Agile movement and review the fundamentals. We then get straight into the practical guide, teaching you how to set up your Agile approach through a series of activities and pragmatic examples. Each key concept has an accompanying exercise for you to practice and learn the thinking behind it.

After we've laid the ground rules and taught the basic techniques, the second half of the book will look at how we can start to expand our understanding. It takes what we've learned and applies slightly different perspectives, such as Lean and Lean Startup thinking. You'll start to see how you can shape or bend the rules to get much more from your Agile practice.

In the final three chapters, we look at some possibilities regarding technical practices, team dynamics, and organizational changes. Here, the intention is to show you where some teams are now. And although some of these may seem distant from where you are on your particular journey, the aim is to show where you may be heading and to inspire you to keep taking the next step.

Agile is a mindset, something we can only achieve by going on the journey ourselves. The hope is that this book will put you on the path to becoming a truly Agile thinker.

Let's go!

Who this book is for

This is a companion guide for those who build software and are about to embark on (or who are already on) an Agile journey. No prior knowledge of Agile is needed. This book fills in the gaps. For those at the very beginning of their journey, this book teaches the foundations to start your Agile practice. For those who are already on the path, this book is designed to give you ideas on where you may be heading. Like any good guide, it gives tips to move you out of your comfort zone and push your thinking to become truly Agile.

What this book covers

Chapter 1, *The Software Industry and the Agile Manifesto*, states that a crisis in the software industry led to a major turning point and the formation of the Agile Alliance. We'll examine the Alliance's origins and discuss how it revolutionized the way we think about building software. We'll also look at the Agile Manifesto, its values and principles, and the impact they have on how software professionals work.

Chapter 2, *Agile Software Delivery Methods and How They Fit the Manifesto*, provides an overview of the mechanics and the rationale behind the three most popular Agile methods: Scrum, XP, and Kanban. We'll look at their similarities and differences, as well as how they look to achieve the Agile Manifesto's guiding values and principles.

Chapter 3, *Introducing Scrum to your Software Team*, provides a step-by-step guide to your first Scrum Sprint. We'll walk you through all of the key activities, including setting up your Agile board, planning to Sprint, a day-in-the-life of a Scrum team, and the differences between the Sprint Review and the Sprint Retrospective. The aim is to give you everything you need to take the first step on your Agile journey.

Chapter 4, *Gathering Agile User Requirements*, explains that working iteratively to incrementally deliver software needs a different approach to requirements gathering. We look at the approach most commonly used by Agile methods, the User Story. We'll look at how to write a well-defined story. We'll introduce Agile estimation using a technique called relative sizing, and we'll play our first game of planning poker.

Chapter 5, *Bootstrap Teams with Liftoffs*, explains that the aim of a liftoff is to set teams up for the best possible chance of success. We'll walk you through the activities of a liftoff, which include communicating the vision, defining mission outcomes, and deciding how you're going to work together.

Chapter 6, *Metrics that will Help your Software Team Deliver*, states that once your team is on a mission, it's important that you know you're moving in the right direction. Taking the right measurements will help us do that. We'll look at various real-world examples that will help your team determine the metrics they should and shouldn't be using. We'll look at negative metrics, positive metrics, metrics that give you quantitative feedback and metrics that give you qualitative feedback. We'll then discuss how to make the information visible and measure the trends over time so that you can see you're improving and moving along the right trajectory.

Chapter 7, *Software Technical Practices are the Foundation of Incremental Software Delivery*, explains that the right technical practices will increase your team's agility. Practices such as Refactoring, Test-Driven Development, Pair Programming, and Continuous Integration give us confidence that what we're delivering is well designed, tested, and meets expectations. We'll look at these practices, as well as others, and offer ideas on how to introduce them to your team's toolkit.

Chapter 8, *Tightening Feedback Loops in the Software Development Life Cycle,* shows how to implement an incremental approach to software delivery. We discuss the important role that user experience plays in helping us tease out what our customer needs. We introduce Lean thinking and show how it seeks to optimize our process so that we can deliver sooner. We also show how to shortcut our learning by conducting a Lean Startup experiment with a real-world example.

Chapter 9, *Seeking Value – How to Deliver Better Software Sooner*, looks at real-world examples to shift the delivery team's perspective from one of just delivering on time, on scope, or on budget, to ways that will actually seek value. We also look at the practical ways teams can use this approach to create feedback loops so that they can measure their value-seeking success as they go.

Chapter 10, *Using Product Roadmaps to Guide Software Delivery*, explains that one of the roles of the Product Owner is to hold the product vision for the team. We show how to discover our key product features using two different techniques: User Story Mapping and Impact Mapping. We show how to prioritize features/User Stories against release milestones to create the initial Product Roadmap. We also introduce Rolling Wave Planning, a technique for adaptive planning.

Chapter 11, *Improving Our Team Dynamics to Increase Our Agility*, states that Agile teams are self-organized, autonomous, and prefer high-bandwidth face-to-face communication. This may seem like a recipe for a high performing, collaborative team, but it doesn't always work that way. This chapter aims to demystify some of the art of fostering good team dynamics by looking at what makes a great team. We also describe the five stages of team formation and give techniques for helping a team become the best it can be.

Chapter 12, *Baking Quality into Our Software Delivery*, looks at several popular approaches that teams take to increase their performance further. We discuss the cross-pollination of skills in cross-functional teams, a total team approach called mob programming, how to live the dream of having no more bugs, and we question the need for estimates in software development.

Chapter 13, *The Ultimate Software Team Member*, speaks about the power of motivation and how to tap into our inner drive to become the best at what we do. We define some of the characteristics of a great Agile team member. We also consider the fact that, as knowledge workers, we're in a constant state of learning, and give some pragmatic suggestions for putting time aside to learn.

Chapter 14, *Moving Beyond Isolated Agile Teams*, explains that in order to become an Agile organization, a change in management style is needed. We look at how the leadership model begins to switch to a supportive role and introduce the concept of the Servant Leader. We look at how modern leadership and different organizational structures create an adaptive, more responsive network of teams. This chapter will help you recognize the signs that an organizational transformation is taking place so that you can take advantage of this transformative approach to work.

To get the most out of this book

1. No software or hardware is needed; just bring your brain and we'll do the rest. All of the activities we describe are easy for you to replicate yourselves, using everyday materials such as coins, spaghetti, and marshmallows.
2. To create your visible workspaces and run a few of the activities, you will need the following in your Agile toolkit: a near unlimited supply of Post-it notes, Sharpies (black markers), index cards, a whiteboard and whiteboard markers, and maybe sticky tape for marking areas on your board.

Download the color images

We also provide a PDF file that has color images of the screenshots/diagrams used in this book. You can download it here:
http://www.packtpub.com/sites/default/files/downloads/TheAgileDevelopersHandboo k_ColorImages.pdf.

Conventions used

There are a number of text conventions used throughout this book.

Bold: Indicates a new term, an important word, or words that you see onscreen. For example, words in menus or dialog boxes appear in the text like this. Here is an example: "Select **System info** from the **Administration** panel."

Warnings or important notes appear like this.

 Tips and tricks appear like this.

Get in touch

Feedback from our readers is always welcome.

General feedback: Email feedback@packtpub.com and mention the book title in the subject of your message. If you have questions about any aspect of this book, please email us at questions@packtpub.com.

Errata: Although we have taken every care to ensure the accuracy of our content, mistakes do happen. If you have found a mistake in this book, we would be grateful if you would report this to us. Please visit www.packtpub.com/submit-errata, selecting your book, clicking on the Errata Submission Form link, and entering the details.

Piracy: If you come across any illegal copies of our works in any form on the Internet, we would be grateful if you would provide us with the location address or website name. Please contact us at copyright@packtpub.com with a link to the material.

If you are interested in becoming an author: If there is a topic that you have expertise in and you are interested in either writing or contributing to a book, please visit authors.packtpub.com.

Reviews

Please leave a review. Once you have read and used this book, why not leave a review on the site that you purchased it from? Potential readers can then see and use your unbiased opinion to make purchase decisions, we at Packt can understand what you think about our products, and our authors can see your feedback on their book. Thank you!

For more information about Packt, please visit packtpub.com.

The Software Industry and the Agile Manifesto

1

Towards the end of the last century, the software industry was in a state of turmoil. There were some significant software project failures, which were having a substantial reputational impact on the industry as a whole. One observation was that software projects over a certain size were more likely to fail.

In this chapter, we'll discuss the factors that led to a crisis and the subsequent major turning-point in the software industry. In the second part of this chapter, we'll introduce the Agile Manifesto and its origins and discuss the way it revolutionized the way we think about building software. We'll explain the Manifesto's values and principles, what they each mean, and the impact they have on how software professionals work.

In this chapter, we will cover the following topics:

- Why the software industry needed to change
- The origins of the Agile Manifesto
- A detailed look at the values and principles of the manifesto and how they translate to today's context
- Adaptive versus predictive planning
- Incremental versus waterfall delivery
- Agile isn't a process, it's a mindset built on guiding values/principles and requires solid technical practices

Why the software industry needed to change

When I was outlining this book, I was in two minds about whether to include a section on the history of the software industry and how Agile came to be. I figured most of you would be young enough not to know any different; you're probably doing something Agile or closely related to Agile already. However, I decided to include this chapter for two reasons:

1. I still see echoes of the past affecting us today
2. "Why" we do something is important to inform "what" we do and "how" we do it

When working as a software developer in the 1990s and 2000s, I worked in a range of different organization types, from software houses to software consultants, from large organizations such as corporate and central government to small three-person startups. In my experience across these different organization types, we used two noticeably different styles of software delivery, either as a product or a project.

Delivery as a software product

When building software products, we tended to form long-lived teams around them. The team would be responsible for the product throughout its life. During the initial build and subsequent revisions, they handled the entire **Software Development Life Cycle** (**SDLC**) end-to-end, including delivery into production. These teams were also often responsible for managing the production environment and providing support.

The scale of the product, and how widely it was adopted, determined whether it was managed by a single software team or by a network of teams all working for one product group. One thing that was noticeable about software product teams, apart from their long-lived nature, was that they often had good relationships with their customers as well as technology and operations staff. Sometimes they even had representatives of these groups within the teams.

Funding these products often took place on a yearly cycle, which coincided with setting the objectives for the product's development that year. A key thing to note is that the budget would often be allocated to fund the team(s) and the decisions on what features would be developed, enhanced, or fixed that year would be managed by the team itself.

Delivery as a software project

When treating software delivery as a project, the approach was often very different. The project team would only form for the duration of the build of the software.

Once built, the software would often be handed over to a separate team, known as the **Business As Usual** (**BAU**) team in business parlance. They would manage the maintenance and support of the product. There was a two-fold intention in handing over to a separate BAU team:

1. They would handle the bulk of changes to the organization, for example, by training all impacted staff on how to use the new software and associated business processes. Once they'd introduced the changes, the BAU team's aim would then be to create and support a stable business environment.
2. The software delivery team would be free to move on to the next project. Software delivery teams were a scarce resource, and this was seen as a way to optimize software delivery.

Software projects required project managers who often operated in the change management capacity as well, although sometimes separate change managers were allocated. In this way, they would also be responsible for seeing that the introduction of the new software platform to the organization and the transition to BAU went smoothly. The project team itself would often be managed by a separate unit who reported directly to the business known as the **Project Management Office** (**PMO**).

Product versus project

What I discovered by using these two contrasting approaches resulted in a profound shift in my thinking: When delivering software as a product, there was much more opportunity to focus on value because the product team was long-lived and was able to adopt an iterative/incremental approach to delivery. We, therefore, had multiple opportunities to deliver, enhance our strategy, and get things right.

However, with software delivery as a project, more often than not the software delivery team only had one opportunity to get it right. Successfully delivering a software project to meet expectations with only one shot just didn't happen that often.

Even when we did deliver, it was often as a result of a considerable effort on our part to get it across the line, including many lost evenings and weekends.

Subsequent revisions of the software were often handled as separate projects and likely by a different software team, often leading to a lack of continuity and knowledge sharing.

As a result, there was a distinct lack of trust between us—the software professionals and the people we were building software for. Unfortunately, "us" often became them and us with unmet expectations being so often the cause of the rift in the relationship.

We tried to solve this problem by making things more precise. Unfortunately, the version of precision the project mindset opted for had only three predictive aspects—scope, time, and budget. All three of these things are very difficult to quantify when tied to a software project where complexity, uncertainty, and sheer volume of work could and did amplify any errors in these calculations.

However, the single most significant problem when you tie down all three of these factors, scope, time and budget, is that something colloquially known as the **Iron Triangle** forms. Refer to the following figure:

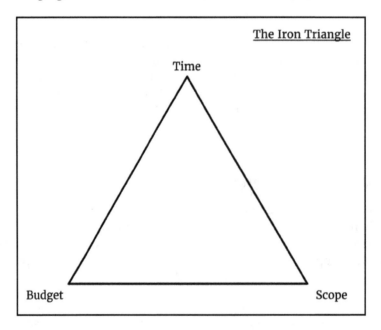

When you set scope, date, and budget like that, there is little room for maneuverability to deviate from the plan. To help mitigate risks, most will create buffers in their schedules. However, the rigid nature of the triangle means that if and when overruns start to eat more and more into the buffers, something else has to give. And what usually occurs when a software development team is under pressure to deliver? One or more of the following qualities of your software product will start to suffer:

- **Functionality**: Whether it works as expected
- **Reliability**: How available it is
- **Usability**: How intuitive it is to use
- **Scalability**: How performant it is
- **Maintainability**: How easy it is to change
- **Portability**: How easy it is to move to a different platform

To understand why precision in predicting the outcome of a software project is so complicated we need to unpack things a little.

Scope was the priority

At the time, many felt that the functionality of the delivered software was the priority and would often seek to lock the scope of the project. We allowed for this by having some degree of variability in the budget and the schedule.

At the time, many project managers would work to the PMI or ISO 9000 guidelines on the definition of quality. Both of these had a reasonably straightforward quality definition requiring the scope of the project to be delivered in a fully functional form.

To meet the scope expectation, we had to estimate, to a fair degree of precision, how long it would take us. In this way, we would be able to determine the length of time needed and the number of people required for the team.

And it was at the estimate stage that we often set ourselves up to fail.

Estimates

One thing that was increasingly obvious in the software industry was that our approaches to estimating or predicting the outcome of a project were out of whack. As a software team, we were often passed detailed requirements to analyze, then do some initial design work, and provide a work breakdown with estimates.

We'd be working on one project and then at the same time asked to estimate on another. The estimates we were told would inform the decision on whether the project was viable and would be funded. Some teams tried to be sophisticated, using algorithmic estimating techniques such as **Constructive Cost Model** (**COCOMO**), COCOMO II, **Source lines of code** (**SLOC**), and Function Point. Most estimating methods incorporated rule of thumb or experience-based factors as well as factors for complexity and certainty.

Sometimes the estimates would be given by people who weren't going to work on the project. This was either because the project leadership group didn't want to disturb an existing project team, or because, without funding, the project teams weren't formed yet. This meant the involvement of someone like an architect or a technical leader who could break down the work and estimate based on the solution they devised. Most complicated problems have several solutions, so if those who had done the solution work breakdown weren't available to provide guidance on how to implement their solution, obviously this could cause trouble later on.

Either way, whoever provided the estimate would give it based on the best solution they could theorize with the information they were given. More often than not, the first estimate that was given would be used as a way to control the project, and it would be pretty much set in stone. This was a pattern that I stumbled across many times. When this continually happened, we tried to improve the accuracy of our estimates by spending time doing more upfront work. But the reality was to get an exact estimate of effort so that time frames and budget can be drawn, you pretty much have to complete all the work in the first place.

Uncertainty buffers

It also became a bit of a standing joke that these estimates were not only painstakingly worked on over days or weeks, but as soon as we gave them to a project manager, they would double the figures. When we challenged that practice, they'd remind us that all software developers are optimistic and that buffers were needed.

But it's not that we're optimistic by nature; in fact, a lot of us had already factored in our own buffer allowances. The explanation is more straightforward; the work we do is novel—more often than not we are working on something entirely different from what we've built before: different domain, different technology stack, different frameworks, and so on.

Some teams would combat this by offering two figures as part of their estimates. The first being the time estimate, the second being the level of certainty that they could complete it within that timeframe. If the task was straightforward, then they would offer their estimate with 100% certainty. If the task was more complicated they would lower the percentage accordingly. The higher the uncertainty, the lower the percentage.

This certainty factor could then be used to allocate a buffer. As certainty got higher, the buffer would get smaller, but even with 100% certainty, there would still be a buffer. After all, there is no such thing as an ideal day as much as we would like to think there is.

At the opposite end of the spectrum, the more the uncertainty in the estimate, the larger the buffer. At the extreme, it was not uncommon to have buffers of 200%.

Estimates became ironic

The chronic misestimation of development effort has led to some Dilbert-esque observations of the way we work.

For example, we would often refer ironically to a task as just a "small matter of programming," when someone with little or no understanding of what was involved was telling us it looked easy.

We also developed ironic laws about underestimation such as the Ninety-Ninety rule, which states the following:

> *"The first 90% of the code accounts for the first 90 % of the development time. The remaining 10 % of the code accounts for the other 90 percent of the development time"*

> *– Tom Cargill, Bell Labs*

This rule was later made popular by Jon Bentley's September 1985 *Programming Pearls* column in Communications of the ACM, where it is titled *"Rule of Credibility"*.

Variability in our estimates

The biggest problem with estimation is the amount of information we assume. We make assumptions on how to solve the business problem, the technologies we're going to use, and the capabilities of the people building it. So many factors.

The level of complexity and uncertainty impacts our ability to give an accurate estimate because there are so many variables at play. This, in turn, is amplified by the size of the piece of work. The result is something referred to as the **Cone of Uncertainty**:

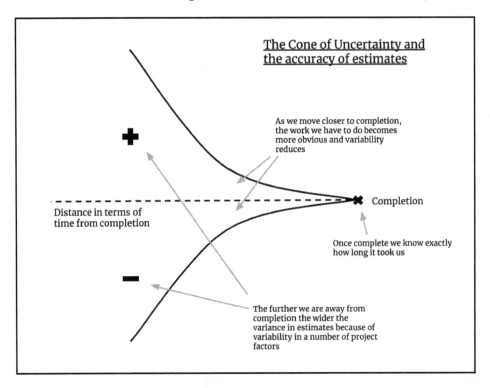

Barry Boehm first described this concept in his book Software Engineering Economics, 1981; he called it the Funnel Curve. It was named *The Cone of Uncertainty* in the *Software Project Survival Guide (McConnell 1997)*.

It shows us that the further we are away from completion, the larger the variance in the estimate we give. As we move closer to completion, the more accurate our estimate will become, to the point where we complete the work and know exactly how long it took us.

So while it was felt that better precision could be gained using a gated process, such as Waterfall, because it led to a tendency to bundle more of the stuff we wanted to get done together, it would significantly increase the size of the work parcel. This, in turn, compounded the problem of getting an accurate estimate.

And then there's missing the point entirely

Sometimes, of course, we'd fail to deliver something of use to our customer and miss the point entirely.

I remember one project I worked on where we were given ideal working conditions. The teams were offsite, in our own offices, which meant we could be dedicated to the project we were working on without being disturbed or shoulder-tapped by others. It felt like the perfect setup for success.

We spent ten months painstakingly delivering precisely to requirements. Everything was built and tested out according to the detailed designs we were given. We were even on budget and time when we delivered. Unfortunately, when the software went live and was in the hands of the people using it, they reported back that it didn't do the job they needed it to do.

Why had we failed? We'd failed because we spent ten months building something in isolation from our customer. We hadn't involved them in the implementation, and too many assumptions had been made. Diagrammatically, this looked a little like the following:

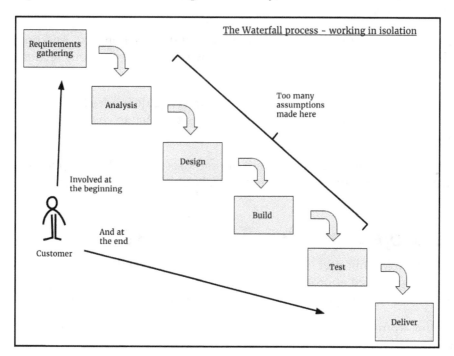

We then spent the next six months reworking the software into something that was usable. Unfortunately, for the partner company working alongside our team, this meant a major variance in their contract, most of which they had to swallow. We eventually did deliver something to our customer that they wanted and needed but at a huge financial impact on us and our partner company.

This, unfortunately, is the path that predictive planning sets you on. You develop a fixed mindset around what is to be delivered because you know if you aren't dogmatic in your approach, you're likely to fail to meet the date, budget, or scope set in the contract.

Where's the business value?

One of the key characteristics to understand about the nature of predictive planning is that the minute someone says, "How much is this going to cost?", or "When can this be delivered?", they significantly constrain the value that will be created. And, at the end of the day, shouldn't it be about maximizing the value to your customer? Imagine if we spent one more month on a project and delivered twice as much value. Wouldn't that be something our customer would want over meeting a date or a particular set of features just because it's been speculatively laid out in a contract?

Instead, we focus on a date, an amount of money, and the functionality. And unfortunately, functionality doesn't always translate to value (as we saw in the previous section when we *missed the point entirely*).

This is why the predictive planning used in Waterfall style deliveries has also become known as faith-driven development because it leaves so much to chance, and usually right until the end of the project.

To focus on value delivery, we have to shift our mindset to use adaptive planning versus predictive planning, something that we will talk about later in this chapter.

So the project mindset isn't good?

It's not that the project mindset is bad, it's just that the mindset drives us to think that we need a big upfront design approach in order to obtain a precision estimate. As noted, this can lead to a number of issues, particularly when presented with a large chunk of work.

And it isn't that upfront design is bad; it's often needed. It's just the big part, when we try to do too much of it, that causes us problems.

There were a number of bad behaviors feeding the big thinking happening in the industry. One of these is the way that work is funded, as projects. For a particular project to get funded, it has to demonstrate its viability at the annual funding round.

Unfortunately, once people in the management seats saw a hard number, it often became set in stone as an expectation. During the execution of the plan, if new information was discovered that was anything more significant than a small variance, there would be a tendency to try to avoid doing it. The preference would be to try to stick to the plan, rather than incorporate the change. You were seen as a better project manager for doing that.

So, we had a chicken-and-egg scenario; the project approach to funding meant that:

1. The business needed to know the cost of something so they could allocate a budget.
2. We needed to know the size of something and its technical scope and nature so that we could allocate the right team in terms of size and skill set.
3. We had to do this while accepting:
   - That our business didn't know exactly what it needed. The nature of software is intangible, most people don't know what they want/need until they see it and use it.
   - The business itself wasn't stationary; just because we recorded requirements at a particular moment in time, didn't mean that the business would stop evolving around us.

So, if we can avoid the big part, we're able to reduce the level of uncertainty and subsequent variability in our estimates. We're also able to deliver in a timely fashion, which means there is less likelihood of requirements going out of date or the business changing its mind.

We did try to remedy this by moving to prototyping approaches. This enabled us to make iterative sweeps through the work, refining it with people who could actually use the working prototype and give us direct feedback.

Rapid Application Development, or RAD as it's commonly known, is one example of an early iterative process. Another was the Rational Unified Process (RUP).

Working on the principle that many people didn't know what they wanted until they saw it, we used RAD tools such as Visual Basic/Visual Studio to put semi-working prototypes together quickly.

But we still always managed to bite off more than we could chew. I suspect the main reason for this is that our customers still expected us to deliver something they could use. While prototypes gave the appearance of doing that and did enable us to get feedback early:

1. At the end of the session, after getting the feedback we needed, and much to our customer's disappointment, we'd take the prototype away. They had assumed our mockup was a working software.
2. We still hadn't delivered anything they could use in their day-to-day life to help them solve real-world problems.

To try to find a remedy to the hit-and-miss approach to software delivery, a group of 17 software luminaries came together in February 2001. The venue was a cabin in Utah, which they chose, as the story goes, so that they could ski, eat, and look for an alternative to the heavyweight, document-driven processes that seemed to dominate the industry.

Among them were representatives from **Extreme Programming (XP)**, Scrum, **Dynamic Systems Development Method (DSDM)**, **Adaptive Software Development (ASD)**, Crystal, Feature-Driven Development, and Pragmatic Programming.

While at least one of them commented that they didn't expect anything substantive to come out of that weekend, what they did in fact formulate was the manifesto for Agile software development.

The manifesto documents four values and twelve principles that uncover "better ways of developing software by doing it and helping others do it".

The group formally signed the Manifesto and named themselves the Agile Alliance. We'll take a look at the Agile Values and Principles in the following sections.

The Agile values

Here is the **Manifesto for Agile Software Development** (http://agilemanifesto.org/):

Manifesto for Agile Software Development

We are uncovering better ways of developing software
by doing it and helping others do it.
Through this work we have come to value:

Individuals and interactions over processes and tools
Working software over comprehensive documentation
Customer collaboration over contract negotiation
Responding to change over following a plan

That is, while there is value in the items on the right, we value the
items on the left more.

Kent Beck	James Grenning	Robert C. Martin
Mike Beedle	Jim Highsmith	Steve Mellor
Arie van Bennekum	Andrew Hunt	Ken Schwaber
Alistair Cockburn	Ron Jeffries	Jeff Sutherland
Ward Cunningham	Jon Kern	Dave Thomas
Martin Fowler	Brian Marick	

To understand the four values, you have first to read and understand the end subtext:

That is, while there is value in the items on the right, we value the items on the left more.

Let's look at how this works by looking at each value in more detail:

- **Individuals and interactions over processes and tools**: In an Agile environment, we still have processes and tools, but we prefer to keep our use of them light, because we value communication between individuals. If we're to foster successful collaboration, we need common understanding between technical and non-technical people. Tools and processes have a tendency to obfuscate that. A good example is the User Story, an Agile requirement gathering technique, usually recorded on an index card. It's kept deliberately small so that we can't add too much detail. The aim is to encourage, through conversation, a shared understanding of the task.

In the same way, we should look at all of the following Agile values:

- **Working software over comprehensive documentation**: As a software delivery team, our primary focus should be on delivering the software—fit for purpose, and satisfying our customer's need.

  In the past, we've made the mistake of using documents to communicate to our customer what we're building. Of course, this led to much confusion and potential ambiguity. Our customer isn't an expert in building software and would, therefore, find it pretty hard to interpret our documentation and imagine what we might be building. The easiest way to communicate with them is via working software that they can interact with and use.

  By getting something useful in front of our customer as soon as possible, we might discover if we're thinking what they're thinking. In this way, we can build out software incrementally while validating early and often with our customer that we're building the right thing.

- **Customer collaboration over contract negotiation**: We aim to build something useful for our customer and hopefully get the best value for them we can. Contracts can constrain this, especially when you start to test the assumptions that were made when the contract was drawn up. More often than not there are discoveries made along the way, or the realization that something was forgotten or that it won't work the way we were expecting. Having to renegotiate a contract, or worse still, recording variances to be carried out at a later stage, both slow down and constrain the team's ability to deliver something of value to the customer.

- **Responding to change over following a plan**: When considering this Agile Value, it is worth drawing a comparison with the military.

  The military operates in a very fluid environment; while they will undoubtedly have a plan of attack, this is often based on incomplete information about the enemy's strength and whereabouts. The military very much has to deal with known knowns, known unknowns, and unknown unknowns.

  This is what we call a **planning-driven** environment; they're planning constantly throughout the battle as new information becomes available.

Plan-driven versus Planning-driven: **Plan-driven** means a fixed plan which everyone follows and adheres to. This is also known as predictive planning. **Planning-driven** is more responsive in nature; when new information comes to light, we adjust our plan. It's called planning-driven because we expect change and so we're always in a state of planning. This is also known as Adaptive Planning

So when going into battle, while they have group objectives, the military operate with a devolved power structure and delegated authority so that each unit can make decisions on the ground as new information is uncovered. In this way, they can respond to new information affecting the parameters of their mission, while still getting on with their overall objective. If the scope of their mission changes beyond recognition, they can use their chain of command to determine how they should proceed and re-plan if necessary.

In the same way, when we're building software, we don't want to blindly stick to a plan if the scope of our mission starts to change. The ability to respond to new information is what gives us our agility; sometimes we have to deviate from the plan to achieve the overall objective. This enables us to maximize the value delivered to our customer.

The Agile principles

The signatories to the Manifesto all shared a common background in light software development methodologies. The principles they chose reflect this. Again the emphasis is on people-focused outcomes. Each of the following principles supports and elaborates upon the values:

1. **Our highest priority is to satisfy the customer through the early and continuous delivery of valuable software**: In encouraging incremental delivery as soon and often as we can, we can start to confirm that we are building the right thing. Most people don't know what they want until they see it, and in my experience, use it. Taking this approach garners early feedback and significantly reduces any risk to our customer.

2. **Welcome changing requirements, even late in development. Agile processes harness change for the customer's competitive advantage**: Instead of locking scope and ignoring evolving business needs, adapt to new discoveries and re-prioritize work to deliver the most value possible for your customer. Imagine a game of soccer where the goal posts keep moving; instead of trying to stop them moving, change the way you play.

3. **Deliver working software frequently, from a couple of weeks to a couple of months, with a preference for the shorter timescale**: The sooner we deliver, the sooner we get feedback. Not only from our customer that we're building the right thing, but also from our system that we're building it right. Once we get an end-to-end delivery taking place, we can start to iron out problems in our integration and deployment processes.

4. **Business people and developers must work together daily throughout the project**: To get a good outcome, the customer needs to invest in the building of the software as much as the development team. One of the worst things you can hear from your customer as a software developer is, "You're the expert, you build it." It means that they are about to have very little involvement in the process of creating their software. And yes, while software developers are the experts at building software, and have a neat bunch of processes and tools that do just that, we're not the expert in our customer's domain and we're certainly not able to get inside their heads to truly understand what they need. The closer the customer works with the team, the better the result.

5. **Build projects around motivated individuals. Give them the environment and support they need, and trust them to get the job done**: A software development team is a well-educated bunch of problem solvers. We don't want to constrain them by telling them how to do their jobs; the people closest to solving the problem will get the best results. Even the military delegate authority to the people on the frontline because they know if the objective is clear, those people are the ones who can and will get the job done.

6. **The most efficient and effective method of conveying information to and within a development team is face-to-face conversation**: Face-to-face conversation is a high-bandwidth activity that not only includes words but facial expressions and body language too. It's the fastest way to get information from one human being to another. It's an interactive process that can be used to quickly resolve any ambiguity via questioning. Couple face-to-face conversation with a whiteboard, and you have a powerhouse of understanding between two or more individuals. All other forms of communication dwindle in comparison.

7. **Working software is the primary measure of progress**: When you think about a software delivery team, and what they are there to do, then there really is nothing else to measure their progress. This principle gives us further guidance around the Agile value *working software over comprehensive documentation*.

The emphasis is on working software because we don't want to give any false indicators of progress. For example, if we deliver software that isn't fully tested, then we know that it isn't complete, it has to go through several cycles of testing and fixing. This hasn't moved us any closer to completion of that piece of work because it's still not done.

Done is in the hands of our customer, *done* is doing the job it was intended to do. Until that point, we aren't 100% sure we've built the right thing, and until that moment we don't have a clear indication of what we might need to redo. Everything else the software team produces just supports the delivery of the software, from design documents to user guides.

8. **Agile processes promote sustainable development. The sponsors, developers, and users should be able to maintain a constant pace indefinitely:** Putting a software delivery team under pressure to deliver happens all the time; it shouldn't, but it does. There are a number of consequences of doing this, some of which we discussed earlier in this chapter.

For example, put a team under pressure for long enough, and you'll seriously impact the quality of your product. The team will work long hours, make mistakes, take shortcuts, and so on to get things done for us. The result won't just affect quality, but also the morale of our team, and their productivity. I've seen this happen time and time again; it results in good people leaving along with all the knowledge they've accumulated.

This principle aims to avoid that scenario from happening. Which means that we have to be smart and use alternative ways of getting things done sooner. This means seeking value, ruthless prioritization, delivering working software, a focus on quality, and allowing teams to manage their work in progress so they can avoid multitasking.

Studies have shown that multitasking causes context switching time losses of up to 20%. When you think about it, when you're solving complex problems, the deeper you are into the problem, the longer it takes to regain context when you pick it back up. It's like playing and switching between multiple games of chess. It's not impossible, but it definitely adds time.

I've also seen multitasking defined as messing up multiple things at once.

9. **Continuous attention to technical excellence and good design enhances agility**: By using solid technical practices and attention to detail when building software, we improve our ability to make enhancements and changes to our software.

   For example, **Test-Driven Development** (**TDD**) is a practice which is as much about designing our software as it is testing it. It may seem counter-intuitive to use TDD at first, as we're investing time in a practice that seemingly adds to the development time initially. In the long term, however, the improved design of our software and the confidence it gives us to make subsequent changes enhances our agility.

   Technical debt is a term first coined by Ward Cunningham. It describes the accumulation of poor design that crops up in code when decisions have been made to implement something quickly. Ward described it as Technical Debt because if you don't pay it back in time, it starts to accumulate. As it accumulates, subsequent changes to the software get harder and harder. What should be a simple change suddenly becomes a major refactor/rewrite to implement.

10. **Simplicity—the art of maximizing the amount of work not done—is essential**: Building the simplest thing we can to fit the current need prevents defensive programming also known as "future proofing." If we're not sure whether our customer needs something or not, talk to them. If we're building something we're not sure about, we may be solving a problem that we don't have yet.
    Remember the **You Ain't Gonna Need It** (**YAGNI**) principle when deciding what to do. If you don't have a hard and fast requirement for it, don't do it.
    One of the number one causes of bugs is complexity in our code. Anything we can do to simplify it will help us reduce bugs and make our code easier to read for others, thus making it less likely that they'll create bugs too.

11. **The best architectures, requirements, and designs emerge from self-organizing teams**: People nearest to solving the problem are going to find the best solutions. Because of their proximity, they will be able to evolve their solutions so that all aspects of the problem are covered. People at a distance are too removed to make good decisions. Employ smart people, empower them, allow them to self-organize, and you'll be amazed by the results.

12. **At regular intervals, the team reflects on how to become more effective, then tunes and adjusts its behavior accordingly**: This is one of the most important principles in my humble opinion and is also my favorite. A team that takes time to inspect and adapt their approach will identify actions that will allow them to make profound changes to the way they work. The regular interval, for example, every two weeks, gives the team a date in their diary to make time to reflect. This ensures that they create a habit that leads to a continuous improvement mindset. A continuous improvement mindset is what sets a team on the right path to being the best Agile team they can be.

Incremental – adaptive versus waterfall – predictive

The Agile Manifesto advocates incremental delivery using adaptive planning. In this section, we contrast and compare this approach with the previously more traditional approach of Waterfall delivery/predictive planning.

In the following section, we'll look at both approaches and some of the impacts on how we deliver software. Before we launch into the detail, here's a quick comparison of the two approaches:

Predictive	Adaptive
Plan driven	Planning driven
Requirements / scope fixed	Requirements / scope flexible
Uses analysis over discovery	Uses discovery over analysis
Big upfront design	Initial upfront design
Architecture pre-determined	Architecture evolves
Estimates given up front	Estimates constantly revised
Forecasting based on upfront estimates	Forecasts driven by work already delivered
Requirements treated as of equal priority	Requirements prioritised by value to the business

The Waterfall process and predictive planning

The traditional delivery model known as *Waterfall* was first shown diagrammatically by *Dr Winston W. Royce* when he captured what was happening in the industry in his paper, *Managing the Development of Large Software Systems*, Proceedings WesCon, IEEE CS Press,1970.

In it, he describes a gated process that moves in a linear sequence. Each step, such as requirements gathering, analysis or design, has to be completed before handover to the next step.

It was presented visually in Royce's paper in the following way:

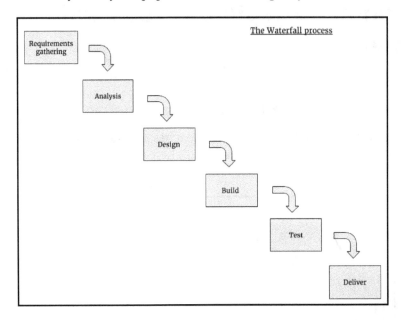

The term *Waterfall* was coined because of the observation; just like a real waterfall, once you've moved downstream, it's much harder to return upstream. This approach is also known as a gated approach because each phase has to be signed off before you can move onto the next.

He further observed in his paper that to de-risk this approach, there should be more than one pass through, each iteration improving and building on what was learned in the previous pass through. In this way, you could deal with complexity and uncertainty.

For some reason, not many people in the industry got the memo though. They continued to work in a gated approach but, rather than making multiple passes, expected the project to be complete in just one cycle or iteration.

To control the project, a highly detailed plan would be created, which was used to predict when the various features would be delivered. The predictive nature of this plan was based entirely on the detailed estimates that were drawn up during the planning phase.

This led to multiple points of potential failure within the process, and usually with little time built into the schedule to recover. It felt almost de rigueur that at the end of the project some form of risk assessment would take place before finally deciding to launch with incomplete and inadequate features, often leaving everyone involved in the process stressed and disappointed.

The waterfall process is a throwback to when software was built more like the way we'd engineer something. It's also been nicknamed faith-driven development because it doesn't deliver anything until the very end of the project. Its risk profile, therefore, looks similar to the following figure:

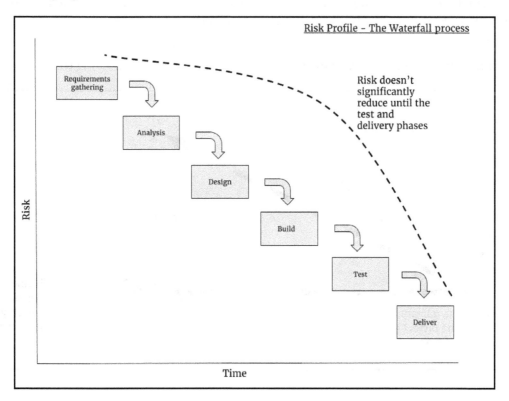

No wonder all those business folks were nervous. Often their only involvement was at the beginning of **Software Development Life Cycle** (**SDLC**) during the requirements phase and then right at the end, during the delivery phase. Talk about a big reveal.

The key point in understanding a plan-driven approach is that scope is often nailed down at the beginning. To then deliver to scope requires precise estimates to determine the budget and resourcing.

The estimation needed for that level of precision is complicated and time-consuming to complete. This leads to more paperwork, more debate, in fact, more of everything. As the process gets bigger, it takes on its own gravity, attracting more things to it that also need to be processed.

The result is a large chunk of work with a very detailed plan of delivery. However, as already discussed, large chunks of work have more uncertainty and more variability, therefore calling into question the ability to give a precision estimate in the first place.

And because so much effort was put into developing the plan, there becomes an irrational attachment to it. Instead of deviating from the plan when new information is uncovered, the project manager tries to control the variance by minimizing or deferring it.

Over time, and depending on the size of the project, this can result in a substantial deviation from reality by the time the software is delivered, as shown in the following diagram:

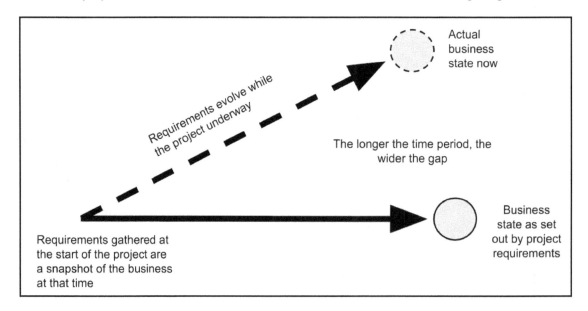

This led to much disappointment for people who had been waiting many months to receive their new software. The gap in functionality would often cause some serious soul-searching on whether the software could be released in its present state or whether it would need rework first.

No-one wants to waste money, so it was likely that the rollout would go ahead and a series of updates would follow that would hopefully fix the problems. This left the people using the software facing a sometimes unworkable process that would lead them to create a series of workarounds. Some of these would undoubtedly last for the lifetime of the software because they were deemed either too trivial or too difficult to fix.

Either way, a business implementing imperfect software that doesn't quite fit its process is faced with, often undocumented, additional costs as users try to work around the system.

For those of us who have tried building a large complex project in a predictive, plan-driven way, there's little doubt it often fails to deliver excellent outcomes for our customer. The findings of the Standish Group's annual Chaos Report are a constant reminder, showing that we're still better at delivering small software projects over large projects, and Waterfall or predictive approaches are more likely to result in the project being challenged or deemed a failure regardless of the size.

Incremental delivery and adaptive planning

Incremental delivery seeks to de-risk the approach by delivering small chunks of discrete value early and often to get feedback and reduce uncertainty. This allows us to determine sooner rather than later, whether we're building the right thing.

As you can see from the following hypothetical risk profile, by delivering increments of ready-to-use working software, we reduce risk significantly after only 2 or 3 iterations:

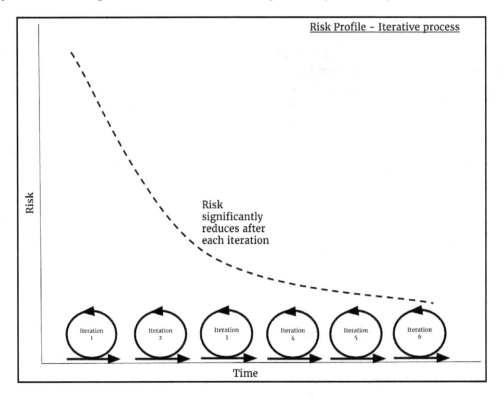

This is combined with an approach to planning that allows us to quickly pivot or change direction based on new information.

With an adaptive plan, the focus is on prioritizing and planning for a fixed horizon, for example, the next three months. We then seek to re-plan once further information has been gathered. This allows us to be more flexible and ultimately deliver something that our customer is much more likely to need.

The following diagram shows that each iteration or increment in an adaptive planning approach allows an opportunity for a correction to the actual business needs:

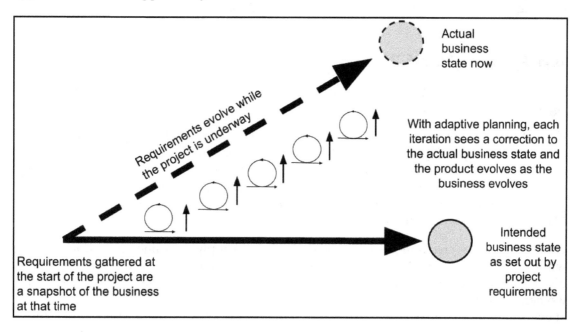

Agile is a mindset

The final thing I'd like you to consider in this chapter is that Agile isn't one particular methodology or another. Neither is it a set of technical practices, although these things do give an excellent foundation.

On top of these processes, tools, and practices, if we layer the values and principles of the manifesto, we start to evolve a more people-centric way of working. This, in turn, helps build software that is more suited to our customer's needs.

In anchoring ourselves to human needs while still producing something that is technically excellent, we are far more likely to make something that meets and goes beyond our customer's expectations. The trust and respect this builds will begin a powerful collaboration of technical and non-technical people.

Over time, as we practice the values and principles, we not only start to determine what works well and what doesn't, but we also start to see how we can bend the rules to create a better approach.

This is when we start to become truly Agile. When the things we do are still grounded in sound processes and tools, with good practices, but we begin to create whole new ways of working that suit our context and begin to shift our organizational culture.

An Example of "Being Agile"

When discussing the Agile Mindset, we often talk about the difference between "doing Agile" and "being Agile."

If we're "doing Agile", we are just at the beginning of our journey. We've probably learnt about the Manifesto. Hopefully, we've had some Agile or Scrum training and now our team, who are likely to have a mix of Agile backgrounds, are working out how to apply it. Right now we're just going through the motions, learning by rote. Over time, with the guidance of our Scrum Master or Agile Coach, we'll start to understand the meaning of the Manifesto and how it applies to our everyday work.

Over time our understanding deepens, and we begin to apply the values and principles without thinking. Our tools and practices allow us to be productive, nimble, and yet, still disciplined. Rather than seeing ourselves as engineers, we see ourselves as crafts men and women. We act with pragmatism, we welcome change, and we seek to add business value at every step. Above all else, we're fully tuned to making software that people both need and find truly useful.

If we're not there now, don't worry, we're just not there **yet**. To give a taste of what it feels like to be on a team who are thinking with an Agile Mindset following is an example scenario.

Scenario

Imagine we're just about to release a major new feature when our customer comes to us with a last minute request. They've spotted something isn't working quite as they expected and they believe we need to change the existing workflow. Their biggest fear is that it will prevent our users from being able to do a particular part of their job.

Our response

Our team would respond as a group. We'd welcome the change. We'd be grateful that our customer has highlighted this problem to us and that they found it before we released. We would know that incorporating a change won't be a big issue for us; our code, testing and deployment/release strategies are all designed to accommodate this kind of request.

We would work together (our customer is part of the team) to discover more about the missing requirement. We'd use our toolkit to elaborate the feature with our customer, writing out the User Stories (an Agile requirement gathering tool we'll discuss in Chapter 4, *Gathering Agile User Requirements*) and if necessary prototyping the user experience and writing scenarios for each of the Acceptance Criteria.

We'd then work to carry out the changes in our usual disciplined way, likely using **TDD** to design and unit/integration test our software as well as **Behavior-Driven Development** (**BDD**) to automate the acceptance testing.

To begin with, we may carry the work out as a Mob (see Chapter 12, *Baking Quality into Our Software Delivery*) or in pairs. We would definitely come together at the end to ensure we have collective ownership of the problem and the solution.

Once comfortable with the changes made, we'd prepare and release the new software and deploy it with the touch of a button. We might even have a fully automated deployment that deploys as soon as the code is committed to the main branch.

Finally, we'd run a retrospective to perform some root cause analysis using the 5-whys, or a similar technique, to try to discover why we missed the problem in the first place. The retrospective would result in actions that we would take, with the aim of preventing a similar problem occurring again.

Summary

In this chapter, we looked at two delivery styles, delivery as a software product and delivery as a software project.

We learned that delivery as a software project was hard to get right for multiple reasons. And giving our team only one shot at delivery gave them little or no chance of fine-tuning their approach. In a novel situation, with varying degrees of uncertainty, this could lead to a fair amount of stress.

There is a better chance of succeeding if we reduce the variability. This includes knowledge of the domain, the technology, and of each of our team members' capabilities. So, it is desirable to keep our project teams together as they move from project to project.

What we learned was that when a long-lived team works on a product, they have the opportunity to deliver incrementally. If we deliver in smaller chunks, we're more likely to meet expectations successfully. Plus, teams that work on products are long-lived and have multiple opportunities to fine-tune their delivery approach.

Those who build software, understand well the complex nature of the work we do and the degree of variability that complexity introduces. Embrace that, and we'll learn to love the new control we can gain from focusing on incremental value delivery in an adaptive system.

In the next chapter, will look at the different Agile methods for software delivery and delve into the mechanics of three of them in particular. See you there.

2
Agile Software Delivery Methods and How They Fit the Manifesto

Some people like a bit of background before they get started, if that's you then you're in the right place. In this chapter, we're going to take a look at the various strands of the modern Agile movement and see how they've come together.

Alternatively, if you're the kind of person who likes to get stuck in first and then get some context later, once you've tried a few things out, skip this chapter and go directly to the next one. In it, we'll discover how to get your team up-and-running using the most popular Agile framework, Scrum. If that's you, see you there.

Here we're going to take a look at several Agile methods, including their backgrounds and how they fit the Agile Manifesto. Or perhaps, more importantly, how the Manifesto fits them because many Agile methods were developed before the Manifesto was written—the practical experience gained by the original members of the Agile Alliance is what gave the Agile Manifesto its substance.

Some have a number of prescribed artifacts and ceremonies; others are much less prescriptive. In most cases, there is no one-size-fits-all approach and most Agile practitioners will mix and match, for example, Scrum and XP. This chapter aims to help you decide which method might work for you.

We'll cover the following topics in this chapter:

- A detailed look at the most common methods: Scrum, Kanban, and XP
- A comparison of specific Agile methods
- Kanban for software is included in this chapter. Although it's technically a Lean approach to software development, Agile and Lean approaches are often combined
- How you can choose the right Agile framework

When the original 17 signatories to the Agile Manifesto came together in 2001 to form the Agile Alliance, they each brought with them ideas about how the industry could be changed for the better based on actual experiences. You see, many of them had already started shifting away from what they deemed heavyweight practices, such as the ones encouraged by Waterfall. Instead, they were putting new ideas into practice and creating SDLC frameworks of their own.

Among the signatories, that weekend were the creators of XP, Scrum, **Dynamic Systems Development Method** (**DSDM**), Crystal, **Adaptive Software Development** (**ASD**), **Feature-Driven Development** (**FDD**), and so on.

They initially called them "light" frameworks, to distinguish them from their heavyweight counterparts, but they didn't want the world to consider them to be *lightweight*. So, they came up with the term *Agile*, because one thing all of these frameworks had in common was their adaptive nature.

They noted at the time that some of their thinking was influenced by industrial product development and manufacturing.

The *industrial heritage* came from, predominantly, three sources:

- Product development and in particular how product development companies in the 1980s had been reducing the time to market for new products
- Engineering technical practices, which provided for better and, in some cases, fully automated quality assurance on a production line.
- Lean manufacturing as developed by Toyota Industries

In the following sections we're going to look at three of the Agile methods, first up is Scrum.

Understanding Scrum

Scrum is the most popular framework among Agile teams; 58% of respondents to *VersionOne's 11ᵗʰ Annual State of Agile Report* use pure Scrum. A further 10% are using a Scrum/XP hybrid.

Background

The following timeline shows a brief history of Scrum:

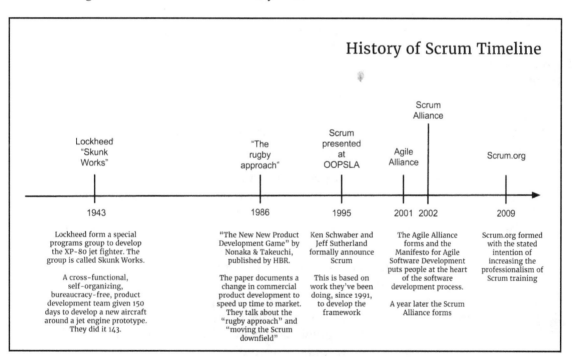

The first mention of Scrum in the context of product development was in *The New New Product Development Game*-Takeuchi, Hirotaka, and Ikujiro Nonaka, Harvard Business Review 64, no. 1 (January–February 1986).

In the paper, the two professors describe efforts by companies to try to speed up their product development life cycles to decrease their time to market. They observed that companies that were successfully doing this were employing some interesting alternative approaches.

These companies were assembling small teams of highly capable people with the right skills, setting the vision for them to build the next-generation product, giving them a budget and timeframe, and then getting out of the team's way to let it do its thing.

Some observed characteristics of these teams included having all the skills necessary to carry out the job they were being asked to do—the essence of a cross-functional team. They were allowed to determine how they best carried out the work, so were self-organizing and autonomous. They used rapid, iterative development cycles to build and validate ideas.

Nonaka and Takeuchi called it the *rugby approach* because they observed product teams passing the product back and forth among themselves as it was being developed, much like a rugby team passes the ball when moving upfield. In a rugby game, the team moves as a unit and even though each team member has a specialty regarding position on the field and gameplay, any member of the rugby team can pick up the ball, carry it forward, and score a try or goal. The same was true of these product development teams—their contribution to the product development was specialist and highly collaborative.

In the section of their paper titled *Moving the Scrum downfield*, they list the common characteristics of the teams they observed as follows:

- **Built-in instability**: Some aspect of pressure was introduced, which encouraged the product development teams to think out-of-the-box and use an innovative approach to solving the problem.
- **Self-organizing project teams**: The teams were given the autonomy to decide how they carried out the task of solving the problem handed to them.
- **Overlapping development phases**: Instead of the normal sequential-phased development that you get with processes such as Waterfall, the teams worked iteratively, building quickly and evolving their product, with each iteration. Multiple phases overlapped, such that the following steps might be informed by the discoveries made in the previous one. In this way, the teams were able to gain fast feedback about what would and wouldn't work.

- **Multilearning**: A trial-and-error learning culture is fostered, which allows team members to narrow down options as quickly as possible. They are also encouraged to diversify their skill sets, to create team versatility. Nonaka and Takeuchi called this multi-learning because they said it supported learning along two dimensions: traversing different layers of the organization (individual, team, unit, and group) and across various functions. This cross-pollination of skills is an aspect of cross-functionality we encourage today.

- **Subtle control**: The approach to managing these projects was very different. To create a space for the team to innovate, they realized command-and-control supervision wouldn't work. Instead, management would check in with the team regularly to check progress and give feedback, leaving the team to manage its work how it saw fit.

- **Organizational transfer of learning**: If and when the development life cycle began to move towards mass manufacture, the product development team would often be strategically placed in the wider organization to seed knowledge and assist with the preparation for production.

The approach described by Nonaka and Takeuchi has similarities to the Skunk Works projects started in World War II by Lockheed's Advanced Development Programs division.

The Skunk Works team were originally tasked with designing and building a highly secret prototype jet fighter aircraft around a new jet engine developed by a British company, deHavilland. The work commenced on little more than a handshake, and the team was formed in a location separate from the rest of the group and given relatively free rein on how to proceed. They were given 150 days to complete their prototype; they finished it in 143.

 Skunk Works was an official alias that originated with the Lockheed special projects development team during World War II. Due to a lack of room at its California premises, the team worked out of a well-guarded Circus Tent next to a manufacturing plant from which strange smells wafted in. The team associated the odor with a famous comic strip of the time called Li'l Abner, in which a mysterious moonshine factory deep in the woods brewed a terrible smelling concoction. The moonshine factory in the comic strip was called Skonk Works; over time this evolved into Skunk Works.

Lockheed's Skunk Works took on many secret projects after the war finished. Their approach gained notoriety among other companies, including Apple who built the Macintosh in a Skunk Works type operation behind a restaurant in Cupertino. It also seems to have permeated through to the product development teams that Nonaka and Takeuchi were observing when they wrote their paper.

Everett Rogers (in *Diffusion of Innovations, 4th Edition*) points to the reason for isolating a project team and allowing them to take this crash approach to product development: it's because companies operate as bureaucracies. The *stability and continuity* that a bureaucratic organization seeks are at odds with the instability needed to foster innovation. Most find it undesirable to disrupt their own, currently successful, business model. The Skunk Works approach fosters maximum creativity by isolating the teams away from the organizational mainstream, allowing them to innovate around both their process and product.

Some of these ideas would go on to influence Jeff Sutherland and Ken Schwaber when they started working on the Scrum framework in the early 1990s. In 1995, they formalized and presented it as a paper at the Business Object Design and Implementation Workshop held as part of *OOPSLA '95* (**Object-Oriented Programming, Systems, Languages, Programming, and Applications**) in Austin, Texas. In the following section we'll introduce Scrum and talk through the basics with an overview of its characteristics, roles and events.

Introduction to the mechanics of Scrum

Here are the basic characteristics and features of Scrum:

- **Planning style**: Empirical/adaptive
- **Delivery style**: Iterative/incremental
- **Iteration length**: Ranges between 1 and 4 weeks; a length within this range is initially chosen by the team and then fixed. The most popular is 2 weeks.
- **Values**: Commitment, courage, focus, openness, and respect
- **Roles**: Product Owner, Scrum Master, Development Team
- **Team size**: small, 5-9
- **Artefacts**: Product Backlog, Sprint Backlog, Sprint progress tracking
- **Events**: Sprint Planning, Daily Scrum, Sprint Review, Sprint Retrospective
- **Special features**: All events are time-boxed
- **Lacks**: A product/project/feature initiation phase and doesn't specify technical practices

There are three roles in Scrum: the **Product Owner**, the **Scrum Master**, and the **Development Team**, which are defined as follows:

The Scrum Team - Roles

Product Owner

- Holds the vision for the product and controls the budget
- Works to maximize value delivered by the team
- Clearly expresses what's to be done, makes the Product Backlog visible and transparent to all
- Sets priorities for the team in terms of which Product Backlog items to work on next
- Should be a single person, not a committee

Development Team

- Create working increments of "done" work
- Self-organizing - team decides how to deliver
- Cross-functional - have all the skills on the team necessary to do the job
- Individuals may have specialist skills, but are accountable as a team for delivery
- Scrum only recognises the title "developer" within the team
- Scrum doesn't ask for or recognise sub-teams within the team

Scrum Master

- Coaches the team in the use of Scrum
- Coaches the organization how to get best value from its interactions with the team
- Facilitates events as requested or needed (Daily Scrum, Sprint Planning)
- Removes impediments to the team's progress
- Acts as a servant leader to the team

Team size is essential in a Scrum. Face-to-face communication is preferred by Agile teams; it's open and has a high bandwidth. The larger the team gets, the harder it becomes for each team member to know everything that is going on.

Scrum recommends a team of no fewer than five and no more than nine. Fewer than five (which includes the **Product Owner** and **Scrum Master**) and it's believed that the team will be limited in what it will be able to achieve. More than nine and the team's communications will become strained, and information may fall through the cracks.

The Scrum Guide defines three artifacts—**Product Backlog**, **Sprint Backlog**, and **Increment**:

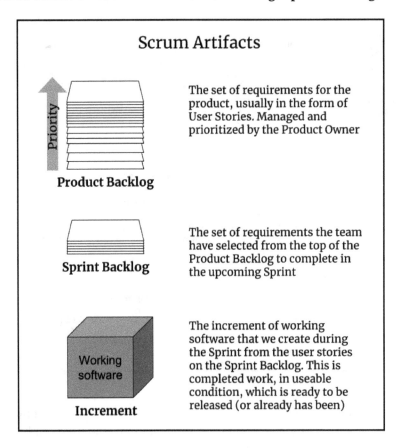

Scrum uses an incremental approach to delivering. It achieves this by working in iterations known as Sprints. The recommended length for a Sprint is between a minimum of 1 week to a maximum of 4 weeks. Most teams opt for a 2-week Sprint:

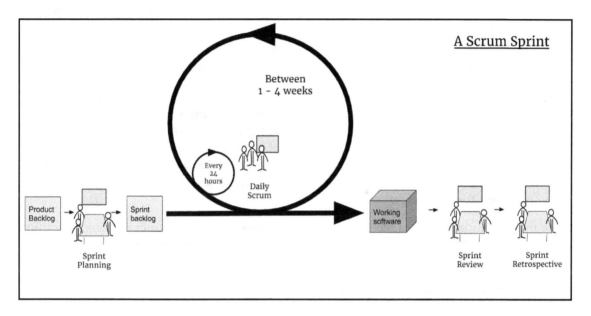

The Sprint isn't the only aspect of Scrum that has a time limit, also known as *time-box*. All of events, such as Sprint Planning, the Daily Scrum, and so on, are also time-boxed. The aim of time-boxing an event is to ensure focus is maintained. The time-box for each event is proportional to the length of the Sprint and is set out in the Scrum guidelines.

Sprint Planning – part 1

The Sprint starts with Sprint Planning, a meeting where the whole team comes together. The aim of the first part of Sprint Planning is for the Development Team to forecast which items, from the top of the already prioritized Product Backlog, they think they can achieve in the coming Sprint.

Several factors influence their decision including the following:

1. The latest product increment.
2. The items in the Product Backlog.
3. The team capacity for the upcoming Sprint; for example, are any members on leave?
4. How did the team perform in the last Sprint?
5. Are there any work items being carried over from the last Sprint?

The usual process will involve the Development Team taking the next story from the top of the Product Backlog and discussing whether they think they can complete it as part of the coming Sprint. Usually, this begins with one of the team reading the story aloud, including the acceptance criteria. The Product Owner should be available for questions if the Development Team needs any clarifications. If, after discussion, our team believe they can complete it in the coming Sprint, they put it on the Sprint Backlog. They then take the next story from the Product Backlog and repeat the process.

Once the Development Team has determined the items from the Product Backlog they think they can achieve, the Scrum team as a whole works to set the Sprint Goal.

Sprint Planning - part 2

The second part of Sprint Planning is for the Development Team to determine how they will do the work. Deciding how involves discussion and breaking down the work into tasks, for each Product Backlog item in the Sprint. At the end of the Sprint Planning Meeting, the resulting set of of work items, including the Sprint Goal is collectively known as the Sprint Backlog.

Once ready, the Sprint Backlog is added to the team's Scrum Board. For Scrum teams, this usually takes the form of physical board, such as a whiteboard or similar, and would look something like as follows:

Product Backlog		Sprint Backlog	To-do	In progress	Done	Sprint Objective
User Story	User Story	User Story	Task Task Task	Task	Task Task	Simple checkout and payment process complete
User Story	User Story	User Story	Task Task Task	Task	Task	
User Story	User Story	User Story	Task Task Task	Task		**Sprint Burndown**
User Story	User Story	User Story	Task Task Task			
User Story	User Story	User Story	Task Task Task			
User Story	User Story	User Story	Task Task Task			

The Daily Scrum

Once the Sprint is in progress, the Scrum team meets each day to coordinate their work. This meeting is called the Daily Scrum.

The Scrum team will congregate around the Scrum Board and discuss what they've achieved since they last met, what they will be working on until they next meet, and whether there are any problems, or if there is anything in their way.

The Development Team will update the board as necessary, moving tasks from left to right as applicable. This Scrum Board's primary function is to help the team to coordinate their work, ascertain progress, and quickly uncover any assumptions or identify any risks in their plan. The team should remain focused on meeting the Sprint Goal; as such, this is a key inspect-and-adapt meeting for the team.

The meeting is timeboxed to 15 minutes to keep it purposeful and focused. Although the Scrum Guide doesn't indicate this should be a standing meeting, many Scrum teams will stand for their Daily Scrum. This is something that's been adopted from the Extreme Programming community. The aim of making it a standing meeting is to keep it short; people are less inclined to talk at length if they're standing.

The Sprint Review

The Sprint Review is the first meeting held at the end of the Sprint cycle. The attendees include the Scrum team and stakeholders for the product. The working software for each completed User Story is demonstrated to the group. The Sprint Review aims to inspect and adapt the business value delivered by this latest increment, to see if we can optimize it further. Based on the feedback gained, the Product Owner can then adjust the backlog (adapt the plan) accordingly.

The Sprint Retrospective

The Sprint Retrospective usually follows on immediately from the Sprint Review and is the last meeting of the iteration. It's an opportunity for the Scrum team to inspect and adapt its process. In general, the Scrum team will ask itself what went well during the Sprint, what didn't go well, and what it can improve. They should consider aspects such as the team dynamics as well as processes and tools. The outcome of this meeting is for the team to come up with actionable improvements that it can carry out during the next Sprint.

Additional events

Most Scrum teams add additional events to their Scrum workflow. A good example is called backlog refinement, an event which some teams hold as regularly as once per week, or at least once per Sprint.

The backlog refinement meeting aims to look at the top stories on the backlog and prepare them to be worked on in an upcoming Sprint. Part of this preparation will include estimating the User Stories, which will tell us whether:

1. We have enough information to able to start working on the User Story
2. We've broken the story down into a small enough chunk; a User Story must be small enough to be completed in one Sprint

Estimates are usually given in Story Points; we'll talk more about those in the following two chapters.

XP - Extreme Programming

Extreme Programming (**XP**) is the second most popular framework, used by roughly 10% of Agile teams. XP stands out as one of the few Agile frameworks that prescribe technical practices.

Background

The following timeline shows a brief history of Extreme Programming (XP):

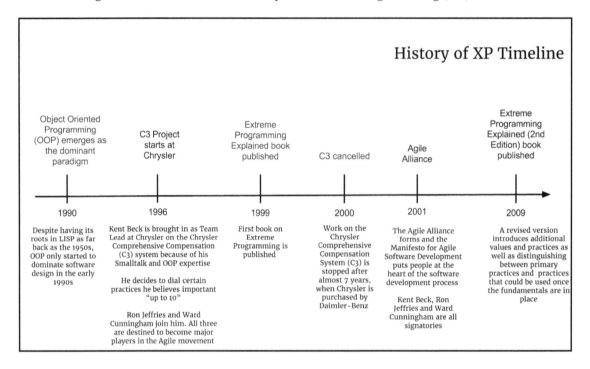

The 1990s was the beginning of another paradigm shift for the software industry as Object-Oriented Programming began to replace Structured Programming. As a way to explore how they would use this new approach, the Chrysler motor company decided to build their payroll system in Smalltalk, an OO programming language.

Initially invited to performance-tune the system because of his knowledge of Smalltalk, Kent Beck was asked to lead their software team in 1996. In Kent's potted history of XP, he says that, before joining Chrysler, he had asked teams to do things he thought were important, such as testing and reviews. This time, at Chrysler, he felt there was a lot more at stake, so Kent asked the team to turn all the *dials up to 10* on the things he thought were essential and not to bother with the ones he thought weren't.

For instance, peer review is considered so important; when *dialed up to 10* we do peer review all of the time. If all code is written while working with another programmer, we are code reviewing continuously. So XP makes the rule that all software that is destined for a production environment must be Pair Programmed.

He applied the same thinking to unit testing. XP deems unit testing so valuable it makes it a rule to write the unit test first before any code is written.

 Writing tests first, also known as **Test-Driven Development (TDD)**, is a practice that supports the creation of simpler code designs because just enough code is written to fulfill the test specifications. The resulting automated test suite also inspires the confidence to make subsequent changes to the specification tests and code, in the knowledge that if the tests still pass, other parts of the system are unaffected by the change.

So this is how XP got its name. It prescribes core programming practices and turns the volume on each up to maximum, taking them to the extreme.

Introduction to the mechanics of XP

Here are the basic characteristics and features of Extreme Programming:

- **Planning style**: Adaptive
- **Delivery style**: Iterative/Incremental, sustainable pace
- **Iteration length**: Ranges from 1 to 3 weeks, with a preference for the shortest possible
- **Values**: Communication, simplicity, feedback, courage, and respect
- **Roles**: Customer, Development Team
- **Team size**: small, 2-10
- **Artifacts**: Release plan, iteration plan, User Stories, tasks, CRC cards
- **Technical practices:** Pair Programming all production code, TDD, metaphor, refactoring, collective code ownership, Continuous Integration, daily builds, Spikes, sustainable pace
- **Events**: Release planning/iteration planning, daily standup
- **Special features**: Prescribes technical practices, gathers requirements with User Stories, promotes working at a sustainable pace
- **Lacks**: Compromise—it's a fully committed, all-or-nothing approach

These are the roles XP recommends for a team:

XP Team Roles

Customer

Writes User Stories, specifies acceptance criteria and helps specify the associated acceptance tests. Engages with stakeholders, sets priorities, manages the budget, explains stories and answers any questions. Works closely with the team throughout the iteration.

Programmer

Estimates stories. Breaks stories down into tasks. Works closely with the customer and other team members to implement stories and tests. Is responsible for ensuring the implemented story meets team standards.

Tester

The tester role often works closely with other team members to help write a range of different tests, including functional and acceptance tests. They will also define and run exploratory tests. The tester is the test champion and advocates for sensible testing plans amongst the team. The tester role will hold the team to account if tests are failing or they aren't up to standard.

Tracker

Tracks the team progress against their current iteration plan. Will keep charts such as the iteration burndown up-to-date. Will take action if things aren't going to plan. These actions include enlisting the support of various team members, including the coach and customer to determine what can be done to get things back on track.

Coach

Coaches the team. Schedules and facilitates meetings. Will record results of a meeting, particularly any actions that need to be taken. Will pass this information to the relevant people. Ensures the proper process is followed. Doesn't tell the team what to do or when to do it.

There doesn't need to be a one-to-one relationship between team members and functions. One person can perform more than one role.

For example, the person who has the **Coach** role could also have the **Tracker** role. Some instances of combined roles are Programmer-Tracker, Programmer-Tester, and Coach-Tracker. Some roles shouldn't be mixed; for example, for the Coach to remain objective, they probably shouldn't combine with anything except Tracker. The same is true for the Customer, where we will also want to avoid conflicts of interest. Plus it's a time-consuming role in its own right.

XP requires that the **Customer** is part of the team; their involvement throughout the product development life cycle is key to its success. In XP, it's assumed that the customer has the most information about the value of what is being built. At the same time, it's expected that the Development Team has the best idea of how to implement that value and how much it will cost.

While this may be a radical shift from your current way of working, you'll be amazed by the results of having the customer on the team—I've seen this work well many times. We may be the experts at building software, but our customer is the expert in their domain and is the person closest to the real-world problem that we're trying to solve.

XP uses iterations to deliver working software incrementally. The iteration length is anywhere from 1 to 3 weeks. The team should pick an iteration length and fix it, only changing it if it's necessary:

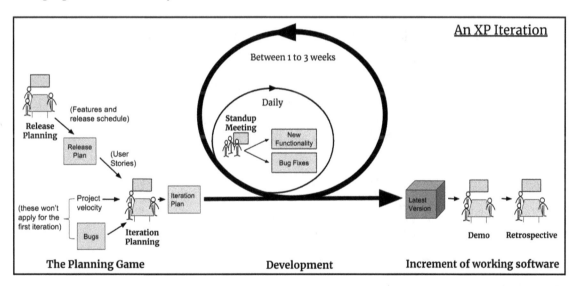

The planning game

We start the beginning of each XP iteration with the planning game, an event in which the whole team participates. It is split into two phases, Release Planning and Iteration Planning, which we'll take a look at now.

Part 1 – Release planning

A new phase of work begins with release planning, a whole team meeting which is used to create a release plan. It commences with the customer/business introducing new problems for the team to solve. At this early ideation phase, the customer will often be thinking in the form of software features. These are written on index cards in the format of users stories.

XP emphasizes that business people are to make business decisions and technical people are to make technical decisions. The Development Team, therefore, leaves the customer to write the User Stories.

The following is an example User Story from a cinema ticketing system:

```
AS A CINEMA GOER
I WANT TO BE ABLE TO PURCHASE TICKETS FOR A
PARTICULAR FILM AND SESSION TIME
SO THAT I CAN SEE THE FILM I WANT TO SEE AT
THE TIME I WANT TO SEE IT.


ACCEPTANCE CRITERIA:
 - I CAN SELECT A PARTICULAR FILM
 - I CAN SELECT A PARTICULAR SESSION
 - I CAN CHOOSE WHERE TO SIT (SHOW AVAILABLE SEATS)
 - I CAN PAY USING CREDIT CARD
 - I RECEIVE MY TICKETS WITH THE CONFIRMATION EMAIL
```

On the top half of the index card, the narrative of the User Story is written. It typically follows the format given here:

As a **<certain type of user>** I want to **<perform some action>** so that I get **<some outcome>**.

In the example User Story given here, the **precise type of user** is the cinema goer. The **action** they want to perform is to purchase tickets and reserve seats for a particular session. Finally, the **outcome** the Cinema goer would like is to watch the movie.

On the bottom half of the index card, the acceptance criteria are written. These help the team to understand what expected behavior is to be delivered as part of this User Story. These are the criteria that the customer will use to determine if the resulting software works as they were expecting.

 User Stories are business problems formulated to fit on an index card. They are deliberately kept in this small format to enable the 3 Cs to happen: Card, Conversation, and Confirmation. In this way, active discussion occurs between the customer and the Development Team during implementation. Leading to fewer assumptions being made when compared to traditional requirements gathering. We'll discuss User Stories in more detail in Chapter 4, *Gathering Agile User Requirements*.

For each User Story, the Development Team will gather enough information from the customer so that they can estimate it. At the release planning level, estimate in **ideal weeks**. An **ideal week** is a week where we can focus entirely on implementing the User Story without any distractions. Estimates should fall between one and three ideal weeks. If the User Story is bigger than three weeks, it should be broken down. If it is smaller than one week, then it may need to be combined with others.

It's not unusual in a release planning meeting to see the User Stories spread around the table. Viewing all the stories like this helps the team absorb the bigger picture and will ultimately make it easier for the customer to identify any gaps.

With index cards, it's easier for both the customer and the Development Team to move the cards around and start to formulate a plan. Priority is given to stories with the highest business value.

The outcome of release planning is the release plan, a deck of User Stories written on index cards, estimated by the Development Team and prioritized by the business.

Work on the release plan begins with the preparation for the next iteration; this starts with the iteration planning meeting.

Part 2 – Iteration planning

Phase 2 of the planning game focuses on planning the next iteration. The release plan is the principal ingredient to this process. If this is the first iteration, that's all we need. If, however, this isn't the first iteration, we'll also need the following:

1. The team's project velocity. Velocity tells the team how much stuff we can get done in one iteration. To calculate it we take the estimates for the work completed in the last iteration and total them. This total is then used by the team to help them determine the right amount of work to commit to for this iteration. User stories are estimated in ideal weeks, so if we completed User Stories with a total of five ideal weeks, our velocity would be 5.

 If the team doesn't have a project velocity, that is, it's their first iteration, they will have to use a degree of gut feeling. It will take at least 3 -4 iterations before their velocity begins to stabilize.

2. As with Scrum, any User Stories that are still in flight from the previous iteration are carried over. This includes any unfulfilled acceptance tests or bugs. Work that is carried over usually takes precedence as it was previously prioritized higher than the other items on the Release Plan. These user stories are placed at the top of the Release Plan for this round of iteration planning.

With all these factors available to it, the team goes about planning the next iteration. It does this by selecting the next story from the top of the release plan and starts to break it down into smaller, more manageable chunks, known as tasks.

Tasks are estimated in terms of ideal days, which is how many days it would take to complete the task if there were no distractions. Half days can be used if necessary. The breakdown of tasks should be done by the people carrying out the work.

The team keeps selecting User Stories from the top of the release plan deck and breaking them down into tasks until they hit their project velocity, or they decide they can fit no more into this iteration.

Some teams assign tasks to developers during iteration planning, some teams don't. It does depend on how you break down User Stories into tasks and whether your team operates as specialists or generalists. It's more fluid if we don't assign tasks and we just let the next available pair pick up the next item to be done.

Implementing the iteration plan

Once the planning is complete, the iteration begins. If a programmer doesn't already have a task, they take the next available one and find a partner. If necessary, design work will be carried out at this stage, including the use of **Class Responsibility Collaborator** (**CRC**) modeling of **Object-Oriented Design** (**OOD**), and other design tools such as UML Sequence Diagrams.

The pair will begin coding in the**TDD** way by writing a failing test. They then write the code that fulfills the test. Once the test is running, they then look to refactor the code, as the following diagram illustrates:

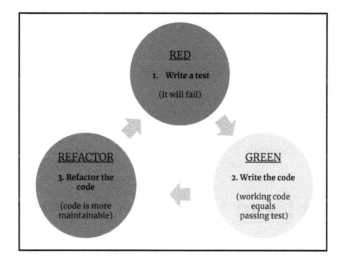

This cycle continues until the task is complete.

Each day the team will meet in the form of a Daily Standup; this is a 15-minute meeting where, as the name suggests, everyone stands. The aim is to coordinate the team's work. Each team member or pair will talk about what they've implemented since yesterday's standup, what they'll look to achieve before the next standup, and what, if anything, is in their way.

XPers aim to integrate early and often; they favor a practice called **Continuous Integration** (**CI**). They will typically commit work every few hours, providing, of course, all of their unit tests pass. Modern CI practices offer an automated way for the latest changes to be incorporated. Teams will often set up their CI server so that it automatically checks out the newest version, builds it, and runs the tests. Their practices and workflow shouldn't allow them to commit code and proceed unless all tests pass.

Once the story is complete, the software is made available for acceptance testing. The customer executes the scenarios they've created around the acceptance criteria of the User Story, so they can determine whether the software is complete. Many teams now automate their acceptance testing as part of their TDD approach, a technique known as **Acceptance Test Driven Development (ATDD)**.

Iteration demo

As with Scrum, the demo is an opportunity to invite stakeholders along so that they can see progress and give feedback. The focus is on a demonstration and inspection of the working software completed during the iteration. Information gathered from the demo can be fed into the release planning ahead of the next iteration, and if necessary changes can be made and the release can be re-planned.

Iteration retrospective

Similar to the idea of the Scrum Retrospective, the iteration retrospective is an opportunity for the team to take stock of how things have gone during the past iteration and determine whether it can make changes to its process for the better.

Kanban and Lean Software Development

In this section, we look at Lean Software Development and its origins in Lean Manufacturing. We'll first discuss the thinking that led to significant breakthroughs in responsiveness and quality on the Toyota production line. We'll then look at how we can apply those to software development.

Background

The following timeline shows a brief history of Lean and Kanban:

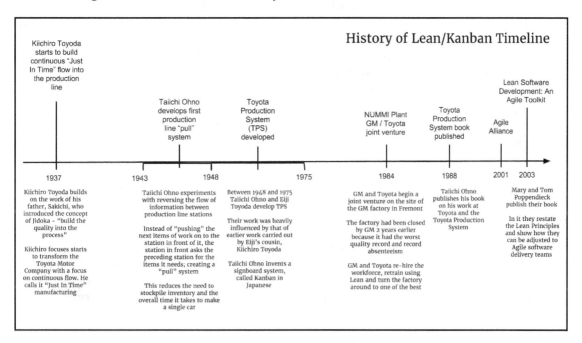

Lean Software Development and Kanban have their history in manufacturing and the work done by one company, in particular, Toyota Motor Corporation. In its effort to economically mass-produce affordable motor vehicles for people after the Second World War, Toyota made profound changes to the way it organized its production line.

Toyota realized early on that there was a significant waste in manufacturing, which added to the overall cost. They implemented two notable changes to typical mass production lines, which had a profound effect on reducing costs and significantly increasing quality.

1. Reduce all waste which didn't add value to the customer
2. Focus on single-piece flow through the production line using a pull system

Reducing waste

Waste was identified at multiple levels, for example, overproduction of a particular part was seen as waste for two reasons. Firstly, space was needed to stockpile the part until it could be used. This cost money not only for storing it but also took up floor space that could be used for production. Secondly, sometimes problems in the manufactured parts weren't found until they were combined with other parts and put to use further down the production line. If a problem were discovered that required the entire batch to be re-machined or re-manufactured, this would add significant time and money.

Single-piece flow

In a production line environment, there are multiple workstations each of which takes the work of preceding stations and combines it or enhances it before passing it on to the next workstation. In this way, each station adds value and passes it further down the production line until the product being built is complete.

In a traditional product line environment, the work was pushed from one station to the next. Sometimes the work was sent in batches. For example, the machine that built widget A, with some amount of retooling, also built widget B. Rather than lose time due to retooling, if you built batches of say 100 at a time, the machine operation was more efficient.

This can create unevenness in the production line, which can lead to fluctuations in the flow; sometimes a station further down the line could be waiting for the previous station to complete a batch of Widget As and retool because it needs two Widget Bs.

To solve these problems, Toyota perfected a system called Kanban. A Japanese word meaning signboard, Kanban is used in lean manufacturing to signal when a piece of work needs to be done. The profound change that Toyota's employee Taiichi Ohno implemented in this signaling system was to reverse the flow of information on the production line. This means that stations further down the production line would send Kanban signals to the stations behind them that they needed certain parts made.

The following figure shows how a **Lean Production Line** works:

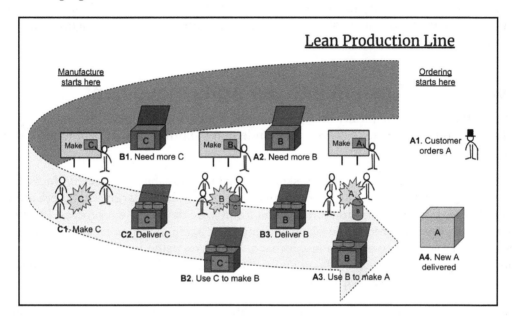

 A **Lean Production Line** waits until there are orders for its product because the communication channel is reversed. The order being placed is a signal to the end of the production line that it needs to deliver more finished products. It does this by sending requests to the stations preceding it in the production line so that they can make and assemble the necessary parts for it to deliver a finished product.

The reversed flow creates a pull rather than push approach to manufacture and changes the dynamic of the system to focus on the whole system's end-to-end flow. In layman's terms, this means that each station on the production line is concerned with carrying out the request it receives as promptly as possible to ensure the next station ahead of it is also able to do so.

Each station only carries out the work when it is requested; this is the **Just in Time** (**JIT**) of lean manufacturing. In any time between servicing requests, the workers at the station can clean their station and prepare themselves for any potentially busy periods ahead. They can also use this time to see if there is anything they can do to improve their process.

It is the responsibility of the entire production line to smooth out any unevenness in the flow. Workers should not try to compensate by deliberately operating their station even though they have no work requests, as this leads to unnecessary overproduction and stockpiling of inventory.

How Kanban/Lean fit into the Agile movement

Kanban, although not technically an Agile method, shares many similar attributes. The Toyota Production System (TPS) was founded on the principle that people were at its heart.

You may find some people are initially skeptical that it is possible to translate practices from Lean manufacturing to software product development. They argue that there are very few similarities between a production line and a software development process. Production lines are doing the same repetitive tasks over and over again in sequence, which is often associated with a predictive planning approach. However, using *Just In Time* manufacturing, Toyota has created and evolved an approach that makes their assembly line much more responsive and adaptive than any other.

The Lean approach to process management has already strongly influenced the thinking of those who formed the Agile Alliance. Many of the methods the practitioners created incorporate aspects of Lean already, such as Scrum's use of the Scrum Board to make work visible. XP and Scrum's use of iterations to manage batch size and create JIT thinking about the requirements and implementation of software products. These are just a couple of examples of how Taiichi Ohno and his work with others at Toyota have influenced how we build software.

Introduction to the mechanics of Lean/Kanban

Here are the basic characteristics and features of Lean/Kanban:

- **Planning style**: Lean/Adaptive
- **Delivery Style**: Flow/Incremental
- **Iteration length**: Doesn't have time-boxed iterations
- **Principles**: Eliminate waste, amplify learning, decide as late as possible, deliver as fast as possible, empower the team, build integrity in, see the whole
- **Roles**: Not prescribed, existing roles
- **Team size**: Not prescribed
- **Artefacts**: Kanban (message board)
- **Events**: Andon (stop the line), Gemba (go and see)
- **Special features:** Kaizen (Continuous Improvement), makes work visible, limits work in progress, works with your existing process, makes policies explicit, evolves empirically
- **Lacks**: A clear process framework of its own; instead it asks that we make our existing process visible and use the principles of Lean to improve it

There are no explicit roles defined by Kanban; assuming you have everyone necessary to do the job you've been asked to do, this is sufficient.

Start with your existing process. Map the workflow on a wall, making it visible so that everyone sees it. Use this sudden wealth of information on how your system works to makes changes and bit by bit evolve it into something that works better.

Getting started with Kanban

There are four steps to implementing Kanban within your team, which we'll cover in the following sections.

Step 1 – Make the team's work visible

This involves creating a board that reflects the current process the team uses to deliver software. The work that the team currently has in progress and the stage it's at also needs to be shown. The easiest way to do this is to write down each work item on an index card and place it in the appropriate area of the board.

For example, a Kanban board for a team with a simple workflow would look something like this:

To-do	In progress	Done
		Work item
	Work item	
	Work item	
Work item		
Work item		

Step 2 – Make the work policies of the team explicit

Teams often handle this by placing entry and exit criteria for each column to make them transparent. This will look something like the following:

To-do	In progress	Done
User story defined Estimated Initial user scenarios	Automated tests written Code reviewed/paired Exploratory tested	Released to staging Acceptance tested Ready to release

The policies form what is commonly known as the **Definition of Done (DoD)**. The DoD is a checklist that the team applies to each work item. It is a way for the team to ensure they've completed the work item to a satisfactory standard and therefore ensure they are the baking quality of their product.

Step 3 – Improve flow

With Kanban, as with the other Agile approaches, we want to add value as soon as we can, by delivering useful software as fast as possible. The reason for this is two-fold:

1. Most people don't know what they need until they see it. It's hard to imagine how the software will look and behave until it's built. Everyone has a different version of it in their head. Once you have something working, you can start to get feedback from your customer. This is when the real work begins.
2. The domain we're operating in is rapidly evolving. In business terms, 6 to 12 months is too long to wait for something. The way the business works and the rules that govern it could have easily changed within such a timeframe.

For work to start to flow across the board, we have to do two things:

1. The first step is to reduce the size of each work item so that it is as small as possible. Taiichi Ohno called this reducing the waste of unevenness (Muri). For us in the software industry, unevenness is reduced by managing and reducing probable variability, which we can also manage by keeping the work item as small as possible. This doesn't mean that we're eliminating all variability, just reducing the amount.
2. The second step is to switch to small batches. This can either be done as Scrum or XP does, using Sprints or Iterations. Alternatively, the more granular way is to start to manage **Work In Progress** (**WIP**) limits so that the team can focus their effort on the items currently being worked on and avoid the loss of time caused by context switching when multitasking. Assuming the items have been prioritized by value, this allows them to focus on completing the high-value items first.

Rather than thinking and working in iterations, the focus in Kanban is on optimizing the flow of work items through the system. To optimize flow two shifts in thinking have to happen. Firstly, we need to think of the system as a whole, the end-to-end process from idea to delivery of that idea. Secondly, instead of pushing the work through the system, we have to think of the system as pulling the work through it. When the system has the capacity, it pulls the next piece of work into it to be worked on.

This requires careful control; the aim is to avoid large batches of work that move as one cohesive block as this only encourages optimization at the local level. Instead, we carefully manage **WIP** and prevent overcapacity by limiting the number of items being worked on at any given moment.

To identify where you might have flow issues in your process, you can map your entire process out so that the entire process is explicit. This is similar to a technique known as Value Stream Mapping, but where a Value Stream Map is a snapshot in time, modeling your Kanban board precisely to your Value Stream allows you to observe and iron out any problems in flow in real time.

The following shows a Kanban board where our team has mapped out every step of the process:

To-do	UX / Design	Code	Unit Test	Code Review	Test	Merge	Deploy Staging	UAT	Deploy Prod	Confirm	Done
Work item		Work item			Work item		Work item				Work item
Work item							Work item				Work item
Work item											
Work item											
Work item											

Visualizing your work in this way will soon help you identify when there is too much work in progress.

For example, the team using the Kanban board in the following figure have identified that they have too much work to test and this is causing a logjam:

To-do	UX / Design	Code	Unit Test	Code Review	Test	Merge	Deploy Staging	UAT	Deploy Prod	Confirm	Done
Work item		Work item			Work item		Work item				Work item
Work item					Work item		Work item				Work item
Work item					Work item						
Work item					Work item						
Work item					Work item						

Blocks like this can have quite subtle effects. One observed result of allowing work to accumulate is to put all of the work items in the column into a single batch. We can then create a single software deployment and carry out testing on all the items at once. We think this will create efficiency in our testing, which it may do at a local level. However, with five work items in that column, the reality is that each work item will delay the others as we wait for testing to complete. If we find any problems with one or two them, the whole batch will be delayed and the overall flow will be significantly reduced.

To tackle this, determine if this is a one-off or whether a pattern is emerging. Either way it is important to take pressure off the people who are currently testing, by swarming on the work as a team. Once the workload is back to normal, the team can prevent this from happening again by placing a **WIP** limit on the test column. The following figure shows a Kanban board with WIP limits set. We'll talk about WIP in more detail in Chapter 8, *Tightening Feedback Loops in the Software Development Life Cycle*:

To-do	UX / Design 1	Code 3	Unit Test 3	Code Review 1	Test 3	Merge 1	Deploy Staging 1	UAT 1	Deploy Prod 1	Confirm 1	Done
Work item		Work item	Work item		Work item		Work item				Work item
Work item		Work item			Work item						Work item
Work item		Work item									
Work item											
Work item											

Step 4 – Kaizen or continuous improvement

Once the team is up and running with the preceding three steps, the next thing for them to implement is Kaizen.

Kaizen is a Japanese word meaning continuous improvement. It is similar in concept to Scrum and XP's retrospective event. The team is encouraged to take time to reflect on their work regularly, and where possible identify improvements to the way they carry it out.

Choosing the right framework

It's no surprise that most Agile transformations start at the team level. Agile is a grassroots movement led by a bunch of software developers who knew, through their trials and tribulations, that there had to be a better way to build software.

In choosing the right framework for your team it will depend a lot on where you are on your journey.

If you're a product/project team, Scrum is the place to start. Especially if you're new to Agile, or if you have a mix of Agile understanding in your team members.

Scrum is simple to pick up because the framework gives you everything you need to get started. Plus, once you begin to master some of the basics of Scrum, it's easy to add practices which enhance your agility.

This is the path that we will follow in this book, in it we will give clear guidance on how to build up our team's practice of Scrum.

What follows in this section is a commentary on the three methods we've just overviewed where we took a quick look at the similarities and differences.

Designed for small teams

All of the Agile frameworks described in this chapter are designed for use by small teams. For Kanban, there is no prescribed team size, but if clear communication and coordination among team members is needed, then keeping the team size small is desirable.

 An Agile team's ideal size is often referred to as a two-pizza team, that is, the team is just big enough that two pizzas would be enough to feed it. This obviously depends on the size of the pizza!

They don't include product discovery phases

The other thing you'll notice about each of these frameworks is they don't explicitly define phases for product discovery/ideation. Few Agile methods do, DSDM being the standout. Instead, most prefer the team to manage this themselves. There are a number of techniques for doing so, including Design Thinking, User Story Mapping, and Impact Mapping. We'll discuss these techniques later in the book in Chapter 10, *Using Product Roadmaps to Guide Software Delivery*.

Not all frameworks prescribe technical practices

Scrum, for example, doesn't specify technical practices. It's rumored that it did initially, to make the framework more effective, but Ken and Jeff pulled them before formally announcing it.

As a result around 10% of Scrum teams, according to VersionOne's *11th Annual State of Agile Report*, incorporate some or all of the technical practices from Extreme Programming (XP).

There are similarities with subtle differences

Scrum and XP both explicitly involve the customer, Scrum with the Product Owner role, XP with the customer/business representative on the team. Lean Software Development emphasizes people are at its heart.

Scrum doesn't explicitly mention release planning, it assumes that the Product Owner will manage the backlog and the items nearest the top of the backlog are the ones of most value to the team. It assumes that the Product Owner will manage the backlog and the items nearest the top of the backlog are the ones of most value to the team.

Scrum and XP form batches of work using iterations. The following figure shows the Sprint Backlog—this is the batch in Scrum:

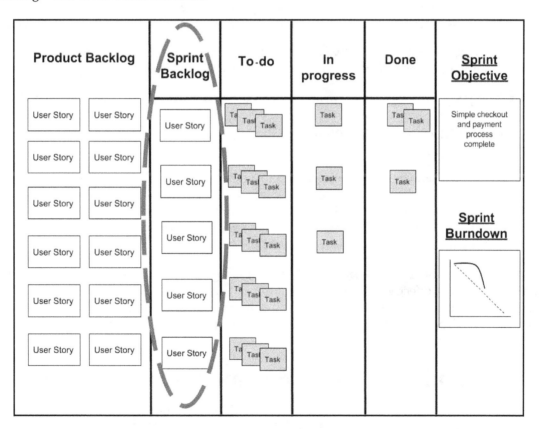

XP encourages its practitioners to err towards the smallest iteration possible. This stimulates incremental delivery thinking and moves teams away from the pitfalls of a mini-waterfall, where you execute a User Story in a series of handoffs just as you would a waterfall project.

Kanban doesn't make use of iterations to batch work. Instead, it focuses on flow; achieved by keeping each work item as small as possible and by limiting the work in progress so that people can focus on one task at a time.

It is designed to work with your existing process, and because of its value-driven mindset, it will start to shift the Development Team's thinking towards delivering something sooner rather than later.

The advantage of using Kanban at a more granular level, work item versus iteration, means that we can be even more adaptive and responsive to change. However, with great power comes great responsibility, and the Kanban approach does require more attention to detail.

For example, to remain this adaptive requires that the customer and team have an innate understanding of the overall objective and whether they are currently tracking towards it.

I often hear people discussing where and when you should use Scrum versus Kanban. For example, because of Scrum's history in product development, it seems the logical choice when developing a new software product or making significant enhancements to an existing one.

For most people, Kanban seems better suited to a more ad hoc backlog, where there is typically little or no coherency between work items. This is often the case when the product is in maintenance mode (some would call this BAU or business as usual). However, we shouldn't let Kanban's apparent simplicity fool us; of the two approaches, Scrum and Kanban, Kanban is probably the more nuanced.

As we'll see in Chapter 8, *Tightening Feedback Loops in the Software Development Life Cycle*, it can be used just as effectively as Scrum to build products, if not more so. Applying Lean thinking to product development increases flow and works particularly well when the top portion of the Product Backlog is prioritized and well defined.

Mixing and matching Agile methods

As we've seen in this chapter, there are a lot of similarities between Scrum, XP, and Kanban. No matter where we start as a team, most will start to combine the practices and thinking of one or more of these methods.

Sometimes we do it without realizing, for example, XP's User Stories have become a universally accepted way to gather Agile requirements. Sometimes we do it explicitly because we want to enhance our Agile adoption with the benefits of a particular practice. An example is when Scrum teams enhance their workflow using Lean principles, something we'll discuss in Chapter 8, *Tightening Feedback Loops in the Software Development Life Cycle*.

When we look at the practices that each method presents, we see a spectrum form. At one end of the spectrum, we have Kanban, a simple but nuanced approach for making work visible and then improving our workflow. At the other end, we have XP, where years of practical experience led the founders of that movement to insist on following a specific, disciplined approach.

XP can be too extreme for some as there are a lot of practices to adopt. This is why in his 2nd Edition book *Extreme Programming Explained*, Kent Beck re-categorized some of those disciplines as primary (ones we can introduce immediately) and others as a corollary (ones that we introduce later when we better understand the context for them).

Lean Software Development and Kanban could be seen as too light—just do what you're doing now, but make it visible and seek to improve it by continuously eliminating waste in our process. Sounds simple, but understanding and optimizing our system isn't as easy as it sounds and requires much practice.

Scrum can be seen as somewhere in the middle. It provides enough of a framework for people to start their journey to becoming great inspectors and adaptors. At the same time, it holds back from prescribing a huge change in technical practices that may cause change phobia.

So, start with Scrum and get used to incremental delivery. Then begin to apply good disciplines that bake quality in from the beginning rather than test for quality later. Do this by conducting a number of experiments to see what works for you in your context. We'll look at how can do this in Chapter 7, *Software Technical Practices are the Foundation of Incremental Software Delivery*.

One final thought, we need to consider that most Agile frameworks focus on the delivery of software. Few include explicit phases, either at the beginning for the initiation of product ideas or at the end of release and deployment. We'll cover techniques for both of these phases in this book, in Chapter 10, *Using Product Roadmaps to Guide Software Delivery* and Chapter 7, *Software Technical Practices are the Foundation of Incremental Software Delivery* respectively.

Summary

The modern Agile movement is the coming together of three different timelines from the software industry's industrial heritage: Product Development, Engineering, and Lean Manufacturing.

We looked at the three most popular Agile methods, and how they represent each of these timelines.

We discussed how all three methods have a degree of crossover or similarity. For instance, Scrum encourages a high degree of transparency, and Scrum teams often communicate this using a visible workspace. This is very similar to the concept in Kanban of making work visible.

We also discussed how many companies are improving their results by mixing and matching from two or more approaches.

In the next chapter, we're going to give a practical overview of how to get our team started with Scrum.

3
Introducing Scrum to your Software Team

This chapter aims to get your new team up and running with an Agile delivery approach as quickly as possible. To do this, we'll use the Scrum framework to show how you can successfully transition a new-to-Agile team to this method of working. We'll use a pragmatic approach, based on real-world examples, offering the steps that you'll need to take.

We will cover the following topics in this chapter:

- Why Scrum is an excellent place to start
- How to efficiently transition to Scrum from Waterfall
- Visible workspaces for managing software delivery
- Measuring and reporting progress with visualization
- Removing impediments
- Managing delivery as a team sport
- The importance of team retrospectives

In the last two chapters there was a lot of theory, now; it's time for the practical guide to begin, and for the navel-gazing to stop. In this chapter, we'll look at how to get your team up and running with Scrum. We'll go through the steps you need to take for you to transition from predictive to adaptive, and from gated to iterative.

At the end of this chapter, your team should have completed its first Sprint. You'll understand that to be successful, managing the delivery of a software product has to become a team sport and not just the responsibility of one person (the person we used to call the project manager). You'll also gain a clear idea of how visible workspaces will help you achieve that. We'll also describe several ways that you can measure the team's progress during the Sprint to help keep them focused and purposeful.

Why Scrum is an excellent place to start

Scrum is a lightweight framework that provides the necessary mechanisms to get your team's mindset focused on the essential aspects of Agile software delivery. If you were to compare learning how to use Agile to learning to ride a bike, then Scrum could be seen as the training wheels that get us moving forward.

That's not to say that Scrum is over-simplistic; as the saying goes, it's easy to learn but will take a lifetime to master. So while Scrum provides enough of a framework to get us started, it will also set us on the path to developing an Agile mindset.

So, Scrum is a perfect place for an Agile team to start its journey. It is by far the most popular framework amongst fledgling Agile teams. This chapter aims to introduce the Scrum framework in a way that will help you to successfully transition a new-to-Agile team to this way of working.

Iterations and iteration length

Scrum is an iterative, incremental delivery process. Each iteration, or Sprint, as they are known in Scrum, lasts between a minimum of 1 week and a maximum of 4 weeks, with the preference being for as short as possible. Shorter iteration lengths are what give our team its agility, as we get feedback at the end of each iteration; the sooner we get feedback, the faster we can adapt our approach.

If your team is new to working iteratively, there's no denying that it will feel odd at first. Based on experience, my recommendation is that your team picks an iteration length that feels slightly shorter than comfortable. Taking this approach will give your team an opportunity to improve their process so that it fits the iterative style, and challenges them to change up their thinking.

What this means is, if you think 4 weeks is comfortable in which to deliver a working increment, choose 2-week iterations. If you believe that 2 weeks would be more than comfortable, opt for 1-week iterations.

The Scrum team should fix the iteration length, so pick an iteration length and stick to it. If after six iterations it isn't getting easier, then perhaps change the iteration length. Remember, the preference is always for the shortest iteration length possible.

 Most teams I've worked with will opt for a 2-week Sprint, with teams occasionally choosing a 1-week Sprint if they feel they can achieve something meaningful in that time. It does depend on the context, but in general, my experience has been that 4 weeks is too long to wait for feedback.

Starting a new Scrum team

A word about time-boxes before we start: all Scrum events are time-boxed. For those that are formally part of the Scrum framework, their time-box recommendations are in the `Scrum Guide` (`https://www.scrumguides.org`).

All other activities or events that we introduce, such as Product Backlog refinement, should also be time-boxed. For these time-boxes, the facilitator of the event should estimate how long they think they need. They declare the time-box at the beginning of the event as part of the setup.

If you hit the time-box and you still have work to do, you can ask the team what they would like to do. Should they carry on, and if so, for how long? Should they reconvene at another time, perhaps?

Remember, meeting fatigue is a real thing, and people may have other commitments. Finding out if they can commit more time to extending the time-box is only polite, plus it's also an opportunity to sense the feeling in the room. If the energy is low, it may be worth taking a break.

Prerequisites

To kick off a Scrum team, you'll need a few items:

- **A timer**: This is used for time-boxing meetings; most smartphones have one of these
- **Whiteboard or wall space**: This will be used to create your visible workspace
- **Tape for marking columns or swim lanes**: If you're using a whiteboard, electrical tape works well; if you're using a painted wall, you'll need to use low tack tape, such as masking tape
- **Index cards**: These are for writing User Stories
- **post-it notes**: These are for writing User Story tasks

If you're putting post-its straight onto a wall, not a whiteboard, buy the post-it® Super Sticky variety. They have much more sticking power, and will save you from having to pick post-its off the floor and trying to figure out where they came from.

- **Black sharpie pens (fine tip)**: These are used for writing User Stories and tasks
- **Planning poker cards**: These are used for estimating User Stories

For those moments when you don't have a spare whiteboard but need to write for the whole team to see, use a post-it® 559 Super Sticky Easel Pad. These are sticky too, so they can be torn off the pad and stuck to a spare wall or window. And no, I don't have shares in 3M (the makers of post-its), but perhaps all Scrum Masters should.

The previous suggestions form a basic Agile toolkit, which each Scrum Master should have. I keep my own toolkit in a clear plastic fishing tackle box.

Preparing to Sprint

Before we start our first Sprint, we'll need to do a little housekeeping first. The primary focus is to make sure we have everything set up for the first Sprint Planning session.

The following activities are set up for team participation. Involving the whole team is the first step in creating a shared understanding and ownership of the product we're building.

Also include stakeholders for a well-rounded picture. Including those with a vested interest in your product will enable you to get their input from the beginning, starting the relationship as you mean to go on.

Here are the pre-requisites for carrying out this series of activities:

- **What you'll need**: Index cards or A5 paper, post-it notes, black sharpie pens
- **Setup**: A large table to work on that the whole team can fit around
- **Remember**: Set a time-box before you start

We begin by first making sure that our Product Backlog is in order, which we'll do using the following activity.

Activity – defining the Product Backlog

One of the hardest parts of our transition to an incremental delivery approach is breaking down our team mission (the problem we're being asked to solve) into manageable chunks of work that will deliver working software.

Fortunately, there are several techniques for creating a backlog from scratch; these include User Story mapping and impact mapping. Both focus on maximizing the value we deliver to our customer.

We'll go into more detail about both of these techniques later in Chapter 10, *Using Product Roadmaps to Guide Software Delivery*, and we'll discuss User Stories in detail in Chapter 4, *Gathering Agile User Requirements*. For now, we'll assume the Product Owner has already created a set of User Stories for us to release, plan, and refine.

Have the User Stories written out on index cards, one User Story per index card. If you're using an online tool like Jira, print each User Story on a sheet of A5 paper.

Having a physical backlog in the form of a deck of index cards has several benefits:

- It allows you to lay out the backlog easily to see the bigger picture
- It's tactile; something you can touch, pick up and examine, or easily move
- By shuffling the order, you can create multiple planning scenarios
- You can easily stick the stories on your Scrum Board, and turn them into a key part of your visible workspace

- Throwing the completed User's Stories in a cardboard box at the end of a Sprint and watching that pile of *done* stories grow iteration after iteration is very rewarding

Activity – release planning

Simply put, release planning is a process in which we determine what order we should implement the User Stories from the Product Backlog. Remember that our aim is to create *customer satisfaction through early and continuous software delivery*, the first Agile principle. When creating a Product Backlog, it's easy for it to become a bit of wish list. Blue-sky thinking happens as part of any requirements gathering process, regardless of the technique used.

Release planning allows us to prioritize the User Stories; the aim of prioritizing a Product Backlog is to surface the stories that will bring the most value and satisfaction to our customer first.

It's entirely plausible that your Product Owner has already prioritized their User Stories. If not, the following are a couple of ways that the team can prioritize the backlog together.

If you do choose to prioritize as a team, who should be present? Well, you'll need your Product Owner. If the Product Owner would like to include key stakeholders, you should include them. Finally, I would recommend including the entire team. I'm always surprised by the amount of information about a product that surfaces during release planning, and your team will benefit hugely from hearing it.

The following activity is a group approach to prioritizing User Stories:

Activity: MoSCoW
What you'll need: The Product Backlog deck, post-it notes, black sharpie pens, and Spare index cards
Setup: A large table to work on that the whole team can fit around
Remember: Set a time-box before you start

MoSCoW is a simple but effective way to prioritize the backlog based on business value and risk. It is an acronym that stands for:
M: *Must* have this
S: *Should* have this, if at all possible
C: *Could* have this if it does not affect anything else
W: *Won't* have this time, but would like to in the future

The lowercase "**o**"s are needed to make the acronym pronounceable. If it weren't pronounceable, it wouldn't be an acronym, it would just be an initialization.

The *Must* User Stories are non-negotiable—if you don't deliver them, then the product won't work and it will be a failure. It's nice to have features classified as either *Should* or *Could*. The *Won't* classification doesn't mean that you won't ever build this functionality, it just means it won't be part of the first release.

The simplest way to play MoSCoW is to set up the table in the following way:

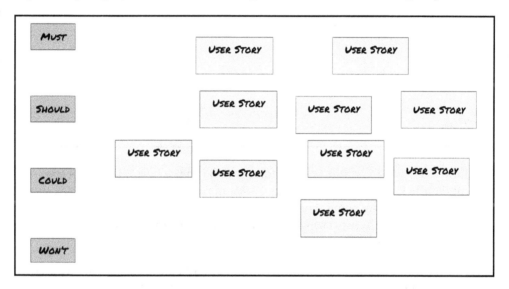

Follow these steps to release plan and prioritize the backlog:

1. Lay all of the User Story cards out on the table and give people time to familiarize themselves with the User Stories. Set a time-box appropriate to the number of stories. This step can be fairly social, people may share stories, or even read them aloud.

2. Next we prioritize the stories, you should ask people to silently work and move the User Stories into the categories they think are the most relevant. Again, set a time-box for this.

Some stories will get moved and then moved again. Most stories will end up in the *Must* category to start with, and the table will likely look as follows:

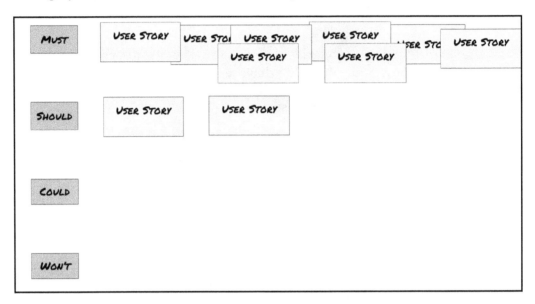

If this situation does arise, remind people that this isn't in the best interests of the product's development. While User Stories marked as *Won't* may be equally important as those in the *Must* category, deferring some work allows the team to get on with other features sooner. To help this thought process, you need to think about which features might deliver the most business value or will reduce risk and uncertainty the quickest.

Ask the team which User Stories in the *Must* category can be moved down while still producing a coherent first release. Ask for suggestions of which stories you definitely *Won't* need, and then place them in *Won't*. Remind people that this is just for the *first* release.

After two or three iterations, you should see something like this:

MUST	USER STORY	USER STORY	USER STORY	USER STORY
SHOULD	USER STORY	USER STORY	USER STORY	
COULD	USER STORY			
WON'T	USER STORY	USER STORY		

Take the opportunity to review the User Stories and make sure you have a coherent set of stories for the *Must* swim lane. If it helps, order the stories from left to right in their logical sequence. The User Stories in the *Must* swim lane are your first release. While this won't necessarily represent a complete set of features, once built, it will give you enough to gather good feedback from your customer, and as such, will act as the beginning of your product's life cycle.

 You'll almost certainly identify additional stories during this stage, so it's important to have extra index cards and sharpies nearby.

Another fun way for the team to work is with *Buy a Feature*. Buy a Feature is a game where team members are each given a certain amount of money. You start by pricing all of the features, making sure that some are more expensive than one person can afford, and only a group can purchase them.

The object of the game is to decide as a team which features you deem most important for your product and need to buy. To do this, you have to collaborate and pool your resources. This game and how to play it is detailed in Luke Hohmann's book, *Innovation Games*.

Activity – introducing the Product Backlog

The first step in this activity is used to familiarize your team with the Product Backlog:

Activity: Introducing the Product Backlog
What you'll need: User Stories written on index cards or printed, post-it notes, and black sharpie pens
Setup: A large table that the whole team can fit comfortably around
Remember: Set a time-box before this activity starts

The first step in this two-part activity involves your Scrum team sitting around the table. Your Product Owner has the Product Backlog; they pass it to the team member on their right. That team member takes the top story and reads it aloud, including the acceptance criteria and any notes.

They then place it in the center of the table so that other team members can read it, ask questions, and discuss the acceptance criteria. You should make any refinements to the story, usually in the form of pencil or post-it note additions.

Once the discussion is complete, the User Story will remain on the table, and the Product Backlog is passed right to the next team member, and the process is repeated.

This activity completes when either the backlog has been worked through or the time-box is over—whichever comes first.

 As a general rule of thumb, it does help if your Development Team has seen the User Stories before they have to consider them during Sprint Planning. Giving your team chance to digest what needs to be done to achieve the User Story will give them greater confidence when planning.

Activity – estimating User Stories on the backlog

The second step in this activity is to estimate the stories on the backlog.

Activity: Using estimate buckets to size User Stories
What you'll need: User Stories written on index cards or printed, post-it notes, and black sharpie pens
Setup: A large table that the whole team can fit comfortably around
Remember: Set a time-box before this activity starts

Once you've had the chance to review the backlog, the second step is for you to refine the User Stories further.

A good place to start any refinement is to try to estimate the stories. When you ask for an estimate, it immediately triggers the thought process, "what do we need to do to complete this story?"

The ensuing conversation from your team will give a good indication if the objective of the User Story is clear and the acceptance criteria are well-defined. If they aren't, you won't be able to estimate the User Story and the team will need to go through a series of refinements with the Product Owner before they are ready to try to estimate again.

Bearing that in mind, and also taking into consideration that not everyone has used relative sizing before, we'll take the following approach:

We'll use a system based on t-shirt sizes: XS, S, M, L, and XL. It's OK; we can translate these to another system, such as Story Points, if we want to at a later stage. In this case, t-shirt sizes make the most sense when starting out with relative sizing.

Lay out the table as follows with a column for each t-shirt size:

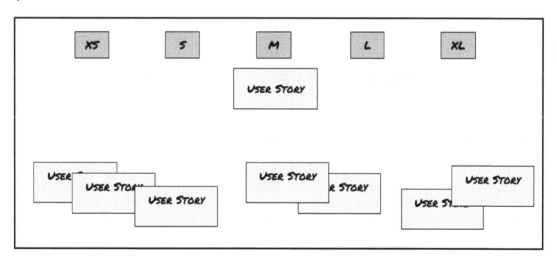

Spread the stories out on the table and take the time to read them and ask questions if necessary. You may refine the User Story or add acceptance criteria at this stage if you wish. The key thing that we're trying to achieve at this juncture is to identify a story which is either small (**S**), medium (**M**), or extra-large (**XL**). Once we've identified the story we think is a good example of one of those sizes, we place it on the table in the appropriate column.

In the preceding example diagram, our team has chosen an example of a "medium" sized story and have placed it in the medium (**M**) column.

Remember that at this stage, it's not important to be exactly right; it's just good to start somewhere.

The next step is to take another User Story from the unsized pile and compare it to one of the stories you've already sized. We should ask ourselves the following:

1. Is it double the effort or more of the already sized story?
2. Is it half the effort or less of the sized story?
3. Is it a similar effort?

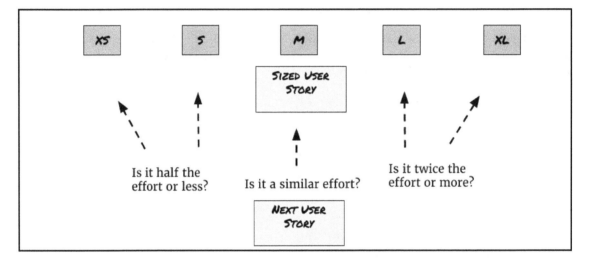

Our team places the story in the appropriate column relative to the already-sized story. You then pick the next story and compare it to the already-sized stories. You decide if it's bigger, smaller, or similarly sized to the currently placed stories. You then put it in the column that's most appropriate and pick the next story card and repeat the process.

Eventually, you will end up with all the stories placed in columns in a similar way to the following diagram:

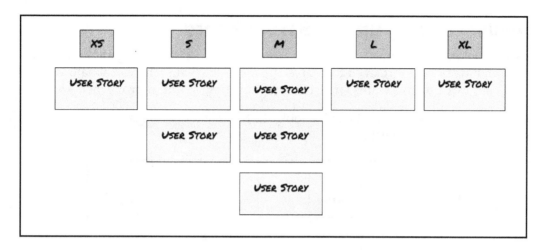

At this point, you should take a step back to admire your work and to decide if you've got it more or less right. Remember that relative sizing is less about precision and more about gut instinct, and most importantly, it's about team agreement.

Once your team is happy with the relative sizing of each story, write its size on the story card in the bottom right-hand corner, as per the following example:

We'll discuss relative sizing in more detail in Chapter 4, *Gathering Agile User Requirements*.

Activity – setting up the Scrum Board

The Scrum Board is the team's information radiator. It enables them to communicate Sprint status with little or no effort, even to people outside of the team. The visual nature of the Scrum Board can also give teams an insight into how they might improve their approach.

We'll initially set up our Scrum Board to look like the following image (using the appropriate tape for your surface):

Product Backlog	Sprint Backlog	To do	In progress	Done	Sprint Objective
					Sprint Burndown

Make sure that you leave enough space in each column regarding width and height. It may be a good idea to use actual index or story cards and post-it notes to make sure you have enough room.

Once in use, the board will look something like this:

Product Backlog		Sprint Backlog	To do	In progress	Done	Sprint Objective
User Story	User Story	User Story	Ta Tas Task	Task	Tas Task	Simple checkout and payment process complete
User Story	User Story	User Story	Ta Tas Task	Task	Task	
User Story	User Story	User Story	Ta Tas Task	Task		**Sprint Burndown**
User Story	User Story	User Story	Ta Tas Task			
User Story	User Story	User Story	Ta Tas Task			
User Story	User Story	User Story	Ta Tas Task			

Discussion – Sprint Zero

At the beginning of a new piece of work, some teams will choose to run a Sprint that focuses purely on setup first. These can include anything from the Scrum Board through to source code repositories, Wikis to staging, and even production deployment pipelines.

This Sprint is often called Sprint Zero, although it is not officially recognized or sanctioned by the Scrum guide. Sprint Zero does deviate from the Agile Manifesto in that it delivers little or no working software at the end of it.

It's also not uncommon for teams to try to expand the Sprint Zero well beyond the usual iteration length—5 to 6 weeks isn't uncommon. This is a sign that the transition from a Waterfall-style delivery to an incremental one is too difficult for some to make.

As a coach with experience, this feels like procrastination. Sprint Zeroes can be used by teams as an excuse not to transition to an Agile approach, but instead stay comfortable with what they know. In this case, procrastination is a form of applied anxiety.

The one thing that I can honestly say is that if we always stick with what we know, we may never discover if the alternative is better.

It's important that we experiment and are not afraid to fail. Scrum is an empirical process, so 'failing' is more of a discovery of what works and what doesn't!

Instead of using Sprint Zero, treat the tooling and infrastructure that you need to set up just as you would each feature: deliver it incrementally. You can do this either as part of each feature, by looking for User Story candidates in which you can include infrastructure setup, or by defining small User Stories that can be interwoven into your Product Backlog alongside feature delivery.

For instance, the first User Story will likely include setting up the source code repository and creating an initial deployment pipeline to a staging environment. Subsequent User Stories will likely include logging and enhancing the deployment pipeline to point to a production environment, and so on.

If you treat your infrastructure setup as you do your feature delivery, you can maintain maximum flexibility by delivering just enough to move forward. To avoid making assumptions, we need to solve the problems we have now, not the problems we don't have yet.

Day one of the Sprint

Now that we have our backlog in order and our Scrum Board set up, we're ready to start our first Sprint. This leads us to our first event of each iteration cycle: Sprint Planning.

Event – Sprint Planning

For Sprint Planning, you'll need the following:

What you'll need: The Product Backlog, post-it notes, and black sharpie pens.
Setup: A large table that the whole Scrum team can fit comfortably around.
Time-box: A maximum of 8 hours for a 1-month Sprint; for shorter Sprints, the event is usually shorter. For a 2-week Sprint, a maximum of 4 hours should be sufficient.

There are two questions essential to Sprint Planning. The first is, "what are we able to achieve in this Sprint?" and the second is, "how will we achieve it?".

What can we achieve in this Sprint?

During this first phase of Sprint Planning, we focus on what we think we can complete in the coming Sprint. It is a forecast by our Development Team that determines which User Stories can be included in this Sprint Backlog. The Product Owner and the Scrum Master aren't allowed to participate in the forecast as such, but they will be advising the team on User Story details and what their priorities are.

Starting with the backlog in priority order, and in a similar way to Product Backlog refinement, present the first story card to your team. The story card should be read aloud and then placed in the center of the table. Your Development Team should then decide if the User Story is achievable as part of this Sprint.

You should continue selecting story cards from the top of the backlog, reading them out and placing them in them on the Sprint Backlog until your Development Team think they won't be able to achieve any more in this Sprint.

At the end of this stage, you will have a line of User Stories sitting in the middle of the table, ordered from top to bottom in priority order.

How will we achieve it?

During the second phase of Sprint Planning, the aim is for the Development Team to determine how they will complete their Sprint Backlog.

Starting at the top of the Sprint Backlog, you should consider how you will implement the User Story. To do this, use post-its and sharpies and break down the User Story into tasks. A lively discussion among your Development Team should ensue as you discuss how to implement this User Story. Write each task on a post-it note. Attach all tasks to the story.

Once one User Story is complete, select the next story from the top of the Sprint Backlog and do the same.

You should consider the **Definition of Done** (**DoD**) as you perform the task breakdown. You don't need to explicitly state items on the DoD as tasks. Instead, you should post the DoD on your Scrum Board so that your team can reference it and ensure they're following it as they implement the Sprint Backlog.

This phase is complete when the team has broken down all the stories into tasks. Your Scrum Master should count the total number of tasks so that they can create the Sprint Burndown chart.

 Sprint Burndown tracks the number of tasks remaining. After each Daily Scrum, the Scrum Master should count the tasks remaining and update the Sprint Burndown. Don't be alarmed if it tracks up before it tracks down; we often discover new information when we start working on a User Story, and so new tasks will inevitably be added.

The Sprint Goal

The final step is for your Product Owner to define the Sprint Goal, an overarching objective that can be met by the Development Team that should provide them with guidance on why they are building the next increment.

It should be a short statement, such as, *"Implement a simple checkout that allows credit cardholders to purchase items in their cart"*.

 Try to keep your Sprint Goal concise, as this will help your team focus on building the right thing. The Sprint Goal should help you decide if our work is contributing to the outcome your Product Owner is seeking. One thing it should not be is a "laundry list" of work, or even a list of User Stories that your team needs to complete.

Event – first Daily Scrum

The Daily Scrum is a time-boxed meeting which lasts 15 minutes. Following the tradition of Extreme Programmers (XP), most Scrum teams stand for the duration. Standing helps keep the meeting short and to the point because you're less likely to chat.

Here, your team gathers around the Scrum Board, as shown in the following figure:

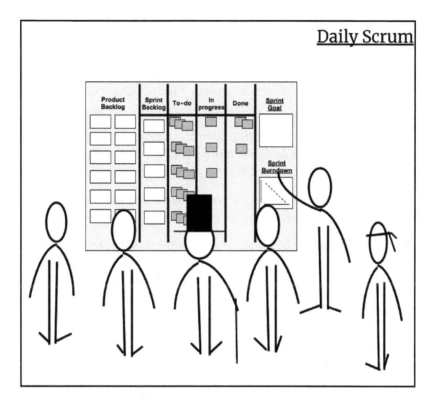

Each Development Team member takes it in turns to answer the following three questions:

- What did I do yesterday that helped the Development Team meet the Sprint Goal?
- What will I do today to help the Development Team meet the Sprint Goal?
- Do I see any impediment that prevents the Development Team, or myself, from meeting the Sprint Goal?

One way for a team member to communicate what they are working on is for them to stand next to the board and point to the User Story or task.

For the very first Daily Scrum, you probably won't need the first question, unless you've already started work on meeting the Sprint Goal.

In the first Daily Scrum, you should be more focused on who is going to work on what, and ultimately how the team will work on things together.

The Scrum Master should keep an eye on the time-box, as its possible the 15 minutes will pass by without notice.

It's worth getting into the habit of taking it in turns to answer the three questions, listen to any updates or feedback from the Scrum Master or Product Owner, and then recognize that the Daily Scrum is officially over.

The Scrum Master should update the Sprint Burndown chart, which measures the total number of tasks left to complete. We'll talk more about the Sprint Burndown in `Chapter 6`, *Metrics that will Help your Software Team Deliver*.

You can then have any breakout sessions, where two or more team members may get together to discuss issues in more detail.

 Some teams call the breakout session after the Daily Scrum the "after party". Some teams even go as far as recording what needs to discussed at the "after party" by making notes during the standup. For examples of this and other visualization ideas, see Jimmy Janlen's book, *Toolbox for the Agile Coach - Visualisation Examples, Leanpub*.

A day in the life of a Scrum team

Each day at the specified time, the team meets at the Scrum Board for the Daily Scrum. Once the Daily Scrum is complete, the team may then catch up with each other to discuss certain work items in more detail, or perhaps to demonstrate the work completed so far to the Product Owner to see if it's heading in the right direction.

Working as a Scrum team requires a coordinated effort that will often extend beyond the Daily Scrum. It's not often that team members operate in isolation from one another. Co-locating your team means you can pick up from the environment how others are progressing, even if people are working individually on a task.

You'll often find Scrum team members completing work before the next Daily Scrum, who will need to find another task on which they can work. If necessary, they can call an impromptu standup around the Scrum Board to discuss things with the team and make sure they are selecting the right thing to work on.

It's also important to keep focused on the Sprint Goal, and you should ask yourselves regularly how confident you feel in reaching it. You could do this as often as every day, for example, at the end of every Daily Scrum. One technique we could use for this is called **Roman Voting**, where you use your thumb to indicate your vote: either up for yes, you're confident, down for no, you're not convinced, or sideways for you're on the fence.

If the majority of team members are not feeling confident or are on the fence, then you should encourage talking as a team to determine if there is anything that can be done to improve confidence in completing the Sprint Goal.

To help determine what course of action to take, you can use visual techniques to help enhance your understanding—something we'll look at in the followings section.

Measuring and reporting progress with visualization

The Scrum Board itself gives a clear picture of how a team is tracking. It's immediately apparent which User Stories are in progress, and on which tasks the team is busy working.

It's possible for us to enhance the information that the Scrum Board radiates in ways that will make the status of the Sprint more evident, and therefore the conversation at the Daily Scrum less about the team's status and more about the work and coordinating around it.

The following subtle visual additions should allow you to reduce cognitive overload, enabling the team to focus more on the work at hand and less on managing the process around it. Of course, these are just suggestions; if you can think of any others, then by all means experiment.

Avatars

Create avatar cards to represent each team member. A picture stuck on a card backed with wall tack will work; laminating them will increase their longevity. You can then place these on a board to represent which task team members are working on, as in the following figure:

Product Backlog		Sprint Backlog	To do	In progress	Done	Sprint Objective
User Story	User Story	User Story	Task Task Task	Task	Task Task	Simple checkout and payment process complete
User Story	User Story	User Story	Task Task Task	Task	Task	

This shows that one team member is working on the third task of the first User Story. Two other team members are working the second task of the second User Story. Using avatars reduces the time taken at the Daily Scrum, as when each person talks, it's clear what they are working on.

It also helps to co-ordinate work outside of the Daily Scrum. For example, when looking for their next task, if a team member can easily see who is working on a User Story, they can co-ordinate with those team members.

Done stickers

Done stickers are simply post-it notes with the word *DONE* written on them. We place them on a User Story to show that it's done—meaning that all work is complete, including those items on the DoD. The following figure shows a 'DONE' sticker on the first User Story:

Product Backlog		Sprint Backlog	To do	In progress	Done	**Sprint Objective**
User Story	User Story	User Story DONE			Tas Task Tas Task	Simple checkout and payment process complete
User Story	User Story	User Story	Ta Tas Task	Task	Task	

Burndowns

At the end of Sprint Planning, after the team has broken down User Stories into tasks, the Scrum Master totals up the number of tasks in the Sprint Backlog. The Scrum Master then creates a Burndown chart.

The following diagram shows a Burndown for a Sprint already in progress:

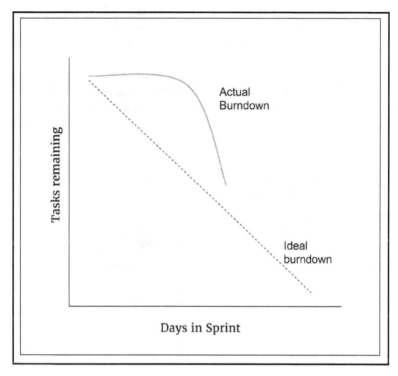

The *y*-axis represents the total number of tasks. The *x*-axis represents the number of days in the Sprint.

The red line on the following Sprint Burndown chart represents the number of tasks left to complete.

The dotted line represents the **Ideal Burndown** rate in order to complete all tasks by the end of the Sprint; as you can see in the preceding figure, the red line (the **Actual Burndown**) hasn't decreased in the way we expected.

In this case, the **Actual Burndown** shows that new tasks were discovered when the team began working on a User Story, and so the total number of tasks has increased. It is not unusual to uncover new information once work commences.

Sprint Goal confidence

In the previous section, we looked at how to run the first Daily Scrum event. We discussed that a Daily Scrum was a good place for a team to review if they felt they could still meet the Sprint Goal by the end of the Sprint. We used Roman Voting to express our level of confidence.

The following figure shows thumb icons on the Sprint Goal; we've used them to record each team member's vote so that we can see from Scrum-to-Scrum how things are changing. We can use this to decide if we need to do anything to improve the process. For example, if there is a sudden drop in confidence, perhaps it's worth re-planning the approach to completing the Sprint Goal:

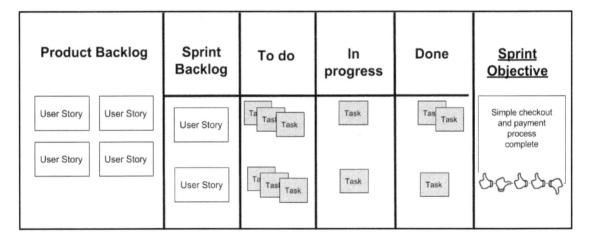

 Thumb icon in the preceding image designed by Freepik from www.flaticon.com.

The importance of visible workspaces

Making work visible in the form of a Scrum Board is one of the most empowering features of Scrum.

We often call visible workspaces *information radiators* because they radiate information to anyone within sight of them, as shown in the following figure:

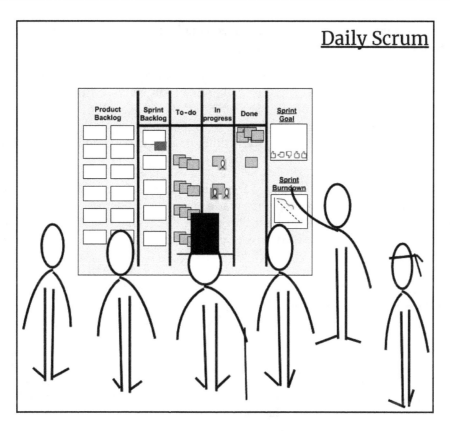

Scrum Boards enable several things to happen:

1. A visible workspace allows a team to debug its process like never before. A team can stand back and take in a complete picture of a Sprint's progress. If you're new to Agile, this gives you information that you've never had before. The visible nature of the work in progress enables you to make better decisions. It's not uncommon to see Scrum teams gathered around the board outside of the Daily Scrum, assessing the state of play and deciding what to do.

2. Stakeholders can also easily assess the work in progress by visiting the Scrum Board. This results in fewer interruptions to the Scrum team.

3. Transparency leads to easier risk management. At a glance, you can determine if an item in progress is blocked and needs assistance, and from the wider perspective, if you're likely to meet the Sprint Goal.

In a non-Agile environment, this information is usually kept online in a project planning tool or spreadsheet, making it less visible.

Online tools can be useful, especially when used for tracking trends over time or when people work remotely. However, we often call online tools, such as Jira, PivotalTracker, Rally, or Trello (to name a few), *information refrigerators* because although they store information well, it's hard to see. You have to go to the fridge, open the door, and poke around. Often, the thing you're looking for is down the back, covered in ice and hard to spot.

The tools that enable you to do this easily are your visible workspaces; in other words, your Scrum Board and your work which is made visible on it. Using the Scrum Board, you can easily track the progress of your User Stories and their related tasks. The completion of a task also feeds into your Sprint Burndown, giving you an idea of how close you are to completion.

We'll look at Sprint Burndown charts and other metrics in more detail in `Chapter 6`, *Metrics that will Help your Software Team Deliver*.

Removing impediments

Part of the Scrum Master's role is to remove any impediments that are in the way of the team carrying out their work. It's sometimes hard for team members, particularly those new to Scrum, to recognize what is and what isn't an impediment.

For example, if you're waiting for your operations team to set up a staging environment for us to perform user acceptance testing and everything else has been done to this point, then this is impeding the completion of this work.

However, the team might not view this as a problem because it's just the way things have always been done. The Scrum Master has to start to develop a nose for this stuff in order to *smell* real impediments.

 We use the term *smells* as a metaphor because, just as in real life, the cause of a smell isn't always what we think it is. Using the term 'smell' allows us to sniff out a potential problem without jumping to conclusions or laying blame. If our nose turns out be correct, we can help our team avoid any nasty bumps in the road. If we're wrong, then it's better safe than sorry.

Bad smells for a Scrum Master include, but aren't limited to:

- A team member talking about something they're working on that isn't visible on the Scrum Board
- A team member not speaking at the Daily Scrum
- A small task that should have only taken hours hasn't made any progress in a day or longer
- The Sprint Burndown is tracking to target—normally, a Sprint Burndown tracks up before it tracks down; new tasks are often added when work on a User Story commences, so if the Sprint Burndown is tracking exactly to the expected burndown rate, something fishy is happening.

Managing delivery as a team sport

When transitioning to Scrum, you may notice that you'll be better able to manage your workload. When you think about it, this makes much more sense; the people who are actually doing the work are the people best placed to understand its progress and value.

When a team forecasts User Stories to be completed during Sprint Planning to create the Sprint Backlog, they're setting up an informal commitment with a Product Owner. Here, we're saying that we will complete this work on the provision that:

1. The Sprint Backlog remains fixed; there are no sudden changes such as altering priorities or swapping out stories.
2. We're given the time, freedom, and space to work.

If we're able to reduce interruptions coming into our Development Team as much as possible, it allows us to focus on what we need to do. Instead of asking a Development Team member to do something "urgently", an urgent task can be placed at the top of the Product Backlog, where it will be picked up in the next Sprint.

Giving a team this latitude within the Sprint boundary means that they will become better at self-management. In fact, they're much more likely to complete the work and achieve the Sprint Goal if they're allowed to determine how to best organize themselves.

Another factor to consider in the successful self-organization of a team is subtle control. For a Scrum team, decisions on what to build ultimately stop with the Product Owner, and these decisions are influenced rather than directed by the wider stakeholder group.

The last day of the Sprint

We will now conclude the Sprint with two events: the Sprint Review, followed by a Sprint Retrospective. Both of these events give us the opportunity to inspect and adapt the work we've carried out during the Sprint.

We always hold the review first because the conversation there is likely to spark further discussions and raise action points at the retrospective.

In the following two sections, we will describe how to set each event up and what to expect.

Event – Sprint Review

The Sprint Review's focus is on the increment of working software that has just been built and how successful the Sprint has been in moving the product's progress forward.

This is how you set it up:

What you'll need: A large screen to demonstrate your working software, the User Stories you've completed, the User Stories you didn't complete, the Sprint Goal, index cards, sharpies, and post-it notes
Setup: A large table that the whole team can fit comfortably around with a view of the screen
Attendees: The Scrum team and stakeholders
Time-box: 4 hours for 1-month Sprints; for shorter Sprints, the event is usually shorter

The central focus of the Sprint Review is for your team to demonstrate the working software they've built as part of the Sprint. They should decide upfront which member of the Development Team is going to show the working software. You may decide that it will be a group effort, in which case, you should decide which team members will show which of the completed User Stories.

The basic flow for the Sprint Review should be along the following lines:

1. The team member who is demonstrating the first complete story reads out the story card, including the acceptance criteria.
2. They then demonstrate the software and explain how it meets the acceptance criteria.
3. They then ask for any questions or observations.
4. The team member who is demonstrating the next complete User Story takes that story card and repeats the process.

The Sprint Review is an opportunity for you to engage your stakeholder group and gather feedback on whether the product is moving in the right direction. Of course, your Scrum Master and Product Owner should be able to recognize that this is the first Sprint and that the software you've delivered won't necessarily show a complete set of features.

Once all complete stories are demonstrated, the Sprint Goal should be read out by the Product Owner, and the team should discuss and review whether they've achieved all, part, or any of it.

The final part of the Sprint Review is to open the room to any questions or observations. For example, the invited stakeholders may be interested to hear what the team has planned next. They may also be keen to offer feedback about the direction the team is moving in, or even suggest changes or a new direction. This feedback is likely to be incorporated into existing User Stories or may even create new User Stories.

The worst case scenario during a Sprint Review is that there is no working software to demonstrate, which can happen if a team hasn't completed any User Stories or if the working software is hit with technical difficulties. If this happens, the team should move directly to the Sprint Retrospective.

Take time to prepare for Sprint Review. It is a demonstration of working software, so the last thing you want is a case of non-working software. Make sure that you've got a working demo before you start. Unfortunately, I've seen Sprint Reviews cancelled on a couple of occasions because the team failed to get their software working. In these instances, there was a room full of stakeholders who left dissatisfied.

Event – Sprint Retrospective

The Sprint Retrospective is an opportunity for the team to reflect on their first Sprint. You should look at what went well, what didn't go so well, and what can be improved.

This is how you set it up:

What you'll need: post-it notes, black sharpie pens, and a whiteboard
Setup: A large table that the whole team can fit comfortably around
Attendees: The Scrum team
Time-box: 3 hours for 1-month Sprints; for shorter Sprints, the event is usually shorter

Your Scrum Master facilitates the Sprint Retrospective. There is a degree of preparation required to run a retrospective, and so we recommend heeding the following format:

- **Setting the stage**: The Scrum Master presents some facts and figures from the last Sprint. They should aim to paint a picture of what happened. Did the team meet its Sprint Goal? What was the team's velocity? How did the Sprint Burndown look?
- **Gather data**: At this stage, the team needs to collect more data about the Sprint. On the whiteboard, the Scrum Master draws quadrants for the four following categories:
    - What went well?
    - What didn't go well?
    - Ideas for change
    - Shout outs (thanking team members for their work)

Using post-it notes and a sharpie, write as many post-its as you can think of (one item per post-it) that fit into either one of those four categories. The Scrum Master will keep the time-box, and the team should work silently. They can then place the post-it notes on the board as they go or wait until the time-box is up.

Once done, you should end up with something like the following:

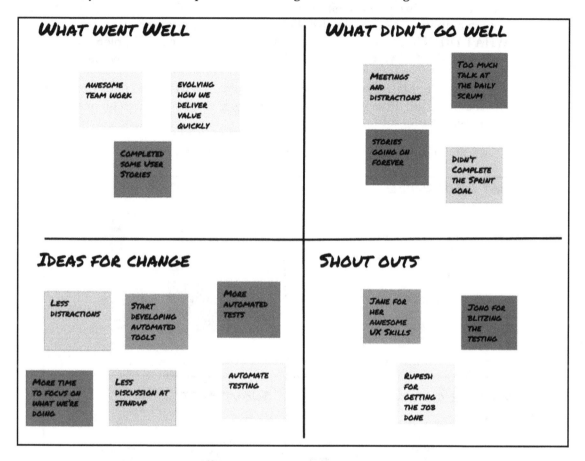

1. **Generating insights**: At this point, you should examine what everyone has written as a group. You can see, for example, that three people have mentioned automated testing in the 'Ideas' quadrant. You can also see that the team agrees that there are too many distractions (referred to in **IDEAS FOR CHANGE** and **WHAT DIDN'T GO WELL**).

2. **Decide what to do**: Next, you need to decide how to improve the next Sprint for the better. For this, you can either take an item from 'What went well' and decide how to amplify it. You could also decide how you can minimize an issue from **WHAT DIDN'T GO WELL**. You could also work out how to implement an **IDEA FOR CHANGE**. Consider the items that will generate the most value.

   The Scrum Master will ask the team to vote on what needs to be done. Team members get three votes each and each vote must be written on one post-it note.

   In the following instance, we use gold stars to vote:

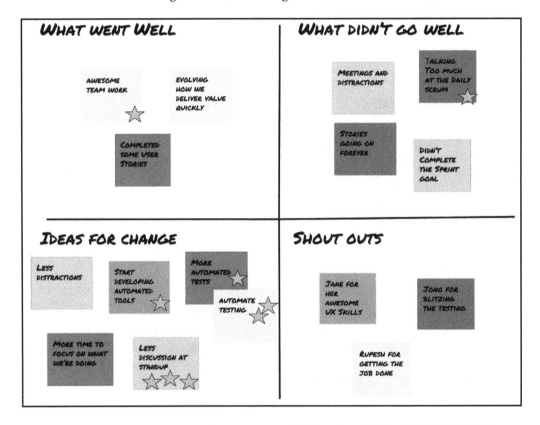

   As you can see, **AUTOMATED TESTS** and **LESS DISCUSSION AT STANDUP** get three votes each in total.

So, now it's time to create actions for each of these. Aim to take two to three actions from each retrospective, and no more. You're aiming for small incremental changes that can be introduced with each Sprint. Your goal should be to make your actions SMART: **S**mart, **M**easurable, **A**greed upon, **R**ealistic, and **T**ime-based.

Here are some suggested actions that fit the SMART approach:

- **ACTION**: Less discussion at the Daily Scrum

  WHAT: Set up an 'After Party Zone' on the Scrum Board. Any topics for discussion should be recorded there so that the team can talk about them in the After Party.

  WHO: The Scrum Master will set up the After Party Zone area on the board and record any relevant topics.

  WHEN: At subsequent Daily Scrums.

- **ACTION**: Automated testing.

  WHAT: Implement a test framework when working on the next story to facilitate learning.

  WHO: Jono and Rupesh.

  WHEN: The next Sprint.

3. **Close**: With the retrospective actions complete, the Scrum Master closes the retrospective. They ask each team member to give one sentence to describe their experience of the retrospective.

The Scrum Master will then place the retrospective action items on the team's Scrum Board to be worked on during the next Sprint.

 Descriptions of the five stages of a retrospective that have been used here, including examples of activities, can be found in an excellent book called *Agile Retrospectives: Making Good Teams Great*, by Diana Larsen and Esther Derby. This book should be part of any Agile team's toolkit.

The importance of team retrospectives

Scrum is an empirical process—we're constantly learning what works well and what doesn't work so well. Scrum requires a team to inspect and adapt its process on a regular basis. In this way, the team can continuously improve its approach, sometimes making profound changes along the way.

Retrospectives are at the heart of this mindset; they teach us to reflect and improve. Just as we would debug our software, we are now learning how to debug our process.

It's important not to accept the status quo! There's always a better, and hopefully more satisfying, way to do something.

Summary

In this chapter, we guided your team through their first Sprint. There were a lot of activities needed to get us this far, and to give us the right foundation for moving forward.

Remember that it will probably take four to six Sprints for a team to hit its rhythm. No matter how successful you are in delivering something at the end of that first Sprint, the important part is that you did it! You and your team have now successfully transitioned and can use an iterative, incremental delivery style.

Congratulations!

In the next chapter, we're going to look at how to gather Agile requirements to better support the incremental delivery of a product. See you there shortly.

4
Gathering Agile User Requirements

Working iteratively to deliver working software incrementally needs a different approach to requirement gathering. This chapter looks at the approach most commonly combined with Scrum: the User Story.

We'll start by briefly looking at why traditional requirements documents don't fit well with an incremental approach. We'll then contrast this with User Stories and how they work to solve some of those problems.

We'll then take a practical approach, using a cinema ticket booking system as an example, to gradually build up a User Story, considering the various elements that contribute to making this technique powerful.

After we've built up a good understanding of User Stories and Agile's requirements, we'll look at how to use relative sizing, an Agile alternative to estimation. We'll use a game called Planning Poker to show how estimation can be easy and fun while teasing out all the important details of what we're about to build.

This chapter covers the following topics:

- The pitfalls of traditional big upfront requirements
- Why User Stories produce better results
- What a User Story is and how to use it
- Card, conversation, confirmation
- Acceptance criteria versus the **Definition of Done (DoD)**
- Telling the team the what, not the how
- Estimating Agile user requirements

The pitfalls of traditional big upfront requirements

In `Chapter 1`, *The Software Industry and the Agile Manifesto,* we took a look at some of the issues that the software industry faced prior to the Manifesto for Agile Software Development and the formation of the Agile Alliance in 2001.

The main issues we saw were related to attempts to control projects through predictive planning, an approach which requires gathering all requirements up front so that a detailed estimate can be made to determine project costs and timelines.

Business Analysts (BAs) often write traditional requirements documents and carry out the analysis work as well, either simultaneously or as a subsequent phase.

A traditional requirements document might contain the following:

- Use case diagrams
- Sequence diagrams describing events and the flow of information
- Data models detailing data and rules
- User Experience (UX) mockups and graphic design elements to give us an indication of how particular user flows might work and look
- Paragraphs and paragraphs of text

As a result of needing to know everything upfront for planning purposes, the document itself would often run into many pages and would require a great deal of time and effort.

Large documents in general also cause something known as "irrational artifact attachment." When a change comes along, which it inevitably does, the reluctance to modify the document is proportional to the size of the investment already made versus the change. This means small changes will often be included, but larger, more fundamental changes might be sidelined until later.

Large-scale requirement gathering and analysis also tend to trigger Big Design Up Front thinking as well. The software design is carried out by an architect who will prescribe the solution, but as they often aren't the people who are going to implement the design, they don't know if it will work.

The following are a few problems that upfront thinking creates in traditional requirements documents:

- Firstly, they're quite difficult to read because technical people write them for technical people. The customer will almost certainly find themselves having to sign off on a document that has little or no meaning to them, and is therefore hard for them to translate and understand what will be delivered.

- Secondly, they often prescribe possible solutions. Prescribing a solution gives the Development Team little or no ownership of the problem; they have to interpret and follow the prescribed designs unwittingly. If they run into aspects of the problem which the design doesn't cater for, the team will find it hard to move the solution forward.

- Thirdly, it's hard to pull out individual requirements because the detail is often buried deep in the hierarchy of a large document, each requirement seemingly linked to the next. These serve to make the requirements difficult to order and prioritize.

  Requirements written in this format are also hard to prioritize because there is little or no indication of the business value. The requirements document tends to get treated like a laundry list, with people often asking for requirements that weren't necessarily important but, once in the requirements document, became as important as everything else.

- Fourthly, human languages can be ambiguous and have multiple interpretations. It was only relatively recently that we started to write things down. Before that, we passed information from generation to generation by word of mouth in the form of stories.

  When stories were handed down in this way, the storyteller was right amongst us, often using body language and actions to act out certain scenes. This is a much richer environment to be in as a communicator, as we were able to directly interact with the storyteller, ask questions, and seek clarification.

  As Mike Cohn puts it in his book *User Stories Applied*, we lost some, or all, of our shared understanding when we started to write things down. In part, this is because we assume accuracy in the written word - more so than when communicated verbally. However, language is ambiguous regardless of the medium. When the nature of storytelling changed to the written word, it became much harder to seek clarification; the author of a document is often not in the same location as you, there's certainly no interactive element as we tend to read documents in solitude, and each reader often forms their own interpretation.

All of the preceding means that large requirements documents don't lend themselves to being broken down into small tranches of work. So, even if the team implementing the design is using Scrum to try to deliver this incrementally, they are unable to negotiate priorities easily. In Agile circles, we call this **Water-Scrum-Fall**. The following figure illustrates this process:

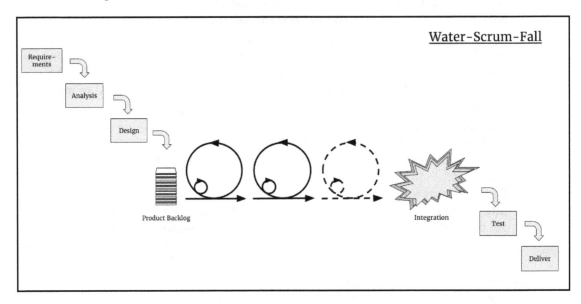

The preceding diagram shows us using waterfall upfront to gather requirements, carry out analysis, and create a design. We then implement the design iteratively, before going through a protracted integration, testing, and deployment phase. Hopefully, we've interacted enough with our customer during the iterative phase, and we've got closer to the original intention of the requirements document than if we were working in isolation. However, this approach only solves some, not all, of the problems Agile was intended to solve.

Why User Stories produce results

To avoid Big Bang integration and delivery right at the end that we get with waterfall and Water-Scrum-Fall, we have to change the way we do requirement gathering, analysis, and design. The aim of a User Story is to break requirements down into discrete chunks of work that will realize some business value in their own right. While it's not always possible to deliver a single User Story in isolation, the aim is to make them as independent as possible.

In fact, independent is the first attribute of the mnemonic INVEST, which we use when discussing the attributes of a good User Story. The letters of INVEST stand for the following:

- **Independent**: Avoid creating dependencies; if we have dependencies between User Stories, we'll create unfinished work, meaning we'll have to wait for other work to complete, before what we're working on can be delivered. This can, and will, create a house of cards as far as delivery is concerned. This is a crucial mindset shift when switching to User Stories and is important to get right.
- **Negotiable**: In this collaborative approach to building software, everything is negotiable. If the Development Team can see a better way to write the User Story or its acceptance criteria, they should negotiate with the Product Owner or vice versa.
- **Valuable**: Each story delivers value which contributes to the overall business objective. Ideally, this should be of tangible value to our customer - something they can see and use. If it doesn't have tangible value, then we're breaking one of the Agile principles: delivering working software frequently.
- **Estimable**: There is just enough information in the User Story for it to be estimated by the team. If the User Story isn't clear or well defined, the team will struggle to estimate it and it will require a conversation to get a clearer picture.
- **Small**: To give you a gauge for the correct size of a User Story, as a rule of thumb a full-size Scrum team is aiming to deliver five stories per Sprint. User Stories break requirements down into small chunks, which if done correctly can increase the flow of work and help aid prioritization, which in turn will help us deliver value sooner.
- **Testable**: Acceptance tests can be written and carried out against the acceptance criteria that tell us if the User Story is completed and the requirement is fulfilled.

Epic User Stories: Sometimes you'll hear the word epic being used to describe a User Story. If you're a literature fan and have read poetry like Beowulf, you'll understand what we mean by epic—it's not small.

We use the word epic to refer to a high-level User Story or feature set that describes a wide-ranging set of functionality. More often than not, stories of this magnitude will need to be broken down into discrete chunks of value so that we can deliver them incrementally.

What a User Story is and how to use it

User Stories are short but well-formed descriptions of some new feature or functionality told from the perspective of the person who needs it.

We write requirements like this to encourage us to think of the actual people that we're making something for; it helps us focus on the value that we're trying to create for them.

The User Story format

The following figure shows an example User Story that you may recognize from earlier in the book. There are three sections to it, shown as follows:

AS A CINEMA GOER *The Actor*
I WANT TO BE ABLE TO PURCHASE TICKETS FOR A PARTICULAR FILM AND SESSION TIME *The Action*
SO THAT I CAN SEE THE FILM I WANT TO SEE AT THE TIME I WANT TO SEE IT *The Value Statement*

The basic template we're using for this User Story is:

- As an <**actor**> I want <some **action**> so that I get <some **value**>

We can either define the **actor** as an actual person, "Kimesha, a cinema-goer", or as a persona, "a Cinema-Goer." The subtle difference between the two is just the name "Kimesha", but this can be surprisingly humanizing. A real person like Kimesha is far easier to picture in our mind's eye, and so we're less likely to objectify our customer when we're building software for them.

It also opens us to the fact that there is more than one type of cinema-goer. Sometimes we want to be specific, and sometimes we want to generalize. It does mean that we're more likely to have conversations among the team that go a little like "Kimesha just wouldn't do that, but another cinema-goer might. Why would Kimesha do something different and how can we accommodate it?"

We should shy away from using the term "user" as the actor, as this is too broad in definition. Being specific will give us much better context and will help us to implement something of worth to that person.

The **action** is what the actor will perform using our software, and is what we'll be implementing for the actor to get the value. The **value** statement is probably the most important part because it's the actual value our customer derives from carrying out the **action**.

In this instance, our actor Kimesha, the cinema-goer, purchases cinema tickets via our software and in return is able to reserve guaranteed seats for a movie.

Crucially, the value statement scopes the work we have to carry out to implement the action. For example, we're building this feature for our cinema-goer to reserve a seat to see a movie, not so the cinema manager can determine how many people are attending a particular session. That's another story (pun intended).

Additional story card elements

The User Story is the key component of our story cards (the index cards that we write our User Stories on), but we'll include additional elements. In this section, we'll take a look at the purpose they serve.

We'll start by taking a look at full story card; we can see an example in the following figure. Each element of the story card is labeled:

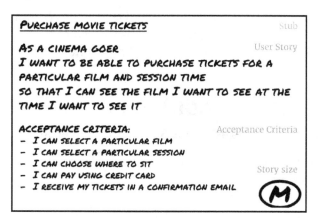

The stub

The stub or title of the User Story is a paraphrased, shortened version of the value statement. Our team will often use it in conversation as a reference to a particular User Story; the User Stories themselves are too wordy to repeat. The stub must convey enough meaning so that everyone knows which story we're talking about, particularly when there are multiple User Stories related to a feature or area of functionality. We'll see how to use stubs effectively in the following section, *Brainstorming a bunch of User Stories*.

Acceptance criteria

The acceptance criteria tell us what our Product Owner is looking for to consider this story complete from a business perspective. The acceptance criteria tell us what aspects of functionality the Product Owner will expect to see and test to verify that it works as expected (also known as user acceptance testing).

Story size

The story size is an estimate of the story's size. In this instance, we're using T-shirt sizes, and we consider the story to be an "M", or medium. We'll talk more about estimating User Stories later in this chapter in the *Estimating for Agile user requirements* section.

Notes

Once the team starts to work on a User Story, it will start to discover all kinds of information that they'll want to make a note of. These are notes that are often included on the back of the User Story, sometimes as additional post-it notes stuck to the story.

Card, conversation, confirmation

Ron Jeffries describes User Stories as having 3Cs: Card, Conversation, and Confirmation.

- The **Card** is the index card that the User Story is written on. The index card format serves two purposes:
    1. To write requirements on index cards, each requirement has to be small and self-contained; this helps us focus on what we need to do for each requirement and means we won't get distracted by things that might not be as important.

2. Having our requirements written on cards enables us to do things that we weren't able to do before, for example, we can now lay them out on the table and see the whole picture of our product. We can shuffle priorities much more easily. We can also easily take a single card or group of cards and discuss them separately from the rest of the requirements.

- The **Conversation** is required to fill in any gaps. Part of the intent of putting User Stories into an index card format is that there isn't room to write screeds of information. Instead, the card contains enough information for us to start and discover more through collaboration as we go.

  The conversation starts when the User Story is first introduced to our team. The story card is read and we seek clarification from our Product Owner. The acceptance criteria are discussed. The team will then try to estimate, and if we don't have enough information we'll ask for more.

  The conversation will carry on throughout the implementation. During Sprint Planning when we break the User Story into tasks. During the Sprint itself, as we begin to build and test it out, we're continually refining the story.

  Conversations will happen up until the point where the story is delivered into the hands of our customer. The final conversations about a particular User Story are most likely to happen in the Sprint Review, which is where we discuss what we've implemented with our stakeholders.

- The **Confirmation** is where we determine if the objective of the User Story is met. At least part of this involves verifying that the acceptance criteria have been fulfilled.

  Confirmation starts as soon as we start to get feedback on our implementation and as we start to write acceptance tests. We'll also seek confirmation by demonstrating working software to our Product Owner and get their feedback. The final step in our implementation cycle is to include feedback in the form of user acceptance testing before deployment.

  The final piece of confirmation comes from our customer that the delivered User Story works as expected.

Acceptance criteria versus the Definition of Done (DoD)

Acceptance criteria help us understand when the functionality is complete for a particular User Story. They're the criteria by which the Product Owner measures and accepts the story as done.

The **Definition of Done** (**DoD**) is a checklist that lets us know we've taken all the necessary steps to deliver any of our User Stories: the criteria by which the Development Team measures and accepts the User Story as done. More often than not, "All acceptance criteria met and accepted" appears on our DoD.

From time to time our team will notice acceptance criteria that regularly pop up on different User Stories. If we spot recurring items in our acceptance criteria, it may be time to consider including them in our DoD.

For example, when completing a piece of work, the acceptance criteria, "Include Google Analytics code to provide feedback for X" might appear regularly, especially if we have a metrics-driven mindset. If it does, then we should consider including this in our DoD.

In the next chapter, we'll show you an example Definition of Done and demonstrate how we can create our own.

Telling the team "what", not "how"

When the military engages in battle, it operates in a fluid environment; all of its best-laid plans can change at a moment's notice. Only after the first point of contact with their opponent will they start to discover the true nature of their counterpart's strategy.

General Patton, and military leaders like him, realized that instead of trying to plan and tightly control the outcome, a much better strategy was to set the minds of his commanders in the field to work instead. If he gave them an objective, then those on the ground were much better placed to determine how to reach its outcome as the battle evolved around them. If things took a turn for the worse while trying to reach that objective, the local commander had ownership of the strategy and was able to adjust it for the better, instead of just following orders blindly.

Our work may seem far from a battlefield, and hopefully, it is. In the same way, however, the nature of the problems we solve are complex and often unfold as we begin to work on them. Often, solutions given upfront will only take us part of the way. If our Development Team has ownership of the solution, as we uncover new information we can evolve our strategy to better fulfill the outcome we've been asked to achieve. Adaptive strategies will often reduce the time taken to reach the outcome our Product Owner desires.

How does this work in practice? Through close collaboration between the Product Owner and the Development Team, we should be able to respond to any challenge we're set. We've deliberately hired a cross-functional team so that they have all the skills necessary to do the job we're asking them to do. Depending on the problem you're trying to solve, this will usually include UX and graphic design, software design, development and testing, and so on.

A common trap that we can fall into as Product Owners is to write User Stories in a way that prescribes how to build something. For example, acceptance criteria such as "Place the checkout button below the form; if the form isn't filled out correctly when the user presses the button, display errors related to the incorrect data."

The preceding example is bad for a couple of reasons:

- Firstly, the user experience of placing the button below the form has been prescribed. But what if placing the button below the form means that the button is at the bottom of the page and out of view for 80% of our customers?
- Secondly, why wait until the button is pressed to prompt our customer to fill in certain fields, or tell them that the information they've entered is incorrect? We could give the customer some indication that certain fields are mandatory on the form instead. We could also give them immediate feedback on incorrectly-formatted information, for example, if they type an invalid email address into the email address field, or type an alpha character into a field expecting a number, such as a telephone number.

By prescribing these simple requirements, we've constrained our team to produce an inferior user experience. Instead, a better way to write the acceptance criteria would have been "The customer can easily complete the checkout form with the required information." This is far less prescriptive and gives the team the ability to decide the best possible approach to achieve the outcome our Product Owner would like.

Brainstorming a bunch of User Stories

This is a team activity which can be used to quickly build a set of User Stories around a product or feature set.

 Activity: Brainstorming requirements with User Stories
What you'll need: Index cards, Sharpies
Set up: A table large enough for everyone to sit around
Timebox: 2 hours

When you're initially setting up for a new piece of work - whether it's a new product or a new feature for an existing product - you'll probably want to pull together your idea(s) and write a bunch of requirements in one go.

A quick way to do this is with the following activity:

1. Either place the index cards in the middle of the table, so that everyone can reach, or pass them around and everyone has a small pile. Do the same with Sharpies.
2. The Product Owner introduces the product or feature that you're there to brainstorm. Include an opportunity for everyone to ask questions.
3. Once everyone has enough information, begin writing User Stories. Start with the stub first, one per index card. Call them out to the group before you start to write to avoid duplicates. Timebox this part of the activity for approximately 15 minutes.
4. Once the timebox is up, move into a more collaborative phase. You should assess what you have in the center of the table as a group. You then need to decide on a coherent feature set that describes either the product or the feature you're trying to build:
    - Try to identify any gaps; write a stub for each on a new index card
    - Look for any overlaps and see if you can create a better separation by writing the overlapping stubs less ambiguously
    - Determine if there are still any duplicates; if so, remove them
5. Once you feel the stubs are a coherent feature set of story cards, it's time to write the User Story for each story card. Use the template we described previously—as an <**actor**> I want <some **action**> so that I get <some **value**>
6. Next, write the acceptance criteria. Remember that the acceptance criteria should describe achievable outcomes without describing how to achieve them.

7. Repeat for as many User Stories as the group can come up with, or until the timebox ends.

Once finished, review the full set of User Stories, and you should now have the beginning of a Product Backlog.

Estimating Agile user requirements

We briefly introduced the concept of relative sizing in `Chapter 3`, *Introducing Scrum to Your Software Team*, in the activity *Using estimate buckets to size User Stories*. This particular technique is useful for sizing a bunch of User Stories at once. It also makes the concept of relative sizing slightly more obvious because we're comparing User Stories to one another. Relative sizing in this setting is a simple question of "Is it bigger, smaller, or is it the same size?"

You're probably wondering why we use relative sizing for estimating, rather than time-based sizing such as hours, days, or weeks. Take a look at the following skyline, you might recognize it:

Photo credit: istock.com/xavierarnau

There is an arrow pointing to the tallest building in this picture. Resist the temptation to look this up and have a guess at how tall the building is to the nearest meter. When you've decided, write down your best estimate. Have you written it down? Are you sure?

Now before we talk about the actual answer, I'd just like you to think for a moment about how you arrived at the estimate you have written down. What were the factors that you considered? Did you think about how many floors there were, or perhaps estimated how tall each floor was and multiplied the number by two? Do you know how tall one of the other buildings is in the photo and did you estimate from there?

Whichever method you used to get your estimate, ask yourself if there were many variables involved or if you just guessed. How accurate was your estimate, did you even get close? What factors influenced the outcome you got?

OK, that's enough suspense. The building is the new Salesforce Tower in San Francisco, and it is 326 meters tall. How close was your estimate?

If you didn't already know the exact answer, I'd expect a range of responses. Some people will have just guessed; they may have been close, but they also may have been way off. If you didn't guess and tried to estimate the height, then your estimate will depend on certain factors. For example, did you count the floors accurately, would you know how much taller the ground floor lobby is compared to other floors? Are some of the top floors shorter than other floors? Is there an uninhabited part near the top where the there are no floors, how tall is that cap? And so on.

To accurately estimate the size of the Salesforce Tower, there are specific pieces of information that you need, which if you don't know you will have to discover. Some of the information you'll be able to discover up front, and some you won't even know you need to know until you start to work through the problem.

However, now that you know how tall the tallest building is, take another look at the photo. Could you estimate the size of the second tallest building, the Transamerica Pyramid?

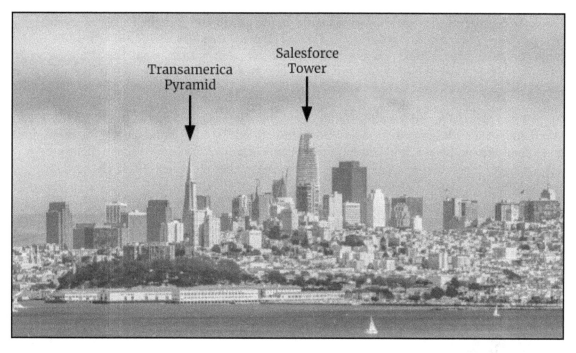

Photo credit: istock.com/xavierarnau

If we compare the two buildings, we can see that the Transamerica Pyramid is smaller, but not by much. In fact, you could probably guess what percentage height it is of the Salesforce building.

What percentage height do you think it is? It's a much easier question compared to the original question we asked, which was to estimate the height in meters. When looking at the two buildings next to each other, we can judge relative/comparative size more easily.

If you guessed that the Transamerica Pyramid was around 80% of the height of the Salesforce Tower, then you'd be very close to its height of 260 meters.

From this point on, now that you know the size of one or two buildings, it becomes easier to estimate the others. It's not an exact science, but it isn't supposed to be. Relative sizing is designed to help us to be more instinctual in our estimates, something that humans are quite good at.

Therefore, before starting with relative sizing, we need to start with a User Story that we know enough about to size. One way to set this is up is to spread the stories out on the table for the team to find what they think is a good example of a medium-sized story. This will involve some level of discussion amongst the team.

Once you've identified a medium-sized story in the group, put it in the center of the table, and put the rest of the User Stories into a pile. The medium story sitting in the middle of the table is now your yardstick, and you'll use it as a comparison to the rest. Take the next story from the pile and compare it to the medium story: "Is it smaller, larger, or is it the same size?"

Repeat this process for all the stories that are in the pile; don't worry about granularities of small, medium, or large at this stage. If it's large, it's on the right-hand side of the table, and if it's small it's on the left. If it's medium, it's in the middle. One way to speed this process up is to hand out stories to each participant and allow them to relative-size the cards themselves.

The advantage of this approach, comparing two or more items against each other, is that we develop a much more instinctual approach to estimation. We're no longer dealing in absolutes because we're looking at things relatively. The law of averages should mean that we don't need to hold the team to the accuracy of their estimates, as we know things will balance out in the long run. All of this, therefore, makes estimation a much more painless approach.

Planning Poker

Planning Poker is a team activity for sizing User Stories.

What you'll need: Planning poker cards, the User Stories that are to be sized, a Sharpie
Setup: A large table to work on and that the whole team can fit around
Remember: Set a timebox before you start

Planning Poker is played any time the team would like to size a User Story. Events it is commonly played at include backlog refinement meetings and during Sprint Planning.

To play Planning Poker you'll need a pack of Planning Poker cards; these can either be ones that you've made yourself or purchased. You'll need enough cards for one set per team member.

The following set uses T-shirt sizes:

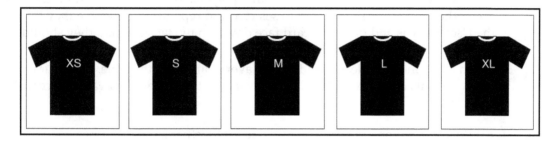

Another approach uses a modified Fibonacci sequence:

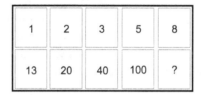

The Fibonacci sequence is used to indicate that size differences aren't always linear. A User Story sized as an 8 is roughly twice the size of a User Story sized as a 5, but it isn't exact, just like estimating in general.

Playing Planning Poker

Pass a set of cards to each member of the Development Team.

 Only the Development Team plays Planning Poker, as its members are going to do the work to implement the User Story. The Scrum Master and Product Owner do not play.

Follow these steps to play:

1. Take the next User Story from the top of the Product Backlog and read it out, including the acceptance criteria.
2. Place the story card in the middle of the table so that others can see and read it if they want to.
3. Ask if everyone has had enough information to size it. If they don't, give the team the opportunity to ask questions. When everyone is ready, move to the next step.

4. Each team member should be holding their Planning Poker cards in such a way that the card values are hidden from other players. You want to avoid influencing each other's choice. Ask the team to select a card representing the size they think the User Story is and place the card face down on the table. Again, they should keep the value hidden from the others.

5. When everyone has selected and each player's card is on the table, the Scrum Master counts down from 3 to 1. On 1, everyone turns their card values face up together.

 We ask everyone to put their cards down together so that no-one influences another individual's decision. We want to avoid "conformity bias," a phenomenon when people want to avoid looking stupid so will go with the first suggestion they see. We genuinely want to hear a diverse range of opinions. Someone might know something about implementing this User Story that could make it easier or harder to complete. If we don't allow them to voice their thoughts on why they selected a particular story size, we might miss something as a team.

6. What happens next depends on what value each team member selected. For example, if you have five Development Team members playing, the following are a few possible scenarios:
   - 5, 5, 5, 5, 5: Everyone selected the same size; that's the story size.
   - 2, 2, 3, 3, 3: There's a tight range, with only one value difference in the selection. Here, you should err on the larger story size.
   - 2, 5, 8, 8, 13: There's wide range. Ask the player who put a "2," why they thought it was that size. Hear them out. Next, ask the player who put "13" why they thought it was a "13." Everyone can contribute to the conversation, but you should allow outliers to share their opinion first. Once you've heard all contributions, play another round and see if the range becomes tighter.

7. Once you reach a consensus, write the agreed size on the User Story. Put the User Story to one side and take the next User Story from the top of the Product Backlog and play again.

If you can't reach an agreed-upon size for the User Story by the time you've played a total of three sizing rounds, you may need to take a different tack. One option is to try to refine the User Story further; this can be done spontaneously if the Product Owner feels that it is possible. The other option is to place the story back on the Product Backlog to be refined and sized at a later date. If one of these approaches still doesn't reduce the team's uncertainty and they still can't reach a consensus when sizing the User Story, you could consider performing a Spike.

A Spike is a particular type of User Story that's used when there is uncertainty over the way forward. Spikes used as an opportunity for the team to gather more information, either from a business or technical perspective. For example, if your team is unable to size a particular User Story via all the usual means, then the final option is to create a Spike User Story and put into the backlog.

When the Spike is selected for the next Sprint, an investigation will be carried out, the outcome of which should inform the way forward for team. The results of the Spike will likely generate further User Stories. Agree on a timebox for the Spike, which once complete is used to ascertain if you've gathered enough information. If you have, the team should stop the investigation and share the results. If more time is needed, you should negotiate with the rest of the team, including the Product Owner, and increase the size of the timebox if agreed.

NOTE: Spikes should be used sparingly. It can be a bad sign if a team is regularly running investigations on how to implement User Stories, as there is always a degree of uncertainty around any of the work that's carried out—a natural part of our process is uncovering more information as we go. Spikes should only be used when there is an unusually high level of doubt.

When using an estimation process such as Planning Poker, group involvement gets a better estimation result because of the benefit of group wisdom. Each member will bring a different experience on what is needed to be done to achieve the story, giving the group the opportunity to improve the accuracy of its estimate very quickly. This method is also a fast way to determine what is and isn't known about a particular story.

Group involvement also serves to inform each member of the team about a particular User Story, and this understanding will help them implement the story more quickly when it's bought into and worked on in a Sprint.

 Estimation and refinement of User Stories should take place regularly. Most teams book a backlog refinement meeting once a week. The general rule of thumb for maintaining a healthy backlog for a team is to keep at least one and a half Sprints, worth of work well refined and ready to go. Some recommend the 20, 30, 50 rules, where the top 20% is well refined and ready to go.

References

User Stories Applied: For Agile Software Development, Mike Cohn, a comprehensive guide on how to write and apply User Stories. Here is the link: `https://www.mountaingoatsoftware.com/books/user-stories-applied`.

Summary

In this chapter, we took a look at why the traditional requirements document doesn't lend itself well to adaptive planning techniques.

User Stories represent a much more human approach to gathering requirements because they focus on the need of the person we're writing software for and less on the technical outcome. They are deliberately designed to generate conversation with the people we are building software for, making the experience much more collaborative.

Defining discrete achievable outcomes for our customer gives us a platform for breaking down requirements into more manageable chunks so that we can deliver them incrementally. This enables us to prioritize work in a way that wasn't possible with the traditional requirements document. This makes the Product Backlog a much more dynamic set of user requirements. Part of the skill of the Product Owner is how they manage the backlog to get the best result from our business and our team.

In this chapter, we went through the different components of the User Story and what they each represent. In particular, we looked the User Story template and its three constituent parts: **actor**, **action**, and **value**. Many traditional requirements documents cater for the actor and the action but omit the value, despite the value element giving the requirements the necessary context and scope. Our Development Team can lose sight of why they're building this particular feature without it and, as a result, the work can take longer to complete.

We also showed you how to brainstorm a bunch of User Stories so that you could create a Product Backlog. The aim here is to start the conversation with your customer on what they want to build, rather than getting everything precisely right. That will come later with further conversation.

Finally, we introduced Agile estimating for User Stories, where we discussed the advantages of relative sizing over absolute sizing. We also looked at how to play Planning Poker, a team approach to estimation.

In the next chapter, we're going to look at how to get our team up-and-running using a Team Liftoff to set ourselves up for mission success.

Bootstrap Teams with Liftoffs **5**

The aim of this chapter is to show our software team how to get the best possible start by using an Agile liftoff. This approach sets the mission objectives for the team and gives you the opportunity to determine how we're going to work together. The aim is to set our team up for success and get us up-and-running as quickly as possible. We will cover:

- What are team liftoffs and why do they work?
- The importance of good vision
- Working agreements and team chartering
- Activities for team liftoff

What's a team liftoff?

When forming a new team regarding a new business problem, there's going to be a fair degree of getting to know the problem as well as getting to know each other.

A team liftoff is a planned set of activities aimed at getting the team up-and-running as quickly as possible. It is useful for two primary reasons:

1. It sets the tone and gives us a clear purpose
2. It's an opportunity for team building, which will accelerate team formation

Team liftoffs can span from half a day to a whole week, depending on the activities included. Dedicating time now to giving our team the best possible start is a shrewd investment as a liftoff will likely enable us to become high performers sooner.

Working closely and collaboratively are habits that we want our team to form as quickly as possible. Choosing liftoff activities that create a shared understanding and foster a positive team culture is key.

We'll run through a set of straightforward activities so that you get an idea of how a liftoff would work.

A simple liftoff timeline looks like the following:

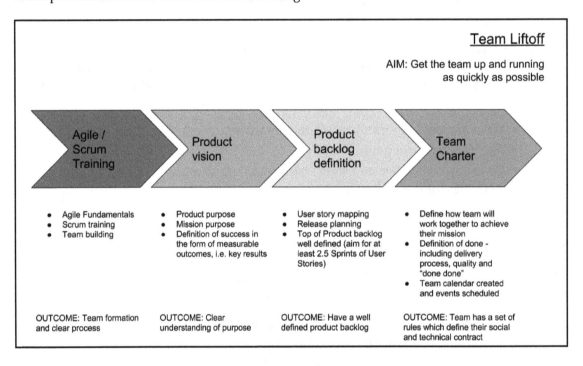

I've outlined the core liftoff events in the following section; each is a separate activity. It does make sense to run certain activities before others, for example, we need to understand product vision before we define the product backlog.

One final thing before we get into the details: it's never too late to run a team liftoff. Even if we've already started on our team mission, running a team liftoff will give a team the opportunity to clarify its understanding and codify its approach. If we feel our current team lacks direction or understanding or cohesiveness, it's probably a good time run an Agile team liftoff.

ACTIVITY – Agile training

Training for the whole team is recommended; this should include coverage of the Agile fundamentals, as well as the basics of setting up-and-running a Scrum. The intention is to provide broad understanding, allow our team to discuss the approach upfront, and have everyone start with the same foundation.

Ideally, this will be carried out by our Agile coach or Scrum Master, an experienced Scrum practitioner who has completed either the Certified Scrum Master (scrumalliance.org) or Professional Scrum Master (scrum.org) course, and who preferably has experience of coaching other teams through their adoption of Scrum.

Recommended training would include the following:

- **An experiential introduction**: The Paper Plane Factory is a great introduction to iterative working. It teaches the basic concepts of Scrum in a 1-hour activity (plus 30 minutes to debrief).
- **Agile fundamentals**: This includes The Agile Manifesto and why Agile is a mindset, not a method.
- **The Agile landscape**: An opportunity to discuss what options, regarding tools and practices, are available to an Agile practitioner. This will include considering what other Agile practitioners are doing in the field.

The Certified Scrum Master course is a 2-day course taught by Certified Scrum Trainers. It is part theory and part experiential, so it will give you grounding in the Agile fundamentals, as well as hands-on experience of forming your first backlog, creating a Scrum board, and role-playing through an entire, short Sprint, including Daily Scrums, a Sprint Review, and a Sprint Retrospective. It may seem over the top to be training everyone as Scrum Masters, but the investment is relatively small compared to the return you'll receive from a high-performing software team, and the CSM course is one of the best introductions to Scrum there is. If this is a route you decide to go down, the quality of training is only ever as good as the trainer, so it is worth seeking recommendations for trainers before you commit.

ACTIVITY – Sharing the vision

The following five steps all contribute to communicating the vision and mission of our team.

Step 1 – Meet the sponsors

It's important that as many of the project/product sponsors as possible attend part or all of our team liftoff. One way or another, they've all contributed to the vision that the Product Owner is holding on our behalf. This is an opportunity for them to introduce themselves, share their hopes and dreams for the product and usher in the next phase of its evolution.

The logical place to actively include them is in the product vision activity (step 3). Getting both their input and buy-in at this stage is crucial. With our sponsors on board, then our likelihood of success is much higher.

Step 2 – The company purpose

The overarching company purpose, also known as the company's mission statement, should be the single anchor for any product development team. Everything the company does should be traceable back to that.

It's important that the organization's purpose is restated as part of the liftoff and that our team understands how our mission contributes to the overall company mission.

It is usually in the form of a simple statement, for example, here are a few high-profile company mission statements:

- Google: *"To organize the world's information and make it universally accessible and useful."*
- Tesla: *"To accelerate the world's transition to sustainable energy."*
- Kickstarter: *"To help bring creative projects to life."*

Step 3 – The product vision

The Product Owner in Scrum is the person responsible for holding the product vision; this is a view of the product overall and what problem, or problems, it solves for your customer. Our Product Owner maintains the bigger picture and shares relevant information so that our team can tie back any decisions they make while on a mission.

There are several ways that the product purpose can be defined; it's usually in the form of a business case. For example, a Lean Start-up would use a Lean Business Canvas. The product vision differs from the product purpose in that it is a shorter, punchier version, something that gets people excited and engaged. Many activities will help us create a product vision and make a business case a little more dynamic; these include the product box, the press release, or an elevator pitch.

The elevator pitch is the most straightforward and can be crafted by the Product Owner. Use the following as a guide to creating one:

Imagine you're the owner of a start-up company with an idea for an exciting new product that is going to change the world. Like all new start-ups, you just need money and are hoping that you can persuade a seed investor or venture capitalist to fund you. One morning, just after buying your coffee, you jump into an elevator on the way to your shared office space and who should be in there but Jeff Bezos (Amazon). He's just pushed the eighth-floor button; you realize you've only got eight floors to persuade him to invest; what do you say?

Step 4 – The current mission

It's also important that the Product Owner maintains a clear view of the current business problem our team is being asked to solve, typically in the form of a simple mission statement.

For example, the following is a real team mission statement:

> *Enabling new methods of content display, navigation, and discovery.*

The mission statement should give our team enough guidance so that we can quickly know if we are on course or if we've deviated. At the same time, it should be broad enough that we can maintain some freedom regarding how we provide solutions. It definitely should not describe how to do something. Instead, it should describe what we are doing.

Step 5 – Define success

As the final stage of setting the vision, we should work with our Product Owner to define how we will recognize success. This not only gives us a clear idea of what the expected outcome of our work is, but also helps us understand where we should put our emphasis.

It's also a time to consider any assumptions that might have been made and to put these out in the open, as ultimately this is what contributes to unmet expectations the most. For example, does this mission require rapid experimentation to see what works in a real-world environment, so we can then learn and build based on our results? Or is it a mission where we have already gained a clear idea of what we need via user research, and we need to build out something that is simple but super reliable?

In the first example, it may seem obvious to our team; they won't have time to performance-test the application. We will assume that performance testing will be carried out in the subsequent phase once the results of our experiments are concluded. However, a Product Owner wouldn't necessarily know or even have thought of this.

They say the most common cause of a relationship breakdown is unmet expectations. This part of the liftoff is an excellent opportunity for the Product Owner to set expectations from the business's perspective, and for our team to contribute from a technical perspective.

A good starting point is the Success Sliders exercise, demonstrated as follows:

Activity: Success Sliders
What we'll need: A whiteboard, whiteboard markers, post-it notes, and a long straight ruler (unless you're good at drawing straight lines)
Setup: A large table that the whole team can fit comfortably around
Remember: Set a time box before this activity starts

Set up the whiteboard to look like the following figure (**note**: all of the post-its are in the **3** column):

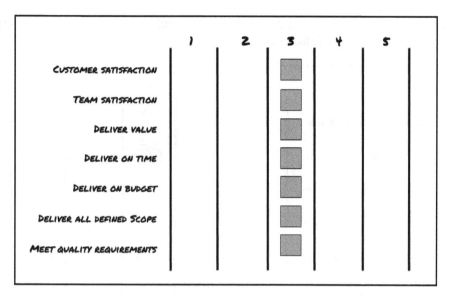

There are seven success criteria listed. The seven post-its represent the sliders for the corresponding success criteria. They can move between 1 and 5, but cannot be taken off the board. Each slider is currently set to a value of 3, and the Success Sliders are in equilibrium; this is a total of 21 (7x3).

The following rules apply:

- We are not allowed to exceed a score of 21, so we can't move all Success Sliders into the **5** column as this would make a total of 35.
- We could leave all Success Sliders where they are, but this would not reflect reality. There is almost always a bias for at least one success criterion over another, for example, delivering on time over delivering all the defined scope (or vice versa).
- We are now free to move the sliders for any of the success criteria; for every slider that moves up, there must be a corresponding downward movement for another slider.

The intention of the activity is to find out what's important for the successful outcome of this mission. After conversation amongst our group, we should move the sliders to the position that reflects the best outcome for this work.

This conversation may be difficult, but it's intended to help us uncover any assumptions and discuss them openly. The following figure is an example of the completed activity:

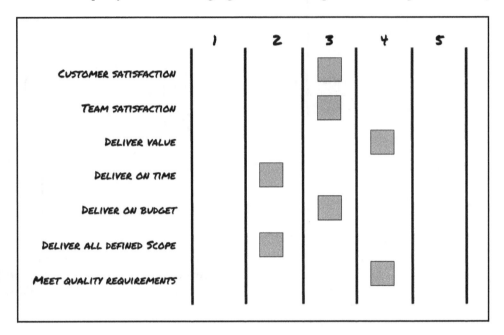

Here you can see that the group has decided that delivering value is a higher priority than delivering all of the defined scope or delivering on time. Maybe the conversation has gone along the lines that they want to get to market sooner with only a core feature set so that they can validate their idea.

As with a lot of these activities, while the outcome is important for our team to base future decisions on, the conversation we have during this activity is just as important as it helps cement our understanding and clarify our purpose.

Defining success metrics

The final step in defining success is to look at our success metrics. These are how we measure whether or not we are moving in the right direction with each iteration. These are typically defined by our Product Owner and shared with the team for refinement. There are several ways of setting success metrics up.

In `Chapter 9`, *How Seeking Value in User Requirements Will Help You Deliver Better Software Sooner*, we'll discuss the following approaches:

- **Hypothesis-Driven Development**: An approach that allows us to take a scientific approach to delivering value.
- **Objectives and Key Results** (**OKRs**): Many companies use OKRs, including Intel Corp, where they originated.
- **Data Insights Beliefs and Bets** (**DIBBs**): Used by Spotify. One of their coaches, Henrik Kniberg, blogged about this at `https://blog.crisp.se/2016/06/08/henrikkniberg/spotify-rhythm`.

Whichever approach is used, we need to make sure our metrics are easily quantifiable and are moving us in a direction that adds value—remember, what we measure is what we get.

Activity – Forming a team charter

The team charter covers several aspects of how our team will carry out its work:

- It's a process definition and agreement about how we will accomplish our work
- It's the social contract defining how we will interact with each other, and how we will work together as a team

Remember, the team charter is a living document; it will evolve as our team evolves its practices. It should be posted somewhere in our team's area so that we can reference it and annotate it as we go.

The following steps take us through the necessary activities to form an initial team charter.

Step 1 – Defining done

First, we're going to look at defining done. We'll need to work together as a team on this so find somewhere quiet where everyone's contribution can be heard. Here's how to set it up:

Activity: Defining done
What you'll need: Post-it notes, Sharpies, a spare wall or whiteboard
Remember: Set a time box before we start

The **Definition of Done (DoD)** is the agreement we use to define how we will know when our work is complete. It looks like a checklist. On it are the tasks that we need to carry out for us to deliver a new feature, enhancement, or bug-fix as part of the next increment of working software.

As a team, we are responsible for defining done. A simple activity to do this requires post-its, sharpies, and a whiteboard. For this activity, we ask our team to think of the steps they go through from the point where they are given a requirement, to the point where they deliver it in the form of working software.

Work collaboratively, write down each step on a post-it note, and share as you go. Put each step onto the whiteboard or wall in a timeline from the left (start) to the right (finish).

The team should consider the quality aspects of what they are delivering, as well as the steps they will take to avoid mistakes and make sure the delivery pipeline runs smoothly.

Once the timeline is complete, discuss it as a group. If our group is happy and there's no more to add, for now, write out the timeline as a checklist.

 It's useful to remind ourselves that done means more than just "coding done" or "testing done" or "review done." To do this, we talk about "done done." "Done done" is when we know that absolutely everything that is needed to take this increment to a production-ready state is completed.

Here's an actual example of a team's **Definition of Done (DoD)**:

> ### DEFINITION OF DONE
>
> - [ ] ACCEPTANCE CRITERIA FULFILLED
> - [ ] UNIT TESTS WRITTEN AND PASSING
> - [ ] INTEGRATION TESTS WRITTEN AND PASSING
>   CODE COMMENTED
> - [ ] CODE REVIEWED OR PAIR PROGRAMMED
> - [ ] USER ACCEPTANCE TESTED IN STAGING ENV AND MEETS
>   PRODUCT OWNER EXPECTATIONS
> - [ ] DOCUMENTATION UPDATED (IF NECESSARY)
> - [ ] CODE COMMITTED TO RELEASE BRANCH, READY TO
>   DEPLOY
> - [ ] RELEASE NOTES UPDATED

Step 2 – Working agreement

Next, we looking at our social contract; this defines ground-rules for working together as a team.

Activity: Creating a working agreement
What you'll need: Post-it notes, Sharpies, a spare wall or whiteboard
Remember: Set a time box before we start

So let's get started:

1. Set up the whiteboard with the banner **WORKING AGREEMENT** and the subtext **WE WORK BEST TOGETHER WHEN...** as per the following figure:

2. Distribute post-its and sharpies to each team member. Explain to the team that they are going to use silent brainstorming to complete the phrase **WE WORK BEST TOGETHER WHEN...** Each idea for finishing that sentence should be written on a post-it note, one idea per post-it only, and as many post-its/ideas as they like. They can use the example topics for inspiration if they need to.

3. Agree on a time box with the team for silent brainstorming and writing post-it notes, somewhere between 5 to 15 minutes. Then set the timer and start the activity.

4. Once we have finished coming up with ideas, or the time-box is complete (whichever comes first), we take it in turns to go up to the whiteboard and place our post-it notes on it. We should do this one post-it at a time, reading them out loud to the rest of the team as we go.

5. Once each team member has placed their post-its on the board, we should gather around the board as a group. The aim of this stage is to group similar ideas or remove any duplicates.

6. The final step is to review the revised working agreement and decide if we can all abide by it. Are there any changes? Anything we should add?

After several rounds, our team should be in agreement, and we should have something that looks like the following:

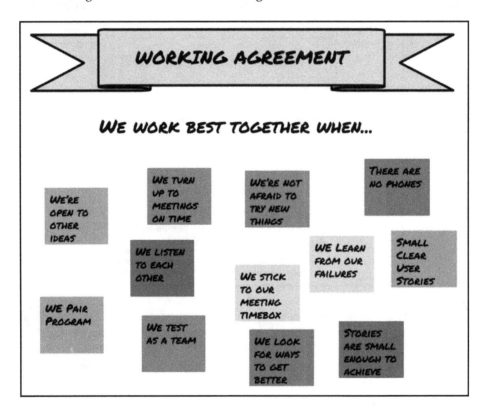

Step 3 – Team calendar

The final step is to work as a team to establish our Sprint calendar. Forming a consensus amongst the group about the days/times that we meet will help ensure everyone can attend and we don't miss out on anyone's contribution.

Activity: Creating a team calendar
What we'll need: Index cards, post-it notes (regular and large), black Sharpie pens
Setup: A large table that the whole team can fit comfortably around
Remember: Set a time box before we start (20 minutes should be sufficient)

Lay out the table as per the following diagram:

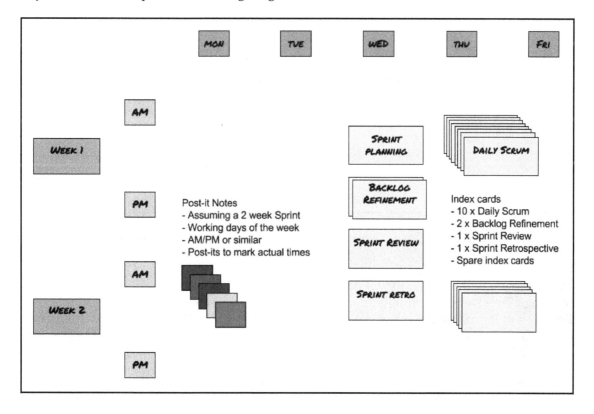

Writing the meetings on index cards means that we're easily able to shuffle them around should we change our mind:

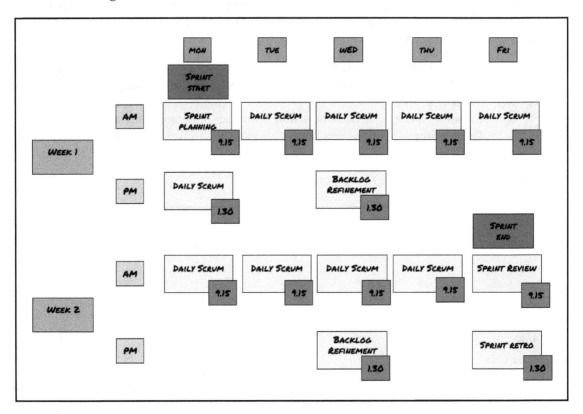

Start the timer, and then ask our team to layout their Sprint calendar using the preceding guide as an example.

Explain that it will be easier to first determine the Sprint start and end dates then set up all meetings. For example, Sprint Planning happens on the first day of the Sprint. Sprint Review and Retrospective are on the last day of the Sprint. The **DAILY SCRUM** should be every day, at a time agreed on by the team, except when it clashes with the Sprint Planning or Sprint Review or Sprint Retro meetings.

In the example, on the first day of the Sprint, our team has chosen to hold the Daily Scrum at 1.30 p.m., after Sprint Planning. Sometimes teams hold their Daily Scrum directly after Sprint Planning; sometimes they don't feel it's necessary. We should use our discretion.

The same thinking applies to the last day of the Sprint; for example, if we decide to hold both the Sprint Review and Sprint Retrospective events in the afternoon, perhaps we should have a Daily Scrum to coordinate our work in the morning.

Annotate the index cards with post-it notes showing the times as in the preceding example.

> Keep team events, such as the Daily Scrum, at the same time each day. This reduces the cognitive load on our team—it means they don't have to think, they'll just get into the rhythm.

Once the team has reached agreement, schedule all meetings at given time slots for the foreseeable future. Cadence is an essential part of Scrum. Establishing a rhythm is key to the success of the incremental delivery approach. The regular iteration cycles give the team a heartbeat by which it operates.

References

Liftoff: Start and Sustain Successful Agile Teams, Diana Larsen and Ainsley Nies, Pragmatic Bookshelf, Second Edition.

Summary

The aim of the team liftoff is to launch our team on its mission as quickly as possible. To do this, we first need to have context; we need to understand our product and its purpose and how it fits in with the company's goal.

Knowing this background helps us better understand the business problem we're trying to solve. It means we will be much more able to make better design and implementation decisions. For example, is this a standalone solution, or does it fit into a wider ecosystem?

The second part of the liftoff is deciding how best to solve this problem together. This gives our team an operating manual/system, which includes our team's technical process (definition of done) and social contract (working agreement). Both of these help us remove any assumptions on how we're going to work with each other.

For a team transitioning to Agile, this should be underpinned with Agile fundamentals training so that we all have a common foundation in the Agile Mindset. This is something we will be able to use in our day-to-day work environment, using our knowledge to guide the decisions we are taking. We should continually reflect on how our choices fit the values and principles of the Manifesto for Agile Software Development.

In the *Define success* section, we discussed the importance of recognizing what success should look like. Without this, we're unable to track our progress and determine if we've completed our mission. We also demonstrated an activity called Success Sliders, which helped us frame which parameters of our mission are important.

In the next chapter, we are going to delve more deeply and look at other measurements that we can track which will help us understand if we're on course to a successful mission outcome. This will include a more detailed way of defining and measuring success.

6
Metrics that will Help your Software Team Deliver

Once our team is on its mission, it's crucial that we know we're moving in the right direction. One question that will help our team know this is: What defines our success? Answering this question helps us discover the measurements we can take to keep us on track.

In this chapter, we'll look at various real-world examples that will help our team determine the metrics they should and shouldn't be using. We'll consider negative metrics, positive metrics, metrics that give you quantitative feedback, and metrics that provide you with qualitative feedback. We'll then discuss how to make this information visible and how to measure trends over time so that you can see you're improving and moving along the right trajectory.

In this chapter, we will cover the following topics:

- Qualitative versus quantitative measurements
- Negative versus positive metrics
- What you measure is what you get
- How will you define success?
- How to run a workshop that will help your team members set themselves up for success
- Team velocity – the engine is working, but it's a negative metric, so be careful
- Sprint and release burndowns
- Code quality

- Code complexity
- Team health indicators
- User happiness index

A brief introduction to measurements for Agile software delivery

Before we take a look at example metrics we can use, there are a couple of distinctions we need to make between the types of measurements and how we should use them.

Understanding measurements

There are many measurements that we can use to give us an idea of how our team is performing. Before we start tracking metrics, it's important to understand that *what we measure is what we get*.

For instance, velocity is a standard measurement used by Scrum teams. It tells us how many User Story Points we're completing on average in each Sprint. As we'll explain further in the *Negative versus positive* section, it's a measurement that is used mainly by the team to help them understand how they are performing. If used out of this context, it can cause adverse effects which can make the metrics meaningless.

A lot of measurements work in the same way; that is, they're meaningful to the team but less useful to those outside it. They don't always mean much in isolation either; we often need to compare and contrast them with other metrics. For example, the percentage of code covered by automated tests is useful if the quality of those tests is also measured.

Qualitative versus quantitative measurements

Simply put, quantitative measurements deal in quantities. They are numeric values such as the total number of members, revenue in dollars, web page views, number of Story Points completed, and so on.

Qualitative metrics relate to the qualities of something. They reflect the sentiments of a person expressed as feelings, opinions, views, or impressions. Examples of qualitative metrics include customer satisfaction and team member happiness.

Sometimes we'll combine both quantitative and qualitative measurements. For example, we judge ease of maintenance for software on:

1. **Cyclomatic complexity**: A quantitative measurement of the number of independent paths through our code; the more paths, the harder it is to maintain
2. **Ease of last change**: A qualitative metric based on the Development Team's viewpoint; the harder it feels to make the previous code change, the harder the codebase is to maintain

More often than not, we can translate qualitative measurements into numbers, for example, rating customer satisfaction with our product on a scale of 1 to 10, one being very unhappy, ten being very happy. However, if we don't also capture the individual's verbal response as to why they are feeling particularly happy or unhappy, then the metric over time may become meaningless. For example, we won't be able to address a downward trend in customer happiness unless we know why people are unhappy, and there is likely to be more than one reason.

Also, "value" means many things to an organization, so we have to measure each aspect of it, that is, direct revenue, reduced costs, return on investment, and so on. Sometimes value is easily quantifiable, for example when a User Story directly produces revenue. Other times it requires feedback from our customer, telling us whether what the team is building is meeting their needs.

Negative versus positive metrics

A negative metric is a performance indicator that tells us if something is going badly, but it doesn't show us when that same something is necessarily going well.

For example, velocity. If our velocity is low or fluctuating between iterations, this could be a sign that something isn't going well. However, if velocity is normal, there is no guarantee that the team is delivering useful software. We know that they are working, but that is all we know. Measuring the delivery of valuable software requires a combination of other metrics, including feedback from our customer.

Therefore, velocity is only useful if it's being used to determine what the team is capable of during each Sprint. It will also aid in scheduling releases, but it is no guarantee that the product under development is on track to being fit for purpose.

Something we should also be aware of with metrics such as velocity is that the very act of focusing on them has the potential to cause a decrease in the performance we desire.
A common request to teams is to increase their velocity because we want to get more done. In this situation, the team will raise their velocity, but it won't necessarily increase output.

Instead, a team may conclude that they were too optimistic in their estimates and decide to recalibrate their Story Points. So now a story that would have been five Story Points is eight Story Points instead. This bump in Story Points means they will get more Story Points done in the same amount of time, increasing their velocity.

In my experience, this isn't something done deliberately by a team. Instead, it's done because attention was drawn to a particular measurement, causing the problem to be analyzed and corrected. Unfortunately for us, negative metrics aren't the ones we should be poking around with.

It may seem an obvious thing to say, but to get more work done, we need to do more work. If the team is already at capacity, this won't be possible. However, if we ask them to increase their velocity, they can do that without achieving any more output. To avoid this scenario, instead think about the outcome you're trying to reach and then think of ways to improve that. For instance, if our interest in increasing productivity is because we want to release value sooner, we can do this without raising capacity or putting pressure on our team. In fact, we'll look at techniques to improve prioritization and increase the flow of work in Chapter 8, *Tightening Feedback Loops in the Software Development Life Cycle* and Chapter 9, *Seeking Value – How to Deliver Better Software Sooner*.

Other examples of negative metrics in software product development are:

- **Lines of code written**: Shows us that our developers are writing code, but doesn't testify to the usefulness or quality of that software in any way. Focus on this metric, and you will certainly get an increase in lines of code written if nothing else.
- **Test code coverage**: The percentage of code covered by automated tests. Shows that tests have been written to run the code, but there's no guarantee of the effectiveness of those tests in terms of preventing bugs.

Examples of metrics that we could focus on:

- **Value delivered**: Is the customer getting what they want/need?
- **The flow of value**: How much and how often is value delivered?
- **Code quality**: Multiple measurements which focus on two critical characteristics of our software:
    1. Is it fit for purpose?
    2. How easy is it to maintain?

    One fit-for-purpose quality that our customer should care about is the number of bugs released into the wild. This includes bugs that result from a misunderstanding of requirements. The further down the value stream we find bugs, the more expensive they will be to fix. Agile methods advocate testing from the get-go.

- **The happiness of our team(s)**: Happy teams are working in a way that is sustainable, with no extended hours or weekend work. Standards and quality will be high. Our team will have a good sense of satisfaction.

In short, negative metrics have their place; however, used unwisely they can have unintentional side-effects and degrade the performance you're looking to enhance.

In the following sections, we'll look at various measurements and how to use them.

Quantitative metrics

In this section, we'll look at measurements that track quantities.

Team velocity

Calculate the velocity for an Agile team by adding together all of the estimates for the completed User Stories in a Sprint. For example, if the team is using Story Points to estimate and complete five User Stories with estimates of 5, 2, 2, 3, and 1 respectively, then their velocity is 5 + 3 + 2 + 2 + 1 = 13.

If our team is estimating T-shirt sizes, it's not possible to say your velocity is 1L + 1M + 2S + 1XS, as this isn't easy to translate from Sprint to Sprint. Instead, assign numbers to each t-shirt size, for example, XS=1, S=2, M=3, L=5, and XL=8. Apply this method to any sizing system that doesn't use numbers.

Velocity is a metric that is used by the team for forecasting. For instance, during Sprint Planning we use it to gauge how many User Stories we think we can compete with in the upcoming Sprint.

We can use velocity in one of two ways. The first is by averaging the velocity from recent Sprints. If we take the last five Sprints it would look like this: (15 + 14 +20 + 12 + 16) / 5 = 15. The second uses the velocity from the last Sprint; an approach referred to as *yesterday's weather*.

From Sprint to Sprint, update the board so everyone can see the current value; here we're using the velocity from the last Sprint:

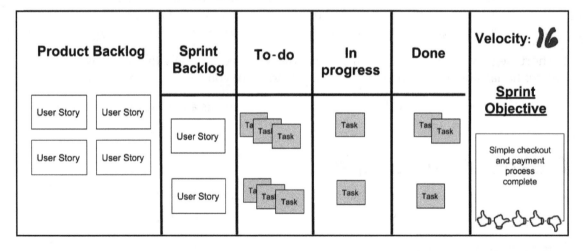

We track the trend over time using a velocity chart; this will look something like the following diagram:

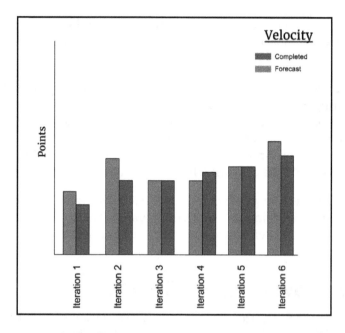

The two vertical bars per iteration represent the work that the team predicted it could complete in Sprint Planning (**Forecast**) and the work the team completed during the Sprint (**Completed**).

Sometimes work "forecast" is higher than work "done," meaning the Sprint didn't go as well as the team predicted. Sometimes forecast is the same as done, meaning it did go as expected. Sometimes done is higher than forecast because the team completed all items on the Sprint Backlog and had time to pull in additional User Stories from the Product Backlog into the Sprint.

The team shouldn't pull other items into the Sprint Backlog at the expense of existing User Stories in the Sprint Backlog. Before we pull in additional items, we should assist our team with any User Stories currently in progress. Being part of a cross-functional team means sometimes we have to perform roles other than our specialty. This is the nature of being a *T*-shaped team player; we do what we need to get the job done.

Velocity will fluctuate from time to time; causes include team members being on leave, or sick, or changing the iteration length. For example, if you have five team members and one is away for the next Sprint, in theory your velocity will drop by 20%. Team leave is one factor to take into consideration when Sprint Planning.

If a team feels the change in velocity is significant and worth discussing, they can use the Sprint Retrospective as an opportunity to understand why and see if the root cause is anything that they can fix.

Also, remember that velocity is just one aspect of our forecasting system. Another method teams often use during Sprint Planning is to break down User Stories into tasks. Some teams allocate hours to tasks and then add up the hours on all tasks at the end of Sprint Planning. They use the total hours to assess if their forecast for the User Stories in the Sprint Backlog is more or less right. Another aspect of forecasting is gut feeling, especially useful when working on small chunks of work which have an air of familiarity.

From an observer's perspective, velocity tells us the team's engine is working, but it doesn't tell us if what the team is working on is delivering value. The only way to measure value is through the software that we deliver meeting our user's needs.

Sprint Burndown chart – TEAM

The Sprint Burndown chart is a useful graphical representation of whether our team is likely to complete all the User Stories in the Sprint Backlog. The following is an example:

The dotted line represents the average burndown rate necessary if the team is to finish every item. The solid line shows the reality that not all tasks are equal; some take longer than others to complete (the plateaus) and some take less time to complete (the vertical drops).

Sometimes the solid line will go up before it comes down; this shows that once the team started working on a story, they uncovered new information and added tasks.

Release burndown charts

Release burndown charts track how much work is left to do before release. To track this successfully, we need to know which stories are in the next release. It is straightforward if we're using index cards to maintain our backlog; we merely separate them into multiple decks representing each release.

To start tracking how long it is before we can release, we first have to estimate all stories in the release. We then add up the number of Story Points to find out how big the release is.

We'll now look at two different types of release burndown chart. For both types, we show the total number of Story Points on the vertical axis and the number of Story Points remaining after each Sprint on the horizontal axis.

Simple Release Burndown chart

The simple Release Burndown chart tracks the total number of points remaining after each iteration. The dotted red line traces the trajectory of the burndown rate, and where it intersects the black horizontal line is the prediction of when the release will complete.

A simple **Release Burndown** looks like this:

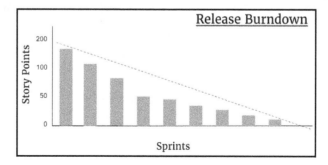

This chart is easy to maintain; it's just a case of adding up the **Story Points** remaining at the end of each Sprint. However, it isn't always apparent from this chart what has taken place in each Sprint. To illustrate, look at iteration five. The velocity for the team was just as high as it was in iteration four. However, the number of remaining Story Points doesn't seem to have dropped as far because new User Stories were discovered by the Development Team and added to the backlog.

Again, in subsequent Sprints, the velocity remains high, but the rate of burndown remains slow. In this instance, it's because User Stories are being re-estimated, which has increased their size.

These are normal activities for a Scrum team to carry out; they often have to replan as new information comes to light. To make the details more visible, we can enhance the Release Burndown chart, as we'll explain in the following section.

Enhanced Release Burndown chart

In the Enhanced Release Burndown chart, we record data both above and below the horizontal line. Above the horizontal line, we show the **Story Points** that were forecast at the beginning of the release. Below the horizontal line, we show any new User Stories added, or any increase in the size of existing User Stories.

A Release Burndown chart is a useful tool that requires all items in the release to be estimated, but note this only applies to the Product Backlog items in the release, not the entire Product Backlog. This fact should help our team focus their effort during Product Backlog Refinement sessions. Of course, if we feel an item on the broader backlog needs to be added to the release, we should do so, and estimate it as soon as we can. Sizing the story may require a small ad hoc Product Backlog Refinement session; after a Daily Scrum is usually a good time. Otherwise, we can wait for the scheduled Product Backlog refinement session, if they happen frequently.

An Enhanced Release Burndown looks like this:

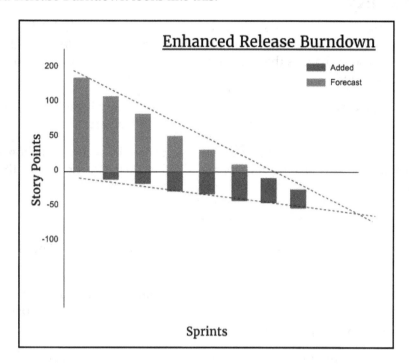

The two dotted lines plot the trajectory of these two groups of Story Points. The top dotted line represents the velocity of our team, and the number of Story Points decreasing as work gets done. The dotted line at the bottom represents the trend of work added to or removed from the backlog. The point at which the dotted lines converge gives the forecast for when the release will be complete.

One thing to note is that User Stories can be removed from the Product Backlog as well as added, and a User Story's size in Story Points can decrease as well as increase. All changes in scope are applied below the baseline.

 New information comes to light all the time in Scrum's fast-paced environment; we'll need to have a robust Product Backlog Refinement process to prevent estimates from going stale.

We can use this approach to forecasting in any situation where we have a bundle of User Stories that represent a milestone when complete. For example, we could also use an Enhanced Burndown chart for tracking when a single feature, or Epic, will complete.

Code quality

Code quality is essential to keep us Agile; poor quality creates technical debt, the sum weight of which will slow us down. Working with low-quality code feels a little like moving through treacle; changes that we thought would be simple turn out to be much harder than we expected.

When considering measurements to help us ensure code quality is high, we should look to measures that help us identify and remove technical debt from our system.

A good analogy is to think of it a bit like weeding a garden. It's a constant chore that we need to keep doing, usually as part of other tasks, rather than a particular job that we do in its own right. Even if we're just walking through the garden on the way to somewhere else and see a weed, we pull it out. Taking the time to do this, little by little, will stop the weeds getting out of control before any of them become bushes.

So, what are the software qualities we should aim for to remain Agile? And how should we measure them?

The simplest way to measure them is first to set some standards for our team to follow. Record this somewhere visible and easily accessible to the team. The ideal space would be anywhere in a visible workspace alongside a Scrum Board.

Feedback on how we're progressing with quality standards is essential, and this can originate from many sources, such as peer review. We should set thresholds, so if one or more of our desired qualities drops too low, the team is warned to take action. There are some handy tools that monitor code quality automatically; examples include **Code Climate** and **SonarQube**.

These are some aspects of quality we should be monitoring:

- **Clear**: Clear code often comes down to the user's coding conventions. We should aim for consistency. A few examples include:
    - Keep function names short and meaningful.
    - Make good use of whitespace and indentation.
    - Keep lines of code to fewer than 80 characters.
    - Aim for a low number of lines of code per function—use functional decomposition, reduce conditional logic to the minimum, and so on.

- **Simple**: This is a two-parter:
    1. We apply the Agile principle *Simplicity - the art of maximizing the work not done* and only write code that we need now.
    2. We make refactoring part of our team's DNA. As Mark Twain once said, *"I didn't have time to write a short letter, so I wrote a long one instead."* He meant that to make something succinct and meaningful, we have to put in time and effort; this applies to our software too.
- **Well-tested**: A broad spectrum of tests which cover unit, integration and UI testing. We should aim for good code coverage and well-written, easily executed tests. If we want to maintain confidence over time, our test suite should be automated as much possible.
- **Bug-free**: Tests are only one part of the equation as they just demonstrate the absence of bugs, not their presence. To aim for a zero defect rate, we have to focus on clear and straightforward code because one of the biggest causes of bugs is code complexity. We'll take a look at this in more detail in the next section.
- **Documented**: We should provide just enough documentation so that those that follow behind us, including ourselves, can pick up the code and have a sound understanding of our original intent. To be frank, the best way to do this is through tests because they are "living" specifications of how our code works. Better still, we can write tests using **Test-Driven Development** (**TDD**), because this gives us specifications up front before we write code. We'll talk more about TDD in the next chapter. Besides tests, we should include code comments, README files, configuration files, and so on.
- **Extensible**: Our software should be easy to build on and extend. Many will use a framework to give it some foundational structure. If we are using a framework to help guide extensibility, then we should adhere to the practices advocated by that framework as much as possible to ensure consistency.
- **Performant**: Performance is key to several qualities, including usability and scalability. We should have baseline measures such as response times, time to the first byte, and so on, which we can use to ensure our software remains useful.

Code complexity

One of the leading causes of bugs in software is the complexity of the system. Simple, well-written code is less buggy and more easily maintainable. Complex code is hard to write bug-free, and subsequently hard to maintain.

One measurement we can use to assess our code's maintainability is called cyclomatic complexity, best described as the number of paths that go through one piece of code. The more paths going through part of our system, the more likely it is to be complex and have to cater to different parameters or conditions. This makes the code harder to read and comprehend, and therefore more likely to contain or introduce bugs.

Unreadable code is the biggest single source of bugs in software, mainly because it's hard to discern all the different paths through it, and what consequences a particular change will have on them. Thus, testing captures most, but not all, scenarios.

Qualitative metrics

In this section, we'll look at measurements that track sentiments.

Defining what success looks like

When working out what to measure, one of the simplest things our team can do is define what success will look like. In doing this, we will identify measurements that we can use to tell us if our team is on the road to a successful outcome.

In this section, we'll look at an activity you can run with your team to help them define success.

Defining our success

In Chapter 5, *Bootstrap Teams with Liftoffs*, we discussed defining success using an activity called **Success Sliders**.

In the Success Sliders activity, we asked the team to consider seven different sliders which represent different facets of success: Customer Satisfaction, Team Satisfaction, Deliver Value, Deliver on Time, Deliver on Budget, Deliver All Defined Scope, and Meet Quality Requirements.

These particular characteristics focus on delivery in a project setting. In a long-lived product environment with iterative/incremental delivery, these could be redefined, for example:

- On time becomes early and often
- On budget becomes cost-effective
- Defined scope becomes useful software or satisfied users

However, all teams are different, and these particular factors may not apply to our team or its mission. So, in this section, we are going to take a look at a team activity that is used to define our own set of success factors.

Activity: What defines our success?
What we'll need: A whiteboard, whiteboard markers, post-it notes, and sharpies
Setup: A large table that the whole team can fit comfortably around
Remember: Set a time box before this activity starts

Follow these steps to define what success will look like:

1. On the whiteboard, write the headline question: how will we define our success?
2. Pass out post-it notes and Sharpies to each team member. Tell them they're going to do some silent brainstorming. Ask them to answer the headline question and write one item per post-it note.
3. Answer any questions, and when everyone is comfortable, set the time box to 15 minutes and start.
4. When 15 minutes is up, assess the room and determine if anyone needs any more time. If everyone is ready, get the team to take it in turns to post their post-its on the whiteboard. Ask each team member to read their post-its out loud as they do so.
5. There will likely be some duplicates and similar themes. Ask the team to come up to the board and do some affinity mapping, involving grouping related ideas together. Move similar post-it notes next to each other then circle the group and give it a name which encompasses the fundamental concept.

The following shows the result that one team came up with:

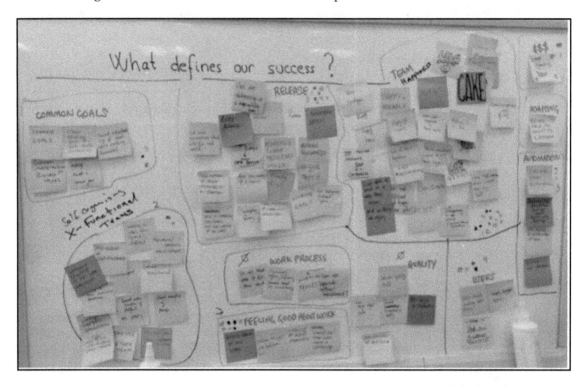

In the image, you can see we've voted on each cluster to indicate which ones our team thinks are priorities. Based on the votes, we only took the top 10, as we felt that there were enough indicators for our team to monitor.

To create our set of Team Success Indicators, we used the post-its within each group to inspire us to write two statements, one positive and one negative, for each indicator. For example, the **Team Happiness** card statements were defined as follows:

We used the preceding template for each indicator and got the following results:

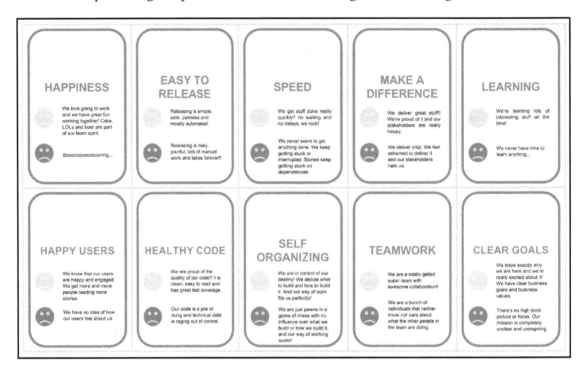

One team's set of success indicator cards

Using our Team Success Indicators

Once we have our Success Indicators set up, it's time for us to see how we're tracking each indicator. At the beginning of a retrospective is one place we can do this.

Set up the whiteboard as follows, with the indicators along the top:

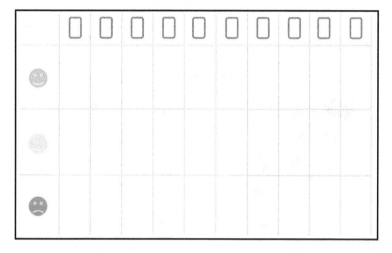

Allow 5 minutes for each team member to vote by placing their X in the happy, sad, or neutral row for each indicator. Neutral indicates they're neither positive nor negative, but somewhere in the middle.

Once everyone has voted, the Scrum Master totals the votes for each indicator. The result will look something like this:

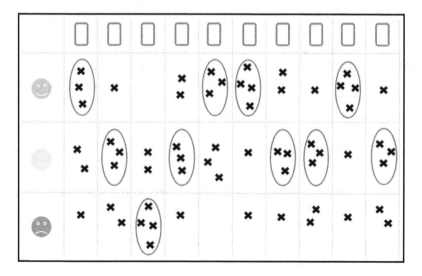

We can use a dashboard to monitor the trends easily. Following is a dashboard for a real-life team, showing their team's health over the past nine months:

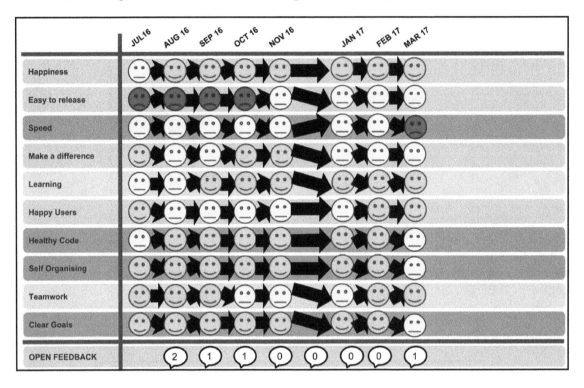

As you can see from the last column, Mar 17, things have taken a bit of a downturn in terms of **Speed**, **Healthy Code**, **Self Organizing**, and **Clear Goals**. The team were learning a whole bunch of new technologies at once while being put under pressure to deliver by their stakeholders. We conducted a retrospective and used it as an opportunity for the team to define actions they felt that would mitigate this.

The larger arrows indicate a gap in which we didn't record our team's health; it's because we were all on holiday.

The speech bubbles at the bottom represent the number of comments our team has made in the **OPEN FEEDBACK** section. This particular dashboard is online, and so are our team health surveys, so we link through so people can read the comments. If we were doing this using a physical workspace, we would post the individual comments on our dashboard for everyone to see.

This process is based on an idea from Spotify, which I've modified slightly from their original. If you'd like to create your own version of this, you can use Spotify's online kit to get you started: `https://spotifylabscom.files.wordpress.com/2014/09/squad-health-check-model2.pdf`. It's available under the Creative Commons Attribution-ShareAlike license.

User Happiness Index

"How satisfied are our users?" is a question we need to ask ourselves often. It is one measurement we can use to determine if we're delivering useful software.

There are many ways to foster engagement with the people for whom we're building software. Here are a few suggestions:

For direct feedback we could:

- Ask for star ratings and comments, similar in concept to the Apple and Google app store rating systems. We could ask for these via our product, or via a link sent in a message or email.
- Observe our user while they use our software. We could ask them to describe what they are currently doing so we can hear the process they have to go through.
- Survey a group; for example, each time we release new feature we could wait for a while to ensure uptake and then poll customers to gauge their impressions.
- Carry out business and customer surveys in person, if possible. This is an excellent way for us to assess the satisfaction of our client.
- Capture feedback from our customers using a tool such as UserVoice.

For indirect feedback we can:

- Look at all calls that have gone to the service desk regarding our software (number and nature)
- Use analytics to find out the level of engagement our user group has with particular features

Summary

Building software products is an empirical process, and similar to a scientific experiment; we don't always know what is going to work and what isn't. The measurements that we take along the way should be designed to help us determine if we're moving in the right direction.

We looked at two distinct measurement categories, quantitative and qualitative. The quantitative group gives us numerical facts, such as the number of Story Points completed. Qualitative data is more subjective but provides us with feedback regarding human qualities such as satisfaction, both at a team level and at a customer level.

We also looked at the difference between negative and positive metrics. We considered that, while velocity is a useful metric to aid the team in forecasting what it might be able to achieve in a given period, it is not a measurement by which the team should be judged or compared. The value delivered from a particular velocity varies from team to team. Velocity only tells you the engine is running; the real measure of a team's performance should come from the value they deliver.

In the final section, we considered types of measurement involving probably the most important group of people: those that use our software. This is the ultimate measure of whether we're building the right thing.

In the next chapter, we're going to look at technical practices that enhance our agility. With a little discipline and the right practices, we can keep our product in good shape, spending less time on bugs and maintenance and more time on the stuff we enjoy doing.

7
Software Technical Practices are the Foundation of Incremental Software Delivery

Delivering working software in small increments every sprint requires a different way of working. To reduce overhead, teams will often look to technical practices to enhance their ability to deliver.

Choosing the right technical practices will increase our team's agility by giving them the confidence that what they are delivering is well-designed, tested, and meets expectations. By improving the team's confidence, we will speed up our ability to deliver.

In this chapter, we'll look at some of those technical practices and how they work with incremental software delivery approaches.

In this chapter, we will cover the following topics:

- Building the thing right versus building the right thing
- Test-driven development
- Refactoring
- Pair programming
- Emergent design
- Continuous Integration/Deployment/Delivery and the DevOps culture

Building the thing right versus building the right thing

The practices that we use are often known as "the intangibles" of software delivery because from an outsider's point of view, they aren't visible as part of the features we deliver but they have the potential to help us build a much better product.

"Building the thing right" means a focus on crafting our software.

"Building the right thing" means focusing on getting good outcomes for the customer.

Unfortunately, sometimes the bias can be towards the latter, the pressure to deliver often being greater than the desire for quality.

Poor quality manifests itself in a few ways: poor performance (slow), doesn't work as expected, takes forever for the team to make requested enhancements, and so on. As a customer, this may only be something that you become aware of after being on the receiving end of poor-quality software.

An incremental approach should help relieve the pressure on the team to deliver. A customer will likely be less nervous about what their money is being spent on if they can see and give feedback on the software. If the customer can use the increments provided so far, it's a win-win.

And although it may seem counter-intuitive, focusing on quality and adopting practices that build it into our software from the beginning will speed up delivery. Why? Because we avoid accumulating something called **technical debt**.

We first mentioned technical debt in `Chapter 1`, *The Software Industry and the Agile Manifesto*, when discussing the Agile principle *continuous attention to technical excellence and good design enhances agility*. We defined it as follows:

Technical debt is a term first coined by Ward Cunningham; it describes the accumulation of poor design that crops up in code when decisions have been made to implement something quickly. Ward described it as technical debt because if you don't pay it back in time, it starts to accumulate. As it grows, subsequent changes to the software get harder and harder. What should be a simple change suddenly becomes a significant refactor/rewrite to implement.

In his blog post *Refactoring - Not on the backlog!* (`https://ronjeffries.com/xprog/articles/refactoring-not-on-the-backlog/`), Ron Jeffries compares software technical debt to the thickets and bushes that might crop up in your previously well-tended field. When you first started out writing software it was fast and easy, just like when you first started mowing the field. We didn't always take the best or straightest path, and in our haste to get the job done, we probably neglected consistency. But when the field was green, we didn't need to think about things like that.

In his blog post, Ron visualizes it something like the following:

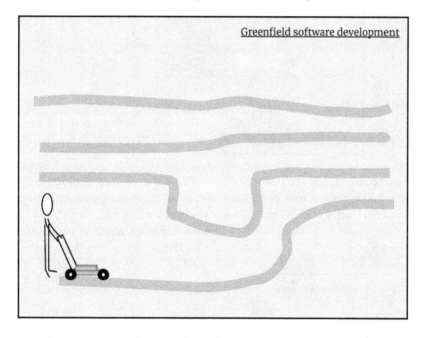

Over time, areas of our code get little neglected and small bushes start to form. One day, we find that we don't have time to remove the shrubs, so we begin to mow around them. This is similar to parts of our code that we find hard to maintain.

Instead of tackling the problem head-on and fixing the code, which would slow us down, we go around it, for example by creating similar code that does a slightly different job. The field starts to look like this:

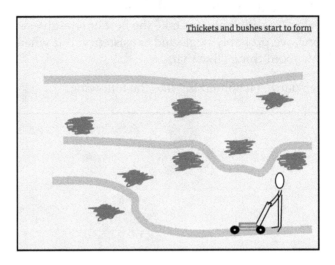

Soon, it gets harder and harder to navigate the area as the bushes get bigger and more numerous. It takes longer and longer to mow the field; at some point, we may even give up trying to mow it at all, only going into that area when we have to. We start to think of this code as "legacy" and consider ways we can replace it. Sometimes, it's just easier to blow it all away and start again:

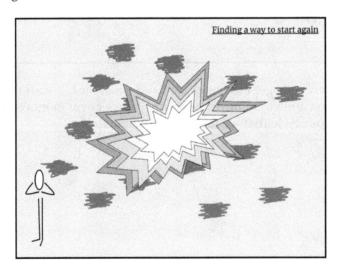

All of the practices that we describe in this section are aimed at preventing those thickets and bushes springing up in our software. If we maintain a disciplined approach to building software using these techniques, it will ultimately speed up our delivery, increase our agility and our product's medium to long-term viability.

Refactoring

In a nutshell, refactoring is the art of small and continual improvements to the design of our code while preserving its behavior. The intention is to create behavior-preserving transformations to our system which ultimately make it more maintainable.

Each time we change parts of our software, we purposely refactor parts of the code that are in our path. To ensure we preserve current behavior, we use automated tests which tell us if our code is still working as we refactor.

Using Ron's analogy of fields, thickets, and bushes from the previous section, instead of mowing around the bushes, with refactoring, we cut a path through each bush we encounter. It looks a little like the following:

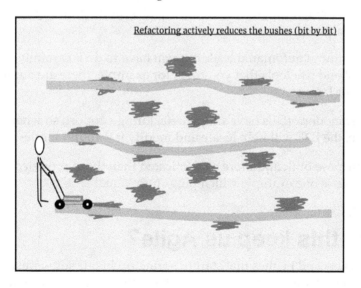

Refactoring actively reduces the bushes (bit by bit)

We do need coding standards when refactoring; a good starting point is *Clean Code: A Handbook of Agile Software Craftsmanship*, by Robert "Uncle Bob" C. Martin. Coding standards are hygiene factors which should be possible to automate using tools such as SonarQube—an open source tool for automating code reviews and the static analysis of code.

One of the principal causes of bugs in our software is complexity, primarily because it makes our code hard to read. If the code is hard to comprehend, it causes developers to make mistakes because they misinterpret how it functions. Over time, it will even affect the developer who wrote it, and they may struggle to maintain their original intentions.

We should always be thinking about how we can make things more easily readable. Sound naming conventions, fewer lines per method, fewer paths, and loose coupling of code are just a few examples.

Remember, it's relative. Some areas may need more attention than others. Definite red flags requiring attention are units of code with many lines; aim to decompose these into more manageable chunks.

Also look for places that have a high cyclomatic complexity. These are hotspots for attention because the code in these locations has multiple paths running through it, often obscuring some or all of its purpose.

You can refactor without automated tests, but you have to do it carefully. You will need to manually test a lot and use tools that you trust, for example, there are automated refactoring tools for Java and C#.

For instance, most modern IDEs have simple refactoring support, so when changing a method signature, the IDE will help locate and modify it throughout the codebase.

Some tools are purpose built and more sophisticated than those provided by an IDE. Re-sharper by JetBrains is one example which plugs into Visual Studio.

How does this keep us Agile?

It reduces the thickets and bushes that start to spring up in our software; it prevents them from taking firm root in our code. This reduces the time it takes for us to introduce additional functionality or enhance and maintain existing features, making us much more reactive to our customers' changing needs.

Things to try

Try following *The Boy Scout Rule,* as described by Uncle Bob in Clean Code. He refers to the Boy Scouts of America as having a simple rule: *Leave the campground cleaner than you found it.*

We can apply this to our code. If we always leave it in a better state than when we found it, over time it will maintain its usefulness. There will be less opportunity for those thickets and bushes to grow.

Remember, refactoring should be treated as making small, continuous improvements to our software.

Test-Driven Development

Test-Driven Development (**TDD**), is a software discipline in which we write an automated test case before we write any code. It is a principal practice of Extreme Programming.

The basic pattern is as follows:

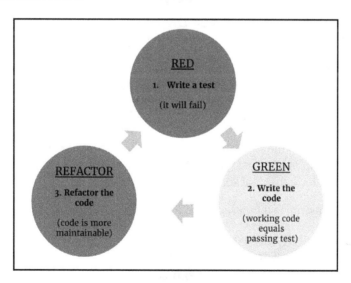

The first step is to write an automated test case for the next piece of simple functionality we intend to implement. The test will fail because we haven't written any code to fulfill it yet.

The next step is to write the most straightforward code implementation to fulfill the test and make it pass.

The final step is to refactor the code so that it meets our coding and implementation standards.

When using refactoring with TDD, they make a powerful ally. The TDD test suite enables us to take the refactor step with the confidence that the behavior hasn't changed, as we make the code simpler and more in keeping with the system design.

So, if we're using a **Model-View-Controller** (**MVC**) framework, then while refactoring our code, we would be ensuring our newly-added functionality is in keeping with the framework's principles.

For example, our quick cut of code to make the test pass may have left some business-related logic in our controller code. During the refactoring step, we would move this code so that the model handles our business rules. This maintains the separation of concerns called on by the framework we're using, and also makes our software more understandable to anyone coming through behind us (including ourselves).

How does this keep us Agile?

Let's just state upfront that the topic of Test-Driven Development can and will cause polarizing responses among software Development Teams. People either love it or hate it.

I believe much of the controversy is caused because we fail to see TDD for what it is: a *specification-driven test harness* for designing and writing more straightforward software. TDD packs so much punch in the Agile community because it encourages a mindset of building what is necessary and nothing more.

Simple software is easier to maintain, more robust, easier to scale, and lacks technical debt or feature bloat. If Scrum is a set of training wheels for better software delivery, TDD is the training wheels for better (simpler) software design.

The many benefits of using TDD include the following:

- It's a specification-focused approach that reduces complexity because we're less likely to write software that we don't need
- It makes our design simpler and our code clearer
- Refactoring refines our design and makes our code more maintainable, a step often haphazardly undertaken if done without TDD's specification-driven framework
- Writing tests as specifications upfront improves the quality of our specifications and makes them more understandable to others

- The automated test suite serves as documentation for our software—the tests act as the specification, and it's easier for new team members to understand what the code does
- Having a suite of readily-repeatable tests gives us the confidence to release our software
- The resulting tests support refactoring, ensuring that we can make the code simpler while maintaining its intended behavior

Some argue that TDD approaches take longer to write code, and this is true in the literal sense because we're designing and writing specifications at the same time. However, when you consider all the other activities involved in software development, other than just "writing" code, this argument breaks down. Plus, the medium to long-term effects on our code base will result in significant cost savings. Plainly put, in my experience, TDD software has far less technical debt and far fewer bugs.

In fact, you should probably see TDD as a way of improving and validating your software design. It's a much more holistic perspective. It's testing++.

Things to try

Select a TDD champion, the person or people who most support the practice within the team. Have them set up the framework and create the initial approach.

Choose one User Story to implement TDD on. Once the User Story is done, have the champion/champions workshop their findings back to the team and teach them how they can implement TDD as well.

The team should then select the next User Story they'd like to TDD and then pick a team member to pair program (see the next section) the solution with the TDD champion.

Alternatively, if the TDD champion is already a confident TDDer, they could introduce the whole team to the Test-Driven Development approach using workshops, or pair or mob programming.

Whichever approach you take, you should work in that configuration as a team until the User Story is "done," that is, delivered into the hands of your customer. A full SDLC end-to-end experiment is necessary if we're to understand the wide-ranging benefits this particular practice has. Remember, building software isn't just about writing code; our work isn't complete until it's in the hands of our customer.

Pair programming

Pair programming is a software practice where two software developers will share one computer. The one with the keyboard is the one programming and is concerned with the details of implementation. The one without the keyboard is maintaining the bigger picture and the overall direction of the programming.

There will usually be a healthy level of discussion between the pair; the one on the keyboard will often describe what they are doing and thinking, while the other will be calling out the next steps and pointing out any issues.

It's a little bit like a rally car driver working with a navigator. The driver is responsible for focusing on solving the immediate problem, the handling of the car around the course. The navigator has the map, keeps track of their location, and ensures the driver has enough information about the direction being taken and any obstacles ahead.

It works well because the developer who is navigating is holding the bigger picture, which ultimately helps the developer who is driving to keep focused on what needs to be done to solve the immediate problem. The navigator is also able to spot potential problems in the design, and even simple things like typos, which will often go unnoticed otherwise.

When turning up the dials on good practice to the maximum for extreme programming, Kent Beck's view was that if we value peer code review so much, why not do it all the time? Extreme programmers will Pair Program all code that goes into a production environment. Pair programming is peer review on steroids.

How does this keep us Agile?

Pair programming keeps us Agile because it shortens the feedback loop when reviewing code. This is feedback at its earliest and means that we're able to incorporate changes immediately, often nipping potential issues in the bud.

It's particularly potent when we follow the driver/navigator scenario, sometimes known as **strong style pairing**, the name attributed to a pair programming approach advocated by Llewellyn Falco. As per his presentation on `https://www.slideshare.net/ llewellynfalco/strong-style-pairing`, he states that *"For an idea to go from your head to the computer it must go through someone else's hands."*

This is cost-effective in the long run because it creates better quality software from the outset. Two sets of eyes are better than one and pairs are also more likely to keep each other honest; for example, due to peer pressure, we won't take shortcuts.

It's also an excellent way to skill or knowledge share, for instance, if one team member knows a particular part of the system well, or wants to coach a practice such as TDD.

Things to try

When initially introducing pairing, it's worth recognizing that it requires more concentration, mainly because pair of programmers are less likely to get interrupted or distracted.

Before starting, discuss pairing etiquette:

- Agree on a start and finish time for the session. Ensure you schedule time for regular breaks.
- Discuss how to avoid distractions. For example, turn off email and instant messenger notifications. Also, have mobile phones turned to silent or preferably off.
- Decide how to manage outside interruptions. For example, explain to the person or persons interrupting that you'll be on a break soon, tell them when that break is and that you can talk to them then.
- Determine who will drive first and how often you'll exchange the keyboard. Make sure you swap the keyboard regularly. Do not allow one person to drive exclusively.
- Accept that pairing is not silent, but like any new skill, we will need to learn how to describe what we're doing while coding. It's often odd at first.

Remember, don't just pair program the "hard bits," pair program for an entire story from start to delivery.

To keep things interesting, try pairing with different members of the team. Also, bear in mind that you both don't have to be software developers to make a pair.

For example, try pairing with a Product Owner, in particular, if the current work involves creating a tangible aspect of the system such as part of the user interface or another form of output. In these situations, they will be able to offer immediate feedback on the direction you're taking.

Activity – pair programming ping pong

Pair programming ping pong combines the two practices of TDD and pair programming and turns them into a fun, collaborative game.

What you'll need: Two software developers, one computer
Setup: The usual pair programming setup

It starts in the usual pairing way, with the two developers using one computer, one acting as the driver, the other as the navigator.

We play ping pong in the following way:

- The first developer writes a new test. It fails because there is no code to fulfill it yet. The keyboard is passed to the second developer.
- The second developer implements the code needed to fulfill the test.
- The second developer then writes the next test and sees that it fails. The keyboard is passed back to the first developer.
- The first developer implements the code needed to fulfill the test and so on.

In the usual TDD manner, refactoring happens after the code to fulfill the test is written.

Emergent design

At the beginning of this book, we looked at the birth of Agile and what provoked this movement. In Chapter 1, *The Software Industry and the Agile Manifesto*, we discussed how, in an attempt to correct our inability to bring projects in on time and budget, we sought to get more precise in our predictions.

It was felt that if other engineering disciplines such as civil engineering were able to be more precise with their process, then so could software engineering.

However, the reality is that we don't build software like we construct bridges or buildings or hardware. With all of those physical things, by the time we get to the actual construction phase, we've already created the design schematics. The construction phase is an endeavor in logistics based on assembling the different components in the right order.

As Neal Ford, software architect at Thoughtworks, describes it, with software, the code itself is our design. Our build phase in software is when we compile/interpret the program code so it can be run. Our program's concrete outputs are the actual results of the design, in the form of pixels illuminated on the screen or messages sent over the ether. That is the tangible result of "building" the design we've written in our software's code.

So, if we're to get better at producing the right output, we have to get better at "designing" our code. Practices we've discussed so far in this chapter will certainly help us evolve our design safely and efficiently.

For example, TDD creates a test harness based on our software's specifications. This allows us to design our software to the specifications prescribed in our requirements (User Stories, their associated acceptance criteria, and possible test scenarios).

TDD's red/green/refactor approach to software development helps us ensure that intended behavior will continue to work as we begin to make changes to our software's underlying structure, for example, improving its scalability.

How does this keep us Agile?

Software design isn't something we do before we start writing code, it's something we do as we write it. When patterns emerge, we can begin to take advantage of them, creating abstractions for reuse.

This helps us avoid being caught by the **You Ain't Gonna Need It (YAGNI)** principle of software design. YAGNI happens when we design software features for some perceived future need and not the actual needs we have now.

It doesn't mean that we just start programming. Having some understanding of the problem and formulating a strategy regarding how we're going to solve the problem is necessary to get us started on the right path. It does mean that we shouldn't try to solve problems we don't have yet.

Things to try

Start with watching or reading some of the videos or articles that Neal Ford has published on the subject. Here's a case in point: `GOTO 2013 - Emergent Design, Neal Ford`.

As he suggests in the video, you can read more about it in IBM's developerWorks library using this link: `https://www.ibm.com/developerworks/views/java/libraryview.jsp?search_by=evolutionary+architecture+emergent+design`.

Activity – emergent design discussion

Hold a time-boxed discussion with the team about software design.

What you'll need: The team, a table big enough for the team to sit around, a whiteboard if you want to record salient parts of the conversation, a timer.
Setup: A round table discussion with a designated scribe if taking notes.

Compare and contrast software to civil engineering. Take a look at how they design, test, and build versus how we design, test, and build.

Discuss the statement, *specifications are our design, the code is our design, testing is our design validation, build/compile is our construction phase, and the output we see on-screen is our building.*

The DevOps culture

Continuous Integration (**CI**), Delivery, and Deployment tackle two problems that we traditionally leave until the end of our software life cycle: integration of code and strategies for deployment.

We've learned that doing something in large chunks, is very risky, especially in a complex software environment. Waiting until the end of your software development process to work out how to combine different parts of the system and deploy them leaves a critical feedback loop open for too long.

Work done during the integration and deployment phase will often include changes to how our software is built. Leaving it until the last moment to receive this feedback will either be costly or will mean it's ignored.

Modern software teams know that the work isn't done until it's delivered to our customer, which for most means it's deployed and operational in our production environment.

They will often look to automate the tools they use to integrate and deploy; after all, it is something they are going to be doing very regularly, so it makes sense to invest time in it. Our Development Team will take on more care and responsibility in the management of our production environments because they know this will allow them to deliver smoothly and quickly.

It's at this point that the lines begin to blur between what was traditionally seen as development and operations. As we move further towards cloud computing, our infrastructure will become increasingly automated, hence the term **infrastructure as code**. This is the rise of the DevOps culture, as we begin to see the cross-pollination of skillsets with a mix of development and operations happening across our teams.

In this section, we'll explain what CI, Delivery, and Deployment are and we'll look at the benefits they bring.

Continuous Integration

When we perform code integration, we're combining the software that we've written with our teams codebase. It's at this point we often discover a few things:

- How much has changed since we last committed?
- What degree of overlap has there been? For example, if shared code has been changed for different purposes.
- How well does our software work together?

During a commit of our software, we will often need to resolve differences in common code, particularly if several pieces of work are being carried out in the same area of the system simultaneously.

Modern source control systems will highlight the areas that need attention and will not allow the code commit to go ahead without first resolving the issues. We will often employ a tool that allows for comparison of the code that is being merged.

Still, this will only go so far in helping us complete the integration. There is still the potential for something to be missed, and if the wrong piece of code is chosen during a merge, then the behavior of the software will change unexpectedly after the commit is complete.

Even if you are in the early stages of the development of your product, it's likely the code is already being used by your customer, so a disciplined approach to code check-in and source control is needed.

The consensus is, the more often our developers commit their code, the sooner they are likely to discover any integration issues and resolve them. Small integrations will resolve more easily and will give each developer involved an idea of the direction the others are taking in the code.

This is why, in the Agile community, there has been a movement away from techniques that prolong the length of time before code is integrated, such as **feature branching.**

Instead, we favor **trunk-based development**—small discrete code commits to the main development code branch, sometimes using feature flags or branch by abstraction to hide code that isn't ready to be consumed yet.

Trunk-based development is better known as CI. It involves making regular code commits, at least once a day. The code is built on every commit, if the build and automated tests are successful, the commit is allowed. If the build or tests fail, the commit is not successful and the developer(s) must fix any problems before attempting to commit again.

In CI, we focus on the integration and validation of code at the unit and integration test-level. To achieve this, it's important that we have a reliable suite of automated unit and integration tests.

How does this keep us Agile?

CI has spread beyond the XP community to other Agile practitioners because it reduces the likelihood of integration issues. It also means we receive feedback earlier regarding how our code performs with that of other developers.

CI has significant benefits over source control strategies, such as feature branching, which creates the tendency to *refine* features until they are ready to release. Leaving the feature branch open for extended periods of time without committing back to the trunk increases the risk of collision.

Things to try

To set up CI, there are a few things that we need to put in place, some of them you'll probably be doing already. My suggestion is that we don't attempt to implement all steps at once unless we have an experienced DevOps specialist in our team. Instead, we'll need to learn as we go. The following stages are suggestions:

Stage 1:

- We use a source code repository to manage our software, its configuration, and documentation
- We check-in code at least once a day
- Both the building and testing of our software is optimized for us to get fast feedback
- Our code is built at every check-in

Stage 2:

- All tests are automatically run at every check-in; any failures are flagged
- The build and test results are obvious to all

Stage 3:

- Tests are executed in a test environment similar to our production environment. Teams usually set up a CI server to manage this; tools such as Jenkins, Concourse, Codeship, and TeamCity are perfect for this job.
- Our software is deployed automatically to the test environment after a successful build.

Continuous Delivery

Continuous Delivery (CD) is an extension of our CI practice and involves setting up push-button deployment processes so that our software can be deployed on request to the production environment. This requires an extra level of discipline on top of CI and means we will need to ensure the following:

- Our software is always kept in a deployable state.
- Our software's environment configuration is automated, which means we can deploy to any environment on-demand.

- It often requires our software's deployment to be *outage-less*, meaning that new features are delivered seamlessly to our customer.
- A deployment pipeline is set up which automatically ensures various steps are taken during each deployment.
- Our team takes ownership and responsibility for the deployment and management of their software in the production environment. This means they are no longer reliant on another team and don't have to wait in line.
- Setting up a Continuous Delivery process requires close collaboration between our development and operations teams. The cross-pollination of skillsets creates more understanding and ownership of our product in its operational environment within both teams. This is often referred to as a **DevOps culture**.
- This level of automation often involves problem detection during deployment; if any issues are detected, the deployment can be stopped and rolled back immediately. This introduces resilience into our release process.

How does this keep us Agile?

The benefits that CD brings us include:

- By deploying to production early and often, we significantly reduce the risk that something might go wrong during that later stage of our delivery cycle.
- We increase resilience in our product, and its overall stability, because we can quickly roll forward and back in our production environment seamlessly. Making changes to production daily irons out any potential problems early and makes deployment to our production environment an insignificant event, and less costly.
- Deployment is treated as part of our development cycle; this solves two problems:
    - Our Development Team has ownership of end-to-end delivery through our deployment pipeline. We no longer have to wait for another team to do work for us.
    - Our business doesn't have to wait to receive the benefits of our good work.
- We close all-important feedback loops by getting our software into our customers' hands as soon as possible.

Things to try

To set up CD on top of the three stages already outlined in the CI section, we'll need an additional stage:

Stage 4:

- Implement a push-button *outage-less* deployment of our software to our production environment
- Confirm success or highlight failure of the release to our human deployment technician
- Implement automatic rollback functionality should a problem be detected during the rollout phase
- Make errors visible to our human deployment technician

Continuous Deployment

Once you have CI and CD in place, the final step is to remove the need for the push button and fully automate deployment to our production environment.

For a variety of business reasons, it sometimes makes sense not to switch on new features immediately. We can use strategies such as feature toggles to hide or show features once they've been deployed.

> Feature toggles enable us to deploy a feature to our production environment behind a toggle or switch, which can be turned on/off at any time without the need to redeploy code. This has a couple of benefits:

> - It's rare for a software team to have a testing environment exactly the same as our production environment; it's too expensive. With a feature toggle, however, we are able to selectively turn on the feature and test it.
> - This will help us ascertain if our software works well with production-only configurations such as load balancing, caching, replication tiers, and so on.

It gives us a more controllable release strategy. With a feature toggle, we can selectively turn on features for certain user groups, for example, in an alpha testing situation where we want our new features to be seen by a select group.

How does this keep us Agile?

The benefits on top of CD include:

- Every change goes into production directly; each increment goes as soon as it is committed.
- The feedback loop is as short as possible.
- By using strategies such as feature toggles, versioning, or branch by abstraction, it is possible to deploy to our production environment without necessarily using the new functionality. This means that our code, even though it isn't finished yet, is already deployed to production, which gives us valuable feedback on the integration and deployment of our new software.

Things to try

On top of the stages required to implement CI and Continuous Deployment, we'll need the following stage:

Stage 5:

- Implement an automated smoke test during production, triggered by a deployment
- Implement a notification system which immediately alerts us of success or failure in production due to a rollout
- Automate the *outage-less* deployment during production, triggered by a successful build/test on our CI server

Summary

We've looked at a few different practices that specifically target increasing our confidence when using an incremental delivery approach.

Refactoring helps us keep our software in a healthy and easy to maintain state. Using the analogy of the field, it's essential that we keep the weeds down because before we know it, we may be dealing with thickets or bushes. To do this, we regularly *garden* our code as we enhance or add to existing areas of functionality.

We can think of **Test-Driven Design (TDD)** or specification driven approach because it changes our thought processes regarding how we write software compared to a test-after pattern.

Refactoring and TDD support an emergent approach to designing our software. So, although we still require some architectural design upfront, we require less big-design thinking overall.

Also, the resulting TDD automated test suite helps us verify and validate our software is still working as intended throughout its development life cycle.

Finally, CI, Continuous Delivery, and Continuous Deployment allow us to avoid the significant integration and deployment issues that plague waterfall projects.

All of these practices for building software keep our focus on delivering small increments of working software. They help us avoid the perils of Water-Scrum-Fall.

In the next chapter, we're going to look at how we incorporate lean thinking into our product development life cycle to help us deliver what our customer needs sooner.

8
Tightening Feedback Loops in the Software Development Life Cycle

Now that we've got you through the foundations of setting up your Agile team, this chapter is where we start to look at the "secret sauce" of Agile.

The adage "people don't know what they want until they see it" is just as true in the software industry as any other. The sooner we can deliver something useful to our customer, the earlier they can use it in a real-world environment, and the sooner we will be able to gather feedback on whether we're on the right track.

People often talk about Agile "speeding up" delivery, which it usually does. But this doesn't necessarily mean we deliver the same set of requirements at a faster pace just by working overtime. Working longer hours is an option, but it is not sustainable over an extended period. Instead, delivery in an Agile context means we become smarter in terms of how to deliver the same set of requirements; this is how we speed up.

How we build and deliver software will make a big difference to whether we successfully give our customers something they need.

In this chapter, we'll look at techniques for getting early confirmation that our ideas are solving the problems we've been asked to address.

We'll look at three different methods, which can be implemented individually or combined, to help us deliver in a smarter way.

These are topics we'll cover:

- Implementing incremental delivery in Agile:
  - Working with software in small, manageable chunks
  - How to make use of inspecting and adapting in your Scrum ceremonies
  - The importance of UX
  - Shifting left
- Introducing some Lean thinking to improve flow:
  - Systems thinking: Optimizing the system as a whole, not locally
  - Changing our workflow by managing the work in progress
  - Developing a mindset for continuous process improvement
- Adopting Lean Startup principles to validate product ideas sooner:
  - Build, Measure, Learn: Learning rapidly by doing and failing fast

Implementing incremental delivery in Agile

In Chapter 1, *The Software Industry and the Agile Manifesto*, we discussed the Agile values and principles. One principle, in particular, has relevance:

> *Deliver working software frequently, every couple of weeks to every couple of months, with a preference for the shorter timescale.*

Working software is a term we use to describe software that is working as it was intended, that is, it has met all of its acceptance criteria and our **Definition of Done** (**DoD**) and is either waiting to be shipped or already has been. The concept of working software is intended to solve several problems we often run into in the software industry:

- It moves the focus from documentation and other non-functional deliverables to what we're being paid for, software. The intention of the Agile value **working with software over comprehensive documentation** isn't to say documentation isn't needed; it's just about maintaining the right balance. We are, after all, a software product development team, not a documentation team.

To illustrate this, if we deliver technical design documentation to our client, it will probably make little sense to them. And unless they are technical, it won't give them any understanding of how their product is evolving. Working software, however, is tangible, much nearer to its final state, and will provide them with a real sense of progress.

- We want to deliver increments of working software so that we build up the product as we go. If we do it smartly, parts of the product can be put to use before the rest becomes fully functional.
- It emphasizes working software because it lets our client preview how things could be and gives them an opportunity to provide relevant feedback based on the real product.

To give you an analogy, imagine we are considering a new kitchen for our house or apartment. We might look in brochures or go to a kitchen showroom to see examples of kitchens we like. We might work with a designer to establish the important key attributes that we're looking for. They might create a computer-generated concept drawing of how our kitchen might look once it's finished. It might even be rendered in 3D, and we might be lucky enough to get to walk around it in a virtual reality environment.

However, until our new kitchen is installed in our space, we won't know if it works how we hoped it would. The only way we'll find out is by using it. The design steps employed by the kitchen designer and our imagination are done to help us envisage any potential problems, but until we're *hands-on* with our kitchen, we won't know if it's right for us.

If it isn't, then it might be quite costly to fix a finished kitchen. The same goes for software; correcting it can be quite expensive. The later we leave it, the more expensive it becomes.

However, with the right software delivery approach, we can reduce the risk of this happening. To do this, we have to think beyond just using iterations; we have to put some thought into how we slice up our product for delivery.

For instance, just completing part of the data layer of an application, without any implementation of the user interface elements that a user will interact with, doesn't deliver anything of real use for our business. Without a technical understanding of how software is built, our customer will find it impossible to imagine how the software might look in its final state and will be unable to give any real feedback.

The sooner we can deliver usable software, the sooner we can get feedback on whether it is useful. This is what we mean by tightening feedback loops. Let's look at how to do this.

Working with software in small, manageable chunks

The easiest way to address the risk of people not knowing what they want until they see it is to deliver usable increments of working software to them as soon as possible. A crucial aspect of this early-and-often approach is that we will get meaningful feedback that we can incorporate back into the ongoing build and delivery.

Using this approach to software delivery means that everyone, including our customer, has to understand the caveats. They won't be seeing or using software that is either necessarily complete or has the final polish applied. In fact, they will see software as it evolves in both function and form. User experience, which includes user interactions, process flow, and graphic design, will also be iteratively applied as we learn more.

How we break down the requirements into small manageable chunks is the first step to achieving this. It's vital that we first deliver the parts of our product that we most want feedback about. These are often our core business processes, the things that directly or indirectly make us money, and therefore involve the most risk.

To achieve this approach, we should stop thinking of building up functionality in layers, as shown in the following diagram:

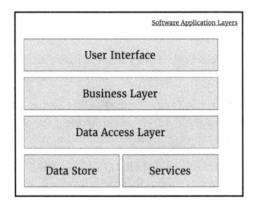

This method may seem sensible because by starting at the backend and developing the data store with its associated business logic, we are creating a foundation to build upon. However, it's somewhat of a construction industry analogy that doesn't apply to how we make software.

Instead, to deliver incrementally, we have to think of each increment as end-to-end functionality that provides some business value to our customer. We often refer to this as vertical slices of software, because every small slice carves through each application layer, delivering aspects of each. The concept of vertical slicing is shown in the following diagram:

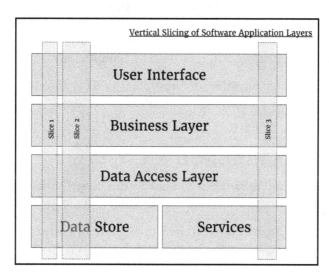

We include the **User Interface** layer so that we provide our client with some way of interacting with our software so that they can make real use of it. If we think of each vertical slice as a feature, we can carve up our features in a way that will make sense as we build out the product incrementally.

For instance, if we are building an online shop, the first vertical slice could be the display of items we have for sale. As well as showing items for sale, we'll probably need some way of managing their details. Again, we can build something rudimentary to start with and then incrementally deliver enhancements as required.

The next vertical slice could be either the checkout process or the search facility. Any of these features can be completed independently of each other, but it probably makes sense to build them in a particular order. For instance, without items for sale the search facility won't work, nor will the checkout process.

If we build up our feature set in a way that makes sense, we get valuable feedback from our customer that we're building the right thing. And as we deliver further increments of working software, they can use these to determine if the software we're developing will meet their needs.

We also get to validate our technical approach by asserting whether or not we're building the thing right. Once we have an end-to-end delivery taking place, we can start to iron out problems in our integration and deployment processes. We will also get to learn sooner how we will configure and manage our production environment.

When building any product, we take the *Goldilocks* approach—not developing too much, or too little, but getting it just right. This, in particular, should influence our decisions in terms of architecture and DevOps; we do just enough to get our current feature or feature slice working. Architecture and infrastructure have to be built incrementally too.

We'll talk more about how to prioritize features later in this chapter, in the *Build, Measure, Learn - Adopting Lean Startup and learning to validate ideas* section.

Inspection and adaption

When Ken Schwaber and Jeff Sutherland created Scrum, they founded it on empirical process control theory, which has three pillars: transparency, inspection, and adaption.

Transparency comes in many forms in our Scrum team, mainly through the tenet of making work visible. The Scrum Board plainly shows what our team is working on. There is no hidden work in Scrum; our team members are open and forthcoming about what they are working on when discussing it at the Daily Scrum or the Sprint Review. Even the Product Backlog is available for all to see.

Scrum provides high-bandwidth information regarding our team, our process, and the product on which we're working. At various points, we can **inspect** the information that we receive and make adjustments to how we work, or what we're working on. If new data comes to light, we **adapt** and change it up.

In empirical processes, all knowledge is gained through sensory experience and custom and tradition should be avoided. In this way, we should encourage our Scrum team to challenge the status quo and prevent any *this-is-how-we-do-things-around-here* thinking. If we do, we will benefit from profound changes in our approach that will significantly increase our chances of success.

In the Scrum framework, there are multiple opportunities to inspect and adapt:

- During Sprint Planning, as the team determine how they will implement the Sprint Backlog
- At the Daily Scrum, when new information is uncovered during the implementation of a User Story

- When a User Story is completed, or a new feature is delivered; we check in with our Product Owner or business owner to verify it is as expected
- At the Sprint Review, when our stakeholders are invited to give feedback
- During the Sprint Retrospective, when we can uncover what is and isn't working well, and we create a plan to take action and change things up

These are all checkpoints for us to consider if new information has come to light since the last time we met and decided what to do.

The importance of User Experience (UX)

Along with our Product Owner, our **User Experience** (**UX**) specialists are usually the first people to engage directly with our key stakeholders to determine what is wanted.

The job of our UX professionals is to help our team turn what our customer **wants** into something our customer **needs**. If the customer needs aren't obvious, a UXer has tools in their toolbox which can be used elicit further information.

Their toolset includes creating wireframes, or semi-interactive prototypes using tools such as InVision, or full mockups using HTML/CSS and JavaScript. Each gives an experience close to the real thing and helps our customers share and understands their vision.

The UX professional, working closely with the Product Owner, is responsible for two aspects:

- What is required?
- How it will work best

 UX covers all aspects of the user interface design. It can be broadly summed up as interaction design and graphic design with a smattering of psychology, but that is just the tip of the iceberg. Although both roles overlap to a certain degree, user interaction design often concerns itself with user interactions and the process flow within the product. Graphic design concerns itself with presentation, particularly information hierarchy, typography, and color.

A UX specialist has to have a good ear, patience, and be willing to go through multiple iterations to get feedback.

If we're to create software that is intuitive and straightforward to use, we have to start with the UX because it drives how we build the application. Different UXs will result in different application architectures. We create software for people; we need to get feedback from these people about whether we're building the right thing as soon as possible

Remember, it's not sufficient to just make software how we think it should work. Instead, we need to turn what the customer wants into something the customer needs.

Shifting left

Shifting left is the concept of incorporating specific practices, which have traditionally been left until late in the process, much earlier in our workflow.

System integration, testing, user experience, and deployment can all profoundly affect the outcome and success of our product; they all validate the product's viability in different ways. If we start thinking about them sooner in our development life cycle and we start to build these strategies as we go, we have a much better chance of success and of avoiding any nasty surprises.

The following diagram shows what we mean by shifting left:

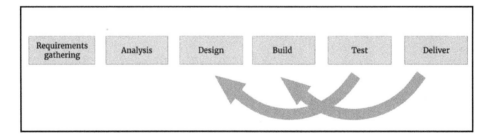

By moving these practices towards the beginning of our product development life cycle, we will start to get feedback sooner that these aspects of our product will work.

For example, in a linear development process such as a gated waterfall approach, we often leave a full integration and system test until the end of the project. This creates several problems:

- Taking the "big bang" approach to system integration often uncovers many false assumptions that were made, and therefore many changes will be required. It will be costly, with days or even weeks of lost time.

- A large-scale test at the end of the development cycle will often find numerous problems that need to be fixed. Sometimes it will discover fundamental issues that require substantial reworking, or even going back to the drawing board.

In the same way, I've seen user interaction and graphic design left until the end of the development cycle. These specialists are often brought in late to the project, with the hope that they will make things work better or make things look nice. Unfortunately, if making things work better or look nice involved significant changes to the user interface, it would also often require a substantial shift in the architecture of the application.

Simply put, by working on the things that could have a profound effect on the outcome of the product sooner, we reduce risk.

The following graph shows the relative cost of fixing deficiencies depending on where they are found in the software development life cycle:

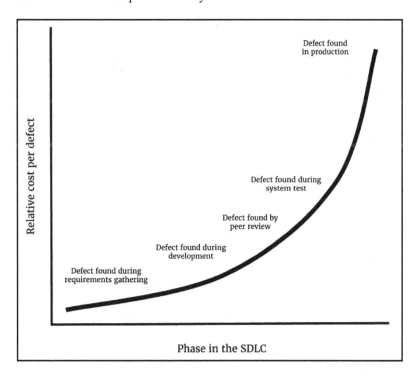

Defects in software are anything that doesn't work as intended or expected, whether it's a miscommunicated, misunderstood, or poorly implemented requirement, or a scalability or security issue.

We uncover defects by moving increments of working software through our system to "done" as quickly as possible. To do this, we have to incorporate all aspects of software development, often starting with UX, as well as testing and deployment strategies from the outset. We don't expect to build all of these in full the first time around. Instead, we plan to do just enough so that we can move to the next increment and the next, iteratively improving as we go.

Shifting right

As well as shifting left, you may be wondering if there is such a thing as shifting right. Yes, there is; it's where we start to think in terms of maximizing the value delivered, and delivering that value to the client as soon as possible.

We'll look at this in Chapter 9, *Seeking Value – How to Deliver Better Software Sooner*.

Introducing some Lean thinking to improve flow

So far, we've looked at breaking work down into small chunks. We've also looked at how we can better inform the work that we carry out by shifting left the activities that we have traditionally neglected until the end of our development cycle.

Now we will apply some Lean thinking to see how we can improve the flow of work.

Just as a refresher, in Chapter 2, *Agile Software Delivery Methods and How They Fit the Manifesto*, we discussed the key tenets of Kanban/Lean, which are:

1. Make the work visible so that we can inspect and adapt.
2. Break down work into similar size units, to smooth flow and reduce the "waste of unevenness."
3. Limit our work in progress so that we focus on improving our end-to-end flow.

In the following section, we talk specifically about how we enhance flow through our system, but first let's try an activity, as there is nothing quite likes a hands-on demonstration of how this works:

ACTIVITY: The coin game.
WHAT YOU'LL NEED: 10 coins, three to eight people, a timing device and a team member to operate it.
SETUP: This game is best played seated around a long table. Arrange the team around the table. Each team member should be easily able to pass coins to the next.

This game is played in three rounds; each round, the coins will start with the first person in the line. The coins have to pass through the hands of every team member. Each coin has to be flipped one at a time before it can be considered "processed" by that team member. The round will end when the last person in the line has flipped all the coins

ROUND ONE: The batch size is 10. Give all 10 coins to the first player. They flip each coin one at a time until all 10 have been flipped and then pass the pile to the next player. The next player flips all the coins one at a time until all are flipped and then gives the pile of 10 to the next player. And so on. Start the timer when the first coin of the first player is flipped. Stop the timer when the last coin of the last player is flipped. Record the time it took.

ROUND TWO: The batch size is split. Repeat, except give the coins to the first player in two batches, one of four and one of six. Flip the coins in the batch of four first. Once the four have been flipped; pass them on to the next player. The next player then flips the stack of four coins one by one. Meanwhile, the first player flips all the coins in the bunch of six. Once they've flipped each coin, they pass the batch of six on to the second player. Again, the timer starts when the first coin is flipped by the first player and stops when the last coin is flipped by the last player. Record the time it took.

ROUND THREE: The batch size is one. For the final round, pass all the coins to the first player. Once again, they flip each coin one at a time, except as soon as they've flipped one coin they pass it to the second player. The second player can then flip the coin and pass it on to the third player. Again, the timer starts when the first coin is flipped by the first player and stops when the last player flips the last coin.

Play the game first, and then we'll discuss the possible outcomes in the results section.

The coin game results

So, how did we get on with the coin game activity? What did we observe?

During the first round with a batch of 10, we'll have noticed that nine people were sitting around doing nothing, while one person flipped coins.

During the second round, with the batches of four then six, we'll have observed that both batches were faster than the batch of 10. We'll also have seen that the batch of four moved faster than the batch of six. If the batch of six had been played first, it would have slowed the batch of four down to its pace.

After the third round, we'll have noticed that, as the batch size comes down, the time to complete the work speeds up quite dramatically. That's because the utilization of every person in the line increases as we reduce the batch size.

We've optimized the system for the coin game; now it's time to discuss the theory.

Systems thinking – Optimizing the whole

When we're part of a complex system, such as software development, it's easy to believe that doing more in each phase of the SDLC will lead to higher efficiency.

For instance, if we need to set up a test environment to system-integration-test a new feature, and this takes a while to make operational, we'll be inclined to increase the size of the batch of work to make up the time lost setting up the environment.

Once we start to batch work together, and because it's complicated and requires so much setup time, the thinking is that it won't do any harm to add a bit more to the batch, and so it begins to grow. While this can lead to local efficiency, it becomes problematic when we discover an issue because any reworking will cause delays. And while this may only affect one particular part of the batch, we can't easily unbundle other items, so everything gets delayed until we fix the problem.

As we saw in the coin game, large batches take longer to get through our system. When a problem is discovered inside a batch, this will have a knock-on effect both up and downstream in the process. Reworking will be needed, so people back upstream will need to stop what they are doing and fix the problem. Meanwhile, people downstream are sitting around twiddling their thumbs, waiting for something to do because the batch has been delayed for reworking.

Gated approaches with handovers cause a big-batch mentality because our local efficiency mindset makes us believe that doing everything in one phase will be more efficient than doing it incrementally. The reality is that doing everything perfectly the first time is just not possible.

In a complex system, when you optimize locally, you tend to de-optimize the system as a whole. Instead, we need to break our big batches of work down into smaller chunks and focus on end-to-end flow through our system, like in the coin game—the smaller batches of coins flow much more evenly.

There is, of course, a balance to be struck; we need to be realistic regarding what is possible. The smallest chunk possible is a discrete piece of functionality that can be delivered and from which we can gain feedback on its applicability. This feature, or slice of a feature, shouldn't be so large that a work item sits in progress for weeks, or months even.

Instead, break items down so that they deliver incremental value. The feedback we get increases in value as it travels down the delivery pipeline. The more input that we gain, whether it's direct from our customer through a working software demonstration, through integration with other parts of our system, or actually deployed; the better our chances of success.

For example, why hold off deploying to the production environment until you have a critical mass? Instead, use feature flags to deploy, but keep the feature switched off in production until it's ready for release. We can do this to get critical feedback about system integration and the final step of the deployment process at production time. Plus, with the right infrastructure tweaks to enable us to switch on certain features for a selective audience, we can test our new feature in production before we go live.

Changing our workflow

When using Scrum, the Sprint Backlog is often seen as the batch size. A pattern we often see, and something that we want to minimize as much as possible, is a Scrum Board that looks like this:

Product Backlog		Sprint Backlog	To-do	In progress	Done	Sprint Goal
User Story	User Story	User Story		Task Task	Task Task Task	Simple checkout and payment process complete
User Story	User Story	User Story		Task Task	Task Task Task	
User Story	User Story	User Story	Task	Task Task	Task	**Sprint Burndown**
User Story	User Story	User Story	Task	Task	Task	
User Story	User Story	User Story	Task Task	Task		

You'll notice that almost every single User Story is in play, which probably means that each member of our team is working on something different. This is often a symptom that our team isn't working together, but as individuals, within their specializations—user experience designer, graphic designer, developer, frontend developer, tester.

Each specialist will go through the tasks of a User Story to determine if there is some work they can do. Once they've moved through all stories on the board and consider their tasks "done," they then look at the Product Backlog to see if there is any further work that fits their specialty.

In this scenario, when a software developer considers the coding is complete for one particular User Story, they then move onto the next User Story for the next piece of coding, and so on. This practice causes a few knock-on effects:

- **Handoffs:** Handing work over between the specializations, in this case between the software developer and the reviewer or tester, is wasteful regarding knowledge and time lost during the transfer. This also includes a transfer of responsibility where, like a game of software development tag, the last person who touches the software becomes responsible.
- **Interruptions:** The team member will need to be pulled off what they're currently doing to fix any problems brought up by either testing or review. There will likely be several iterations of reviewing, testing, and bug fixing.
- **Waiting in queues:** Queues of work start to form. For instance, all the coding is getting done super quickly because all of the developers are so busy coding. So busy, in fact, none of them are stopping to review each other's code or fix any problems the testers have raised. This leaves each of those User Stories open, with a status of "in progress" on the board, when in fact nobody is working on them.
- **Multitasking**: Despite all best intentions, the lack of synchronization between team members will cause people to be pulled from one task to another to perform handovers or reworking.

When a team works this way, if we lay out each task in sequence it will look a little like a production line, except instead of having just one production line, we have one for each User Story. The previous person in the line believes they've completed their work and hands it over to the next person to do theirs; they then start the next User Story and open a new production line. However, making software is not a linear process, and it won't be long before each team member is being pulled from one User Story to another.

Handoffs are especially apparent to the test role. They are often the last people in the process before deployment, and therefore the ones under the most pressure—pressure to get testing done and pressure not to find problems (or if they do, depending on how significant the problems are, to accept that they could be dealt with in another round and to let the software go out in a compromised form).

Thinking in terms of job specializations tends to put us into boxes. It makes us think that business analysts only gather requirements, software developers only write code, and testers only test it. This isn't team thinking; this is individual thinking.

At worse, it causes an abdication of responsibility, where people only feel responsible for their part of the User Story, rather than the User Story as a whole. This approach is little more than a mini-waterfall. It still shares the same problems associated with cascading work, albeit on a smaller scale.

To accommodate "vertical slices" of useful software, we have to change our workflow. Each User Story becomes the whole team's responsibility. Remember, Scrum intends us to work together to get the ball across the line. The distinction between frontend, backend, UX designer, and tester starts to blur.

To focus on flow, we have to consider the system as a whole, from the point when we start to work on an item to the point where we deliver it. We look to optimize the end-to-end delivery of items in our flow through the close collaboration of our roles.

 You might hear end-to-end flow also referred to as **cycle time**. The cycle time for a User Story starts when work begins on it, and is the number of days to completion, or "done."

One way to improve team cohesiveness and focus is by limiting the amount of **Work In Progress (WIP)**. How do we do this? There are two schools of thought:

- Reduce work in progress limits to a minimum; allow the team to get a feel for flow over several items of work, then if necessary increase WIP gradually to see if it increases flow or decreases flow.
- Don't set any WIP limits and watch what naturally happens; if a logjam starts to form, reduce the WIP limit for that particular column.

The aim of limiting WIP is to reduce the amount of multitasking any one team member has to do. As we've already mentioned in Chapter 2, *Agile Software Delivery Methods and How They Fit the Manifesto*, one definition of multitasking is "messing multiple things up at once."

This isn't just an approach we use for Kanban. We can apply this to Scrum as well, by merely applying a WIP limit in our in-progress column.

We can start to measure flow by annotating our User Stories with useful information. Apply the start date to mark when work began. Add the finish date when the job completes. The number of working days between the start and end date is the cycle time of the story. At each Daily Scrum, if the story is in progress but isn't being worked on; mark the story card with a dot. This shows the wait time in days. By reducing delays, we will also increase flow.

There are team configurations that will help us naturally limit WIP:

- **Pairing**: Two Development Team members work together on one User Story, taking it from end to end across to the board. See `Chapter 7`, *Software Technical Practices Are the Foundation of Incremental Software Delivery* for more on Pair Programming.
- **Swarming**: A temporary burst of the whole team's power, used to get over humps. For instance, to move all the User Stories waiting to be tested, everyone rolls up their sleeves and starts testing. Once we've gotten over the hump, the team then tends to return to their standard configuration.
- **Mobbing**: The whole team's power applied to one User Story at a time. Unlike swarming, the team tends to stay in mob configuration to see a piece of work through from start to end. Some teams work in mobs permanently, giving them a WIP of one User Story at a time. See `Chapter 11`, *Improving Our Team Dynamics to Increase Our Agility* for more on Mob Programming.

In each of these approaches, people work much more closely together. Software development is about end-to-end delivery. Cross-pollinating and understanding each other's skill sets by literally working together creates better software and most likely sooner. Working this way also avoids hand offs and context switching as much as possible

This is a move from optimizing our "resources" to optimizing our workflow, which at the end of the day achieves what we wanted—increasing the flow of value we deliver to our customer, which in our case is in the form of working software.

Kaizen and developing a small, continuous improvement mindset

We first discussed Kaizen in `Chapter 2`, *Agile Software Delivery Methods and How They Fit the Manifesto*. It is a Japanese word meaning "change for the better." It is commonly referenced as meaning "continuous improvement," and made famous through its incorporation in the **Toyota Production System (TPS)**.

On the Toyota production lines, sometimes things go wrong. When they do, the station where the problem has occurred gets an allotted time to fix it. If they exceed the time buffer, there will be an impact on the rest of production, and they will need to stop the entire line. At this point, workers, including the managers, gather at the problem site to determine what seems to be the problem and what needs to be done to fix it.

All too often, when a problem occurs, we see the symptoms of the problem, and we try to fix it by fixing only the symptoms. More often than not, the cause of the problem goes deeper, and if we don't fix more than just the surface-level observations, it will occur again. So, if the production line starts up again in this situation, it won't be long before the problem recurs and it needs to be shut down once more.

To solve this problem, Toyota introduced *Root Cause Analysis*, which uses techniques for getting to the bottom of why something has happened. Two popular methods are Five Whys analysis and Ishikawa (Fishbone diagram).

I'll explain the simpler of these, *Five Whys* analysis, using a real-world example.

At my current place of work, we encourage our teams to take ownership of their deployments during production. This strategy doesn't come without risk, of course, and the teams do have a lot to learn in the DevOps space. Fortunately, we have coaches who work explicitly in this area, helping us come up-to-speed. Even so, sometimes the teams can be overly cautious.

That is why we introduced the concept of Fail Cake, inspired by a ThoughtWorks team who did something similar; we could see that we needed to encourage the team to take strategic risks if they were going to advance their learning.

Here is the story of Fail Cake and learning fast.

Fail Cake

Several of the teams I worked with identified specific circumstances which would trigger a Kaizen event (Continuous Improvement Meeting). These triggers included one particularly dire situation: releasing a priority-one bug to production. If this happened, they would fix the problem immediately. Fortunately, they had a deployment strategy that meant they could usually quickly recover if they couldn't isolate the problem straight away.

Inspired by a ThoughtWorks blog post, `https://www.thoughtworks.com/insights/blog/` `make-failure-taste-better-failure-cake`, they would then buy a cake for everyone and invite them to a meeting. While eating the cake, they'd perform a root cause analysis to determine what went wrong in their process and how they could prevent it ever happening again. The purchase and eating of the cake was deliberate; it was intended to give the team space to reflect and also encourage others involved in the incident to attend and give feedback. As a result of following this process, they very rarely released any priority-one bugs into production.

Here's a real example of one of our teams reflecting on how to improve their process using the Five Whys method.

Root cause analysis with the Five Whys method

Now we will see how a team used the Five Whys technique to solve a real-world situation:

Background: The team noticed that User Stories were taking longer to complete; they wanted to understand why. We had the presence of mind to understand that we'd been unconsciously increasing our batch size, so we conducted a Five Whys root cause analysis to try to understand it more:

- **Why were the team increasing their batch size?** Because the time dedicated to the weekly release train meant we might as well bundle more things together.
- **Why was the weekly release cycle so costly regarding time?** Because there was a business-critical part of their system that was written by someone else and had no automated tests, so they had to test it manually.

- **Why didn't we write automation tests?** We had tried, but certain parts of the code were resistant to having tests retro-fitted.
- **Why didn't we do something different from a full regression test?** We had tried multiple different strategies, plus a recent increase in the number of teams meant they could spread the regression test out amongst the group and rotate turns. However, this had the effect of only spreading the pain, not mitigating it entirely.
- **Why didn't we try a replacement strategy?** We could for certain parts of the system; in fact, we had come up with several plans to do so. But we couldn't do everything without making some changes to the existing code, and so it would still require regression testing. Plus, the weekly regression sapped our time and energy.

After conducting the above analysis, our team decided to change up our approach in the following ways:

- We would write an automation test suite for the parts of the application we could easily and reliably test. This would reduce the regression test effort.
- We would look at different strategies for manually regression-testing the rest so that we could find the optimal approach.
- We would re-architect the system, designing it with the intention of making it automation-testable from the get-go. We would gradually move away from the existing architecture, replacing parts as we went, using Martin Fowler's Strangler Application pattern.

Adopting Lean Startup methods to validate ideas

The Lean Startup method was devised based on the company start-up experiences of its author, Eric Rees. It aims to shorten product development times by using a hypothesis-driven incremental delivery approach, which is combined with validated learning.

In the following section, we'll provide a brief introduction to Lean Startup thinking and how this might apply generally, not just to organizations that are in their start-up phase.

Build, Measure, Learn

We mentioned just now that Lean Startup is a *hypothesis-driven* approach; let's pull this apart a little for more understanding. The hypothesis-driven approach involves setting up an experiment to test out if a theory we have has legs or not. It could be as simple as writing a statement with the following template:

- We believe that by creating *this experience*
- For *these people*
- We will get *this result*
- And we'll know this is true when we see *this happening*

A hypothesis has four parts:

- **The belief**: This is something that we think we know based on either evidence from our data, the needs of our customer, or a core competency (something we know how to do well, or are particularly good at)
- **The target market**: Our audience for this particular hypothesis
- **The outcome**: The outcome we believe we will get
- **The measurement**: The metrics that will tell us if our outcome is taking us in the right direction, towards our business objective

Using the hypothesis template, we then build out enough of a product feature set so that we can test out our theory. This is usually done incrementally over a number of iterations. This first cut of our product is known as the **Minimum Viable Product** (**MVP**) and is the smallest possible feature set that makes sense for us to validate with real-world users.

To do this, we take a feature-driven approach, where we prioritize certain features over others and get them to a viable offering state as soon as possible.

Prioritization is carried out using a release planning strategy that targets our primary, secondary, and tertiary user groups. Our primary user groups are the key users of our software product, the people who will tell us if our business idea is worth pursuing. So we'll build software which targets their needs first. This allows us to focus our efforts and target the most important aspects of our product.

We don't have to fully develop a feature to make it viable; we can target certain segments of our market first and test it out before we further enhance it. The aim is to create "light" features which, although limited in their functionality, will allow us to validate our ideas as quickly as possible.

Our *validated learning* comes into play as we start to measure the success of the experiment to determine if we're on the right track. We use *actionable metrics*; these are metrics that we've set up to help inform us of what business actions we should take when certain measurements are recorded.

To illustrate, if we're testing a feature that drives new membership sign-ups, we need to measure exactly how many new members signed up as a result of using our feature. If the non-member to new-member conversion rate is above a certain percentage threshold of people who used our feature, then we can most likely say it's a success, and we can carry on enhancing it further.

Another example is when building a checkout process for our online shop; we are validating two key aspects of our product. Firstly, do our customers want to buy what we're selling? Secondly, do they trust us and our checkout process enough that they will complete a purchase?

We can test this out in a number of ways without building out the full product feature, providing we capture people's actions and their reactions to measure our success.

In the Lean Startup approach, this constant testing of our assumptions is known as the **BUILD, MEASURE, LEARN** cycle as shown in the following diagram:

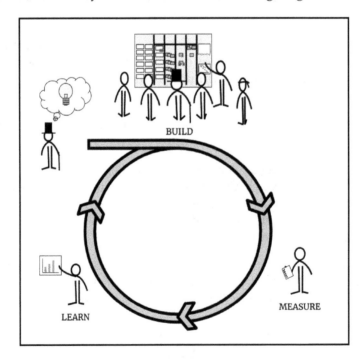

A Lean Startup is a metrics-driven approach, so before we start building features, we need to think about how we are going to measure their success.

The trick is to use the MVP to learn what does and doesn't work. The measurements we take from the learning phase, and the insights that we generate from them, we then feed into the next increment.

If the measurements indicate we're moving in the right direction and adding value, we continue to build on our current ideas.

If the measurements indicate we're not moving in the right direction, then we assess what to do. If we determine that the experiment is no longer working, we have the option to **pivot** in a different direction and try out new ideas.

The aim is to build up the increments until we have a **Minimum Marketable Product (MMP)**.

An example of Lean Startup MVP

We can use the Lean Startup mindset whether we're setting out to build a new product or creating a new feature for an existing one. The core concepts remain the same; first put together the hypothesis, and next create a release strategy which focuses the first release on the minimum core feature set that we need to validate our idea with.

We then build it and test it out with a user group that will give us constructive feedback. This group is often known as our "early adopter" group because they love using new technology, and if it solves a problem that they care about they won't be too concerned about the little "problems" an early product might have.

In the next section we give an example of a real-world MVP and how we can use the *build-measure-learn* cycle to validate an idea as quickly as possible. It illustrates how we can use the principle even on existing products.

Background

Our current product offers specific features that can only be accessed if you're a signed-up member. We were on a mission to increase our membership community and so decided to test out a few ideas to see if we could encourage people to sign up. This is the story of how we validated one of those features.

Hypothesis

Here's the hypothesis for our membership experiment:

- **We believe** that by *creating a virtual scrapbook in which web page clippings of text and photos can be placed*
- **For** *our audience of dedicated readers*
- **We will get** *more of our audience to sign up as members*
- **And we'll know this is true when we see** *more of our audience engaging with our new clippings feature and signing up as part of the process*

Approach

These steps outline the approach we took:

- **STEP 1: Brainstorm the experience from the user's perspective**: We first brainstormed as a group what the virtual scrapbook and clippings feature might look like. This took the form of a workshop guided by our User Experience specialist. She encouraged us to draw a storyboard to show the flow when using the web clippings tool.
- **STEP 2: Test the basic user experience**: Our UX specialist then took our collective ideas away and assembled some wireframes which we could test out with people on the street (Guerrilla usability testing).
- **STEP 3: Breakdown of User Stories**: Once we worked out the basic flow of clipping and pasting to a scrapbook, we broke the feature into User Stories. We used the User Story Mapping approach described in `Chapter 10`, *Using Product Roadmaps to Guide Software Delivery*, to create a simple story map.
- **STEP 4: Identify areas of risk or uncertainty**: We reviewed the story map and identified areas that were likely to impact our strategy. In particular, we were concerned that building a scrapbook that was robust and secure would take too long for our purpose of quickly validating this new feature. We proposed a spike (a mini-hackathon) to identify possible alternatives.

- **STEP 5: Shortcut to validation, build the minimum!**: We realized during our spike/mini-hackathon that we wouldn't need to build out the full scrapbook feature. Instead, we could use a slightly sneaky approach where we offered the clipping tool alone, and then once the audience member had clipped the text or picture, we would ask them to sign in or sign up before proceeding. If they clicked either option, we knew we had them, and they would likely use the feature. We also showed them an apologetic message: "Thanks for trying this new feature, but it isn't finished yet, we're just trying to discover the level of interest. Leave us your email address, and we'll be in contact soon." This shortcut is known as the "button to nowhere" because even though it's a dead-end for our user, we still manage to validate our idea.
- **STEP 6: Measure and learn**: So, while feeling somewhat dastardly because we hadn't given our audience a fully working feature, we spent the next five weeks with the "button to nowhere" feature live on our website. We felt less guilty after our analytics reported less engagement than we hoped for. We tweaked the user experience of the new feature to attract people's attention as they scrolled down the page but to no avail. Few people clipped an item, and even fewer clicked to sign up or sign in when asked.

We had failed and failed quickly, with relatively little effort in comparison to a full build, a failure that was a win for the Lean Startup MVP and the build-measure-learn mindset!

Learning rapidly by doing and failing fast

By using a hypothesis-driven approach such as Lean Startup, we can validate an idea quickly. The measurements we make give us feedback telling us whether we're moving in the right direction. We can use these numbers as we tweak and enhance a feature to see if it will make a difference and improve the outcome.

Failure is an option as long as there is learning and we adapt to the incoming information. The secret is to recognize the failure as early as we can.

To respond to rapid changes that are happening in the technology sector, above all else we need to become a learning organization.

Summary

Mostly, when moving from a waterfall-style delivery to an iterative/incremental delivery style, we struggle with a couple of things:

- **Breaking the work down into small chunks**: As a rule of thumb, a full-size Scrum team is aiming to deliver around five User Stories per Sprint. Most will struggle with delivering one in their first iteration.
- **Having the appropriate mechanisms for delivery setup**: If coming from a waterfall-style delivery background, most people will be used to work being carried out in separate phases. Unfortunately, we can apply this thinking to Scrum too, expecting development to be done in one sprint, integration and testing to be done in another, and deployment to be done in yet another. This isn't Agile thinking, we should avoid this approach at all cost.

In this chapter we've looked at ways to slice up our product into features that we can then prioritize and deliver in a way that provides value for our customer sooner. Why wait for the product to be complete before we start to share its usefulness?

We also discussed *shifting left* some of the technical practices, which gives us confidence that we can deliver—quickly and reliably—each vertical slice of a new feature. In this way, we rapidly increase our delivery capability, hopefully flooding our customer with regular feature updates.

With Scrum and other Agile frameworks, we make our customer part of our team and include the broader stakeholder group. We regularly seek their feedback based on the demonstration of each working increment of our product.

In the last section, we looked at Lean Startup and its approach to incremental delivery. It aims to build the *earliest testable product,* a product with a minimal feature set, known as the MVP (Minimum Viable Product). We used this to confirm, with our customer, and in a real-world setting, that it's what they need. The aim was to seek the highest value from our product and deliver something that our customer would truly be delighted with.

In the next chapter, we'll look at methods for seeking out value sooner so that we can first focus on the ideas we think our customer will need the most.

9
Seeking Value – How to Deliver Better Software Sooner

Traditionally, we have managed projects with a budget, date, and scope in mind. Although Agile techniques can deliver on any of these constraints, an Agile incremental delivery system is more powerful when it is used to focus on value. Focusing on value allows a Product Owner to be highly effective in their prioritization; they can pinpoint what is the best return on investment to the organization. A value focus reduces scope creep, enabling an Agile team to deliver what the business needs sooner.

In this chapter, we'll look at how product thinking combined with an objective-driven approach will help us narrow down what is important to our customer, sooner.

To do this, we'll look at real-world examples to shift the delivery team's perspective from one of just delivering on time, within scope, or within budget, to one of seeking value. We'll also take a look at practical ways that teams can use this approach to create feedback loops so that they can measure their value-seeking success as they go.

In this chapter, we will cover topics such as:

- Moving from project to product thinking
- Seeking value versus budgets or dates
- Product ownership becoming a team responsibility
- Telling the team *the why* and not *the what*
- Setting objectives
- Objectives and Key Results (OKRs)
- Hypothesis-Driven Development (HDD)
- Data Insights Beliefs Bets (DIBBs)

Moving from project to product thinking

To create a shift from project to product thinking, first we have to think about why we would want to do this.

As discussed in the early chapters, there has been a tendency in the software industry for us to use predictive forms of planning, mainly because we feel like this would give us the best chance of controlling a successful outcome. Up front requirements for gathering and design are needed to ascertain a budget, resources, and a completion date. This helps determine levels of comfort with the project before requesting a budget and moving forward with the implementation of the idea.

However, predictive planning requires **Big Design Up Front** (BDUF) which, even if using an iterative Agile method such as Scrum, will result in *Water-Scrum-Fall*. We carry out the initial ideation, requirement gathering, analysis, and design up front. We then implement the plan iteratively, before going through an extensive integration and deployment phase.

Water-Scrum-Fall solves some but not all of the problems Agile was intended to address. In fact, it reduces our agility significantly because we fix scope at the beginning of the work during the planning phase. When changes arise, there is little flexibility and a certain degree of reluctance to modify the plan. I've seen this happen many times, particularly in large projects where there seems to be a reluctance to change course, even when the obvious is staring us in the face.

 This is the **Sunk Cost Fallacy** in full swing. In a nutshell, sunk cost refers to how much money, time, and effort we've already invested into something. The more invested, the more likely we are to pursue something because of our predisposed position of not wanting to waste time, effort, or money already spent. However, this can create an emotional state which makes us unable to see whether we should cut our losses or not. We refer to this lack of objectivity as the Sunk Cost Fallacy. It points to our tendency to be biased towards pursuing those things we've already invested in. When considering whether to continue work on a product, we should focus on the value it will return when finished, not the money and time already spent.

If we shift from predictive to adaptive planning, we'll be able to avoid the feeling that we have to keep spending and we'll be able to chase value. To understand why we need first to understand the nature of the problem with which we're dealing. In the next section, we'll look at a framework that helps us make more sense of the situation.

Cynefin – A sense-making framework

Cynefin is a sense-making framework; it offers us a perspective from which we can assess a situation and identify a strategy to deal with it.

 Dave Snowden is the creator of the Cynefin framework. He started working on the model in 1999, while at IBM. He then went on to found and direct the IBM Cynefin Centre for Organizational Complexity in 2002. The word Cynefin itself is Welsh, pronounced *kun-ev-in*, and means haunt, habitat, acquainted, accustomed, or familiar.

The framework has four defined quadrants: **OBVIOUS**, **COMPLICATED**, **COMPLEX**, and **CHAOTIC**. Each quadrant defines a classification of a problem. In the center, there is a bubble of **DISORDER**; this is where issues that are yet to be classified reside.

The four classifications and some descriptions of each are shown in the following diagram:

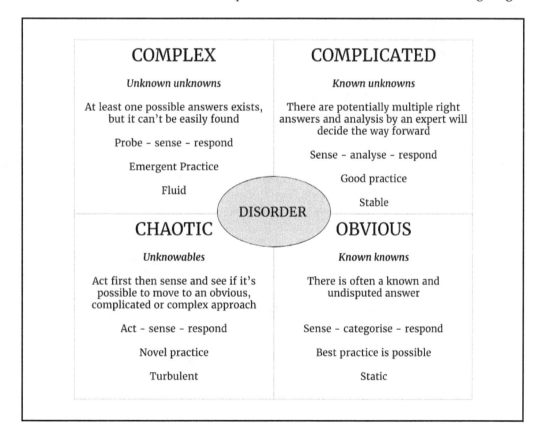

If we use the Cynefin framework to frame how we solve business problems, then one way of describing each quadrant would be:

- **OBVIOUS**: The solution to the problem is evident to all.
- **COMPLICATED**: The solution isn't obvious to everyone, but an expert in the domain would be able to analyze the problem and guide us to a solution.
- **COMPLEX**: This type of problem involves too much complexity for us to solve it through analysis alone. Instead, we have to conduct experiments (sometimes called Spikes) to determine what might work. We evolve our hypothesis based on each test's results.
- **CHAOTIC**: This type of problem catches us entirely by surprise. We have to act first, for example, to remove ourselves from immediate danger. We can then assess how to break down the problem into one of the three other classifications and deal with it.

For a software delivery team, it's rare that we're tasked with something **OBVIOUS**, especially as we're often using new technologies and solving complex business problems.

Sometimes we slip into the **CHAOTIC** quadrant, which can come in multiple forms, for example, a security breach in our production environment. Hopefully, this is also rare.

We quite often operate in the **COMPLICATED** quadrant which requires, at the very least, a degree of analysis and guidance toward a solution, usually by an expert in either the domain or the technology, or both.

However, if we're using new technologies and working on novel ideas, which we often are, then we're operating in the **COMPLEX** quadrant. This requires a different approach; analysis will only take us part of the way. Sometimes we just have to do something to discover how it might work. This is where Agile incremental delivery approaches will help us validate our ideas quickly.

Innovation with new technologies and business ideas creates a high degree of complexity due to the uncertainty of success in either the product or technical direction. We often talk in terms of developing resilience in these situations rather than developing the perfect solution. To do this, we need to operate the **COMPLEX** quadrant's empirical, hypothesis-driven, fail fast/learn rapidly approach.

The advantages of a product team

These are some of the benefits of working with a product team over a project team:

- **Better quality**: Project teams are often under pressure to deliver on budget or on time; this is how they are usually managed. If the project comes under pressure in terms of either of these, the scramble to complete it will result in a lower-quality product. If integrating with other systems, this can lead to high dependency (tightly-coupled reusability) or total autonomy (no reusability, which will probably involve us reinventing the wheel several times) rather than the sweet spot of getting just the right level of coupling and reuse.

- **A sense of ownership**: There is a sense of ownership that comes built-in with product teams; they've been responsible for their product from concept to delivery. Project teams know they will be moving on to the next project, and although they will try to their best as professionals, they will have little opportunity to provide a sense of ownership and responsibility once they've transferred to their next project.
  A software development team responsible for maintaining its product and keeping the lights on in the production environment will do all they can to minimize the effort they have to put into that, usually by automating repetitive tasks so they can put their energy into developing product features.

- **A learning mindset**: Shifting right to realize value sooner isn't just about moving from predictive to adaptive planning, but this does help. Building a complex system requires both a learning process and time for us to get things right, as we discussed in `Chapter 1`, *The Software Industry and the Agile Manifesto*. Even Winston Royce back in the 1970s was saying that we need to develop software iteratively/incrementally so that we can learn and improve. We learn as we go, and by making the product team long-lived, for the life of the product, we keep the learning within the team.

In a nutshell, this helps us start to develop what is known as **business agility**—that is, our agility moves beyond just our software teams themselves and begins to permeate through our business. Often, beginning with our product management team and through the use of data, insights, and measurements, we start to become a **learning organization**.

At the beginning of our journey towards business agility, we recognize that our business and the software that supports it are inextricably interlinked. Being able to adapt our software rapidly will help our ever-evolving business keep doing just that, allowing our company to keep up with change and maintain its competitive edge. *The only constant is change*, and with technology advances accelerating on an exponential curve (Moore's Law and then quantum computing) we need our business to be Agile too.

Moving from project to product

To shift to product thinking, we first need to look at some of the side-effect of project thinking.

We discussed project versus product thinking early on in Chapter 1, *The Software Industry and the Agile Manifesto*. We concluded that although project thinking wasn't all bad, if not managed correctly it tended to focus on the wrong outcomes—meeting time and budget requirements instead of delivering something of value, often settling for something that was somewhat useful rather than something that truly delights our customer.

Even projects that we run with an incremental delivery approach can suffer from this, as we often get put under pressure to deliver on time or within budget, or both, which can result in a significant slip in quality.

Project thinking works for particular categories of software development, mainly those that are small. The general rule of thumb is: the smaller the project, the higher its chance of success of delivering on time, within budget, and within scope, as there is less variance in the estimate. This thinking was shown by the *Cone of Uncertainty* in Chapter 1, *The Software Industry and the Agile Manifesto*, which shows that the further you are from completing something, the less certainty you have.

Larger-scale projects often introduce significant changes to the organization, and you can view the project manager as the curator of that change. We seek to minimize the disruption that large change brings by using a change management process. As we introduce the change, we will need to provide excellent communication and staff training.

Once everyone in the organization is up to speed, our project team then hands over maintenance and support to the support teams. This includes business support, that is, helpdesk, operational/infrastructure support (the operations team), and enhancement/bug fixing support. Although not always the case, each support team usually looks after multiple systems. Once our project is in the support phase, this is known as **Business As Usual (BAU)** and the support teams will be collectively known as BAU teams.

The project team is then free to disband or move to the next project. Some transfer of knowledge will take place between the project team and the BAU team, but just like any handover, this approach often results in us losing much collective knowledge of the finished product.

However, a fundamental shift has taken place—our business is no longer supported by digital systems. Instead, our digital systems are interwoven into our business; they are either core product offerings for our customers or our operational backbone. Viewed in this light, the knowledge we gain about our core products is one of our organization's chief assets.

Project managers are concerned with time and budget, and to an extent, product managers are too, but our product management teams are also focused on delivering return on investment to the organization. They use a different set of metrics to determine the success of a product.

Decisions that product managers make will include being able to identify when peak value has been achieved from a particular work stream. It's also vital for a product manager to know if more value is likely; for example, maybe by extending this particular work stream by another month, they might be able to double the organization's return on investment.

Our organization needs to become empirical in that it should fund work on product(s) based on data. We treat everything as experiments, and we measure our successes and failures honestly and brutally. We become a learning organization.

To shift from project to incremental product delivery, we turn our focus from managing date, budget, and scope to managing outcomes. Change management is also handled incrementally, giving the people working with our product a sense of evolution rather than abrupt, sometimes disruptive change.

Regardless of our organization's size and how it is structured, we want to create the sense that we're all on the same team, moving in the same direction, regardless of product management, the project management office, technology, marketing, and so on. We need to break down the silos as much as possible.

The first step is to create an alignment of purpose; the outcomes for our product(s) should align with our organization's overall mission and purpose.

By shifting our focus to outcomes, we will start to look at our products and our associated teams as **long-lived**. One way to start is to foster ownership amongst our technology teams regarding our core products.

In the next section, we'll look at ways to create alignment within our teams.

Setting objectives to create alignment of purpose

Giving teams relative autonomy by operating a system using subtle control means we have to devise ways of creating alignment within our organization. If our team is to be successful, it has to understand its purpose and how it fits with the rest of the group.

The following diagram shows a typical organizational hierarchy of strategic intent:

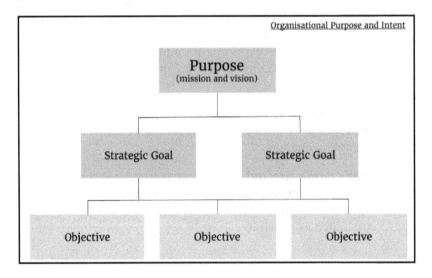

An organization's mission or purpose is the reason it exists. It rarely changes and is often defined in a single sentence. We mentioned a few prominent companies and their purpose in `Chapter 5`, *Bootstrap Teams with Liftoffs*; here are those examples again:

- **Google**: *To organize the world's information and make it universally accessible and useful*
- **Tesla**: *To accelerate the world's transition to sustainable energy*
- **Kickstarter**: *To help bring creative projects to life*

An organization's vision is a short statement indicating how it intends to realize its purpose or mission. A vision statement is usually relevant for several years and defines the current organizational strategy for carrying out its mission.

The strategic goals are often set annually, activities that will likely tie into the beginning of the financial year as it will usually involve a funding round. The annual goals should answer the question: How are we going to enact our strategy this year?

Objectives are quarterly milestones on our strategic roadmap, which we send to our teams to align them with our strategic intent.

Jason Yip, an Agile Coach at Spotify, defines alignment as *Intent + Rationale + Constraints* (`https://www.slideshare.net/jchyip/enabling-autonomy-at-spotify`).

The following diagram gives an example of alignment for an online retail company:

Intent ➕	**Rationale** ➕	**Constraints**
(the what)	(the why)	(any restrictions on the how)
Halve the number of returned items	It will increase customer satisfaction and reduce overheads	We have to do this in a way which increases customer satisfaction
		For example, we can't have a no returns policy

In this section, we'll look at how we can set objectives for creating alignment and get feedback on our success by tracking our progress against meaningful measurements.

Using Objectives and Key Results (OKRs)

OKRs were first introduced by Andy Grove at Intel Corp when he was CEO. They were then taken to Google by Grove's former colleague, John Doerr. Since then, many high-tech companies have used them including Uber, LinkedIn, Netflix, and so on.

The **Objectives** state the problem we're trying to solve, and the **Key Results** tell us if we're on the right track in terms of meeting the objective. We should look at OKRs as a way of aligning our people to our organization's purpose and its current strategic plan. They are a way of empowering our people to find solutions that will solve the challenges that we face.

The OKRs themselves should be challenging; we deliberately set the objective to stretch the team, making it only around 60% or 70% achievable.

So while OKRs are aspirational, we definitely shouldn't see them as a stick to beat our teams with. Instead, see them as a way to instill a sense of purpose and passion.

An example OKR for an online shop is shown as follows:

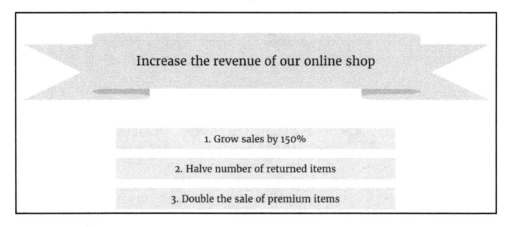

OKRs can be cascaded through to multiple teams. For instance, using the Objective and Key Results in the preceding diagram, we could cascade its three key results as objectives to three teams, as the following diagram shows:

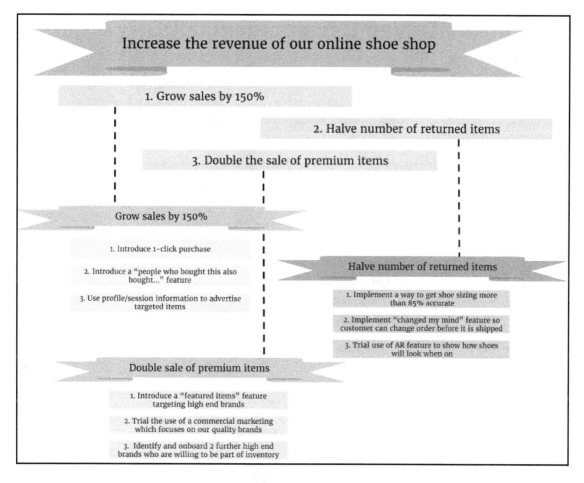

This top-to-bottom connection between objectives, the strategic goals, and the organization's vision and mission helps our teams create alignment regarding purpose. Effectively, it gives them the *why* of what they are doing and any solution they create will consider the broader context.

OKRs are revisited quarterly. Therefore, each key result should be set up so that it's possible to achieve tangible results in fewer than three months. The success of the key results will inform us in terms of whether we continue with the objective or alter our course to try something different.

Hypothesis-Driven Development (HDD)

We briefly introduced HDD in the last chapter when we discussed the Lean Startup's Build-Measure-Learn cycle.

As with OKRs, HDD is influenced by our organization's vision, mission, and strategic goals. We set the hypothesis at the feature/epic level; this will span multiple User Stories, sometimes across several teams.

A bit like OKRs, we can also cascade the hypothesis through to the team level, adjusting it accordingly to fit into each User Story's context. We can use the same simple template for both the feature/epic and User Story, which is as follows:

The template

We believe <by doing something>

For <these people>

We will <get this result>

And we'll know this is true when we see <these things happen>

An example

We believe by halving the returns of sale orders

For our online customers

We will increase our customer satisfaction and our revenue

And we'll know this is true when we see:

1. A significant increase in successful first times sales

2. Our overall revenue increases due to the lack of overheads such as return postage,

3. Our customer satisfaction index increases by 100%

The HDD and User Stories are similar in that they focus on an outcome and the people that we're creating that outcome for.

The significant difference between the User Story format and the HDD approach is that while the User Story has an acceptance criterion that often describes aspects of functional and non-functional requirements, the HDD approach has measurable outcomes.

Teams often use the acceptance criterion as the basis for their scenarios for **user acceptance testing** (**UAT**). It's possible to augment the HDD approach with an acceptance criterion if our team finds that helpful.

Data, Insights, Beliefs, Bets (DIBBs)

At Spotify, their teams are called **squads**. These small cross-functional teams, similar to a Scrum team, are often grouped in what they call tribes of up to 100 people. A tribe usually focuses on one aspect of Spotify's business, for example, a tribe that focuses on native mobile apps. A tribe's collection of squads will often co-locate in the same area.

There are many tribes at Spotify, spread across many different locations around the globe. This distributed nature presents a challenge for an organization that needs to move coherently across its music player product range.

Creating alignment is key when we have a high degree of autonomy in our teams so that we can move quickly, unencumbered by a chain of command.

After several evolutions of alignment-by-objective frameworks, including using OKRs, Spotify developed an argument framework called DIBBs. The following is a hypothetical example of a DIBB:

DATA	INSIGHTS	BELIEFS	BETS
A set of measurements	Our interpretation of those measurements	What we believe that means	Things we can try to test our beliefs
Premium / Free	ONLY A QUARTER OF USERS PAY FOR OUR SERVICE, BUT OUR MEMBERSHIP SIGNUP RATES HAVE PEAKED.	IF WE MAKE FEATURES WHICH ARE ONLY AVAILABLE FOR OUR PREMIUM MEMBERS WE'LL GET MORE SUBSCRIBERS.	1. ENABLE PREMIUM MEMBERS TO DOWNLOAD MUSIC TO PLAY OFFLINE.
Premium Signups Year-to-date	HOW CAN WE CONVERT MORE FREE MEMBERS TO PREMIUM?		2. GUARANTEE PREMIUM MEMBERS EXCELLENT PLAYBACK QUALITY.
			3. OFFER DAILY MIXES TO OUR PREMIUM MEMBERS, A BIT LIKE A MIXTAPE JUST FOR THEM

The Spotify DIBB is data-driven, for example, by interpreting analytics taken from the website and mobile apps we can generate possible insights. The beliefs about these insights are then used to create a series of bets. Each bet is then distributed to the appropriate tribe to execute.

DIBBs are cascaded through the organization, as the following diagram shows:

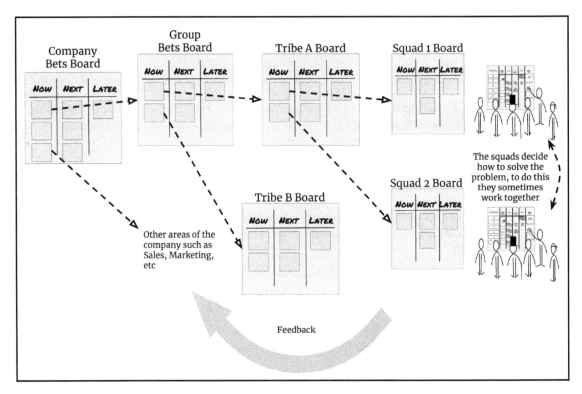

Each squad is autonomous; it will make decisions regarding how to implement the particular bet it has been asked to carry out. Sometimes it will need to work in close collaboration with other squads; sometimes those squads might be part of another tribe.

Bets are similar in concept to bets that we make on a sports game or race. However, these bets differ because with a framework such as DIBBs we can adjust our bets as we get new information.

Therefore, feedback should happen on multiple levels, with each squad measuring the success of its own work. The tribe will also gauge the success that its squads are having, and in turn, they will feed this up the line to the group and so on. Adjustments to bets can be made at any level and cascaded up or down the line.

Seeking value

OKRs, HDD, and DIBBs are all ways to create alignment with our organization's purpose by setting objectives that tie back to its strategic intent. Alignment helps establish the mission, but how do we choose the things that are of the highest priority/value to work on?

All are data-driven approaches, which help us focus on our customer. By setting measurements by which we can determine our success, we can inspect and adapt our approach. In essence, this allows us to optimize the value that we return to the organization.

When we talk about seeking value in a software product development context, we mean maximizing our customer or organization's return on investment. We can do this by prioritizing the delivery of features and User Stories so that we get the best return on investment for our customer (or company, if they are the same thing).

Adaptive planning allows for **Plan Do Check Act** (**PDCA**) cycles, where we can quickly adjust our return by prioritizing what is important to the business based on feedback from the previous period.

One thing that isn't easy is comparing one feature to another and determining objectively which will likely return the most value to the organization. Most companies still use very qualitative processes to estimate business value, for example, gut instinct. This approach creates unresolved arguments about one project versus another or one feature versus another and what gets funded.

To reduce the debate, we need to level the playing field so that all types of value are quantifiably measured. In the next section, we'll look at some different ways of measuring value.

How to seek value

Back in `Chapter 3`, *Introducing Scrum to Your Software Team*, we looked at product backlog definition and release planning and introduced a prioritization technique called **Must have**, **Should have**, **Could have**, **Won't have** (**MoSCoW**) as a quick way of prioritizing our backlog.

This technique, just like the *buy a feature* technique, aims to place value on features, often based on the Product Owner's gut instinct.

Buy a feature is a planning game where each feature is given a monetary value. Our stakeholders are given a pot of cash less than the total feature cost so that they are forced to prioritize features. Sometimes they have to club together to afford a feature, which fosters stakeholder collaboration. Find out more about buy a feature and similar games in Luke Hohmann's book *Innovation Games: Creating Breakthrough Products Through Collaborative Play.*

There are alternative ways of prioritizing features and User Stories that put an explicit emphasis on value.

Value comes in several forms, direct revenue, the most obvious, being just one of them. Comparing features that increase direct revenue with features that reduce costs, or enhance our product's brand, can be like comparing apples and oranges.

This disparity often makes it hard to objectively decide which features should gain priority on a product roadmap and which we could put on the back burner for now. We often favor the ones that increase our direct revenue because they're easier to quantify.

Cost of Delay (CoD) is one way of determining if whether we should do something now or later. Don Reinertsen, in his book The Principles of Product Development Flow, says it's one of the key measurements we should make use of when building a product.

In the simplest terms, we can think of it in terms of a $/week value for every week we delay releasing a new feature.

For instance, if we have two features that we'd like to develop:

- Feature A would generate us $1,000/week in additional revenue.
- Feature B would reduce costs by $750/week.

In other words, for every week we delay releasing Feature A, we miss out on extra $1,000 revenue, and for every week we don't release feature B, we spend $750 more than we have to. Assuming the time taken to develop both is the same, then Feature A, with its higher cost of delay, would be the obvious choice.

However, not all features are the same, and it's unlikely that both features will take exactly the same amount of time. In fact, imagine that Feature A takes 16 weeks, while Feature B will take 4 weeks.

Feature A: $1,000/week will take 16 weeks to build

Feature B: $750/week will take 4 weeks to build

Which feature should we build first? If we look at doing these sequentially with one team, there are two options—we build A then B or we build B then A.

Build Feature A then B: B's cost of delay while implementing A is 16 weeks at $750, so **$12,000**.

The following diagram shows the cost if we build A then B:

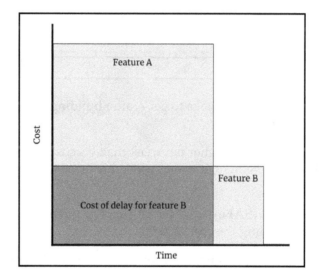

Feature B then A: A's cost of delay while implementing B is 4 weeks at $1,000, so **$4,000**

The following diagram shows the cost if we build B then A:

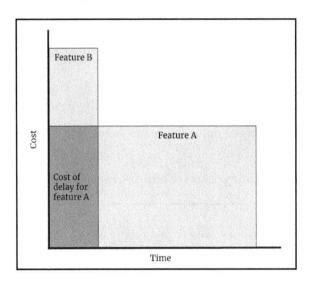

We only have to wait for four extra weeks to get A after building B. If we built A first, we would have to wait 20 weeks for B.

So even though A's cost of delay is higher per week than B's cost of delay, when we factor in the duration each takes to implement, it makes economic sense to build Feature B before we build Feature A.

The **Scaled Agile Framework (SAFe)** suggests we quantify three aspects of the value of a product feature when calculating the cost of delay:

1. **User value or business value**: How much value will this feature give to our customer or business?
2. **Risk reduced or opportunity enabled**: Will this feature reduce the risk to our business? Or will it enable a new opportunity?
3. **Time Criticality**: Is there a timing factor that is too important to ignore, for example, a change to existing legislation that needs to be implemented by a cutoff date?

There are several ways we can quantify these variables. The simplest is to use a deck of planning poker cards, such as t-shirt sizes (XS, SM, M, L, XL) or the modified Fibonacci sequence (1, 2, 3, 5, 8, 13, 20, 40, and so on).

We estimate in a group, likely product managers with technical representatives such as architects, tech leads, infrastructure and operation teams, and so on.

Once we've assigned the three values for *UV|BV, RR|OE* and *Time Criticality* using rounds of planning poker (see `Chapter 3`, *Introducing Scrum to Your Software Team* for the rules). We then add the three figures together to arrive at a single figure, which is our cost of delay:

$$Cost\ of\ delay = UV|BV + RR|OE + Time\ Criticality$$

If we then factor duration into our calculation, it will help us manage our production pipeline more economically. So, as a final step, we also estimate the size of each feature, again using planning poker. If we then divide the CoD total by Duration (*CD3*), this gives us a single value which we can compare to others:

$$CD3 = Cost\ of\ Delay\ /\ Duration$$

The feature with the highest CD3 is implemented first. So, using our example, the business value (BV) for feature A and B is $1,000 and $750:

Feature A: *1000 / 16 =* **_63_**

Feature B: *750/ 4 =* **_188_**

The highest CD3 is Feature B, so we'd build that first. This comparison technique is also known as **Weighted Shortest Job First** (**WSJF**). We can use it to prioritize the feature that will return the highest value in the shortest time frame.

Telling our team "the why" not "the what"

When solving complex problems, those who are directing the work sometimes prescribe solutions. They do this for several reasons:

- Because they want to help, and if the answer seems obvious to them then it seems the right thing to do
- Because they feel it will help them get the outcome they want sooner
- Because that's always been the way they do things—management directs

To some extent, this makes sense if the solution is obvious. However, it may cause unexpected side effects both for our software team and the outcome that we desire. An answer may seem obvious, but simple problems have a knack for hiding complexity. Also, our solution might not be the best.

The *New New Product Development Game*, Takeuchi and Nonaka, HBR, 1986 discusses the need for **subtle control** when managing product development teams. By setting the purpose for our team and giving them the intent, rationale, and any constraints, we can operate a much more fluid style of management which empowers our team to work how they see fit within those boundaries. Boundary setting enables team self-organization.

Those closest to solving the problem, the ones working on it, often have the information necessary to make decisions. If they don't always have to go up and down the chain of command to get answers from superiors, this will prevent long waits. And besides, our management teams are often removed from the day-to-day context of the problem in the first place.

This doesn't mean that management doesn't have an interest in what our teams are doing—far from it. Management will still check in with the team to see if things are progressing in the direction they hoped for. However, giving our team a degree of autonomy will rapidly speed up the decision-making process.

We've hired smart people to solve problems; as professions go; most software development team members are a highly educated bunch. Rather than telling them what to do, we should work collaboratively. This collaboration will help our team understand where the value of our product lies and means they will be more focused on a solution that realizes value sooner.

By telling our team why we want to do something and then leaving our team a degree of autonomy as to how they do this, we may be pleasantly surprised by the results.

Summary

In this chapter, we've looked at the somewhat inevitable shift that is taking place from project to product thinking as technology becomes core to our business. Information technology is no longer a cost center; it's either our operational backbone or our critical money-making channel, or both. Without it, our business likely wouldn't exist, and without constant evolution, we wouldn't remain competitive.

To keep our products competitive, we shouldn't think in terms of time, budget, and scope. Instead, our thinking needs to shift to the return on investment of each feature that we develop. This mindset leads us to the unceasing endeavor of seeking value.

By linking our objectives to vision and mission, we align our purpose and provide the context for our team from an organizational perspective.

If we then explain *why* we're doing something and not *what* we're doing, we empower our team to help us create the solution. The whole team can collaborate to build a product of worth, with each member, including the Product Owner, contributing their area of expertise.

If we obtain direction regarding the highest value items in our Product Owner's prioritization, everyone in the team can seek value that contributes to the product's overall success.

When we have a team who take shared ownership, and in which **product ownership becomes a team responsibility**, this is when we know we've switched from project to product thinking.

In the next chapter, we're going to look at how the Product Owner can hold the bigger picture for our team to help us stay focused on our mission.

10
Using Product Roadmaps to Guide Software Delivery

One of the roles of the Product Owner in Scrum is to hold the vision for the team about what needs to be built. This high-level vision statement allows the Product Owner to make decisions about where the product should be heading and what the priorities should be. They will often translate the vision for the product into a Product Roadmap, which can then be used to communicate to the team, including the broader group, where the product is headed and what level of investment is needed to deliver the features specified in the roadmap.

In this chapter, we look at several techniques for Product Discovery—User Story Mapping and Impact Mapping. Both of these methods are used to create an initial feature set which we can then break down into User Stories. We'll then look at several techniques for prioritizing features/User Stories against release milestones, which will then allow us to create the initial Product Roadmap.

Finally, we'll look at Rolling Wave Planning, an adaptive planning technique where we only keep the immediate horizon (3 to 6 months) for the Product Roadmap very clear. This enables us to maintain flexibility for the less immediate horizon (beyond six months) so that we can respond to change.

In this chapter, we'll cover the following topics:

- The importance of product roadmaps
- Product Discovery to create roadmaps
- User Story Mapping

- Using Impact mapping
- Using Spikes to reduce business unknowns
- Using Rolling Wave Planning for an adaptive delivery

The importance of Product Roadmaps

In the previous chapter, we looked at ways of creating an alignment of purpose between our teams and the organization. A Product Roadmap is another tool in our Product Manager's toolbox to help paint the bigger picture for our team in terms of the direction our product development will be heading in.

A practical roadmap communicates the product vision and areas that need to be tackled to get there, but it doesn't have to be set in stone.

The Product Roadmap is a living document which is usually set out at the beginning of the product's life and is kept updated as new information becomes available and we learn more about our product. If we take a planning-driven approach to product strategy, we can maximize learning and take advantage of new opportunities.

The roadmap is a result of forming a product strategy around the vision and mission, usually by performing an initial Product Discovery to determine what shape our product will take. We'll describe two techniques for carrying out a product discovery workshop: User Story Mapping and Impact Mapping.

Product Discovery to create roadmaps

Product Discovery is the phase at the beginning of a piece of work where we're working out what we're going to do.

This phase is used to explore a new idea or "customer problem" we are trying to solve so we can dig into the details a little more. We don't have to reserve Product Discovery just for new products; it's something that we can use to determine how we're going to build new features for an existing product too.

The aim is to keep the process light and gather just enough information to inform what we're going to build. Remember, we won't know exactly what our customer wants until they have something in their hands, working.

If we adopt the *build, measure, learn* philosophy used by the Lean Startup during the implementation phase, we can validate our ideas through working software early and often, and Product Discovery will become an incremental learning process as part of that cycle.

User Story Mapping and Impact Mapping are two techniques for fleshing out the details of what we're going to build. In this section, we'll look at how to use each technique case by case. We'll then look at ways we can prioritize and begin to create our high-level roadmap and associated Product Backlog.

User Story Mapping

Back in `Chapter 4, Gathering Agile User Requirements`, we discussed an activity for very quickly putting together a Product Backlog by brainstorming a potential set of User Stories for our product.

The first step was to write down a simple sentence or **stub** on an index card—one idea per index card—so that we could create a broad picture of the product. We then started to flesh out the ideas, creating fully-formed User Stories with Acceptance Criteria and so on. We aimed to get as much of our product on paper (index cards) as possible, so that we didn't lose any of our ideas.

When we use this technique for creating a physical Product Backlog for the first time, we may notice a few things about it that make it very powerful. The nature of having the backlog on index cards spread out before us on a table, or perhaps a wall or the floor, means that suddenly we can see the complete picture.

Also, our product suddenly feels somewhat tangible; this is its first physical incarnation. It suddenly becomes much more straightforward to pick up User Stories, examine them, and shuffle the cards around to group them by feature, Epic, or workflow. We can easily rearrange the cards to prioritize and lay out our release strategy to maximize value creation. For example, if we're using the Lean Startup approach, we can use the index cards to map out a possible **Minimum Viable Product (MVP)** and its subsequent **Minimum Marketable Product (MMP)**.

The simplified technique we briefly describe here, and in more detail in `Chapter 4`, *Gathering Agile User Requirements*, is known as **Task Brainstorming** and is one way to start a **User Story Map**. It's mainly useful when we know what we want to build or can easily imagine it.

However, it's not always easy to know where to start. Sometimes we have to put ourselves in the shoes of the people who are going to use our software and work out, from their perspective, what we need to build.

One way to do this is to imagine ourselves using our software and to build up a narrative or story timeline, which focuses on how our user carries out a particular end-to-end journey.

This approach is known as **User Story Mapping**, and the result is known as a **User Story Map**. As well as being a potent visual prioritization tool to shape the initial Product Backlog, it also lays out our Agile Roadmap in such a way that we can comfortably manage it.

 User Story Mapping is the brainchild of Jeff Patton, his book *User Story Mapping: Discover the whole story, build the right product* is an invaluable guide to making the most of this important technique.

The following illustration shows a User Story Map for the checkout process of an online retail store:

FINDING OUR WEBSITE		SEARCHING FOR ITEMS	VIEWING DETAILS ABOUT ITEMS		BUYING ITEMS			
OPEN WEB BROWSER	BROWSE TO OUR ONLINE STORE	SEARCH FOR SHOE BRAND	VIEW DETAILS OF SHOE	SELECT SIZE + COLOUR	DECIDE TO PURCHASE STRAIGHT AWAY	ENTER DELIVERY ADDRESS	ENTER CREDIT CARD DETAILS	ORDER CONFIRMED
		USE KEYWORD TO SEARCH FOR SHOES	VIEW PICTURES	SEE SIZING GUIDE	PUT IN SHOPPING CART	USE EXISTING DELIVERY ADDRESS	USE EXISTING CARD DETAILS	
		USE FILTER TO SEARCH OF SHOES		SEE WHAT DIFFERENT COLOURS LOOK LIKE	CONTINUE BROWSING	SIGN-IN TO CUSTOMER ACCOUNT		

Here's the same User Story Map, this time annotated so we can see what each area represents:

The tasks that are on the timeline tell the story, which in this instance begins with **OPEN WEB BROWSER** and ends with our **ORDER CONFIRMED**.

We sometimes call this a User Journey because it describes a step-by-step journey that our customer must go on to achieve a particular outcome. The User Journey forms the backbone of the User Story Map.

One last thing to note before we get started: if you already have a product, but don't have a User Story Map for it, don't worry, you don't have to begin by creating a complete User Story Map before you can start using this technique. You could use this method just to map a small part of your system, such as a new feature that you want to create.

Even if we have a set of features already in mind, taking time to flesh out the key user narratives for our product is still a worthwhile and valuable exercise.

In the following section, we'll learn, in detail, how to create a User Story Map.

Activity – creating a User Story Map

This activity requires a good cross-section of the people invested in building our product. We'll need to make the activity work with enough people to benefit from group wisdom without crowding out good ideas, so probably with a maximum of 8 to 10 people in one session. Of course, multiple sessions can be run and the results combined.

Where possible, we should have representatives from the following groups present: the key stakeholders, user experience, development (software devs, testers, BAs), our Product Owner, and the people who will use our software.

What we'll need: Index card, sharpies, a big table, and wall space with a way to pin or tack story cards and post-it notes.

Step 1 – User roles

Before we start creating our User Journeys, we need to consider the people that we are building our software for. We usually think about the people that interact with our software from the perspective of three degrees of use:

- **Primary Actors**: The key group of people we provide our product for. In this instance, they are our online shoppers. Our Primary Actors are the key reason our product exists, so this will be a significant focus.
- **Secondary Actors**: The people who work with our system to administer our product. For example, our team of content administrators putting merchandise for sale on our website, or those writing marketing content.
- **Off-Stage Actors**: The people who work indirectly with our system; they usually derive data from third-party tools. For example, analysts who use Google Analytics to generate insights on our sales or the team that monitors and manages our website to keep it operational.

At the start of the session, we should make it clear which user group we are going to define the User Journey for. If we're starting a new map, we will start with the **Primary Actors**. Once we've defined the initial user journey for our primary actor, it then becomes easier to determine how our **Secondary Actors** and **Off-Stage Actors** might be involved in setting up that journey. For instance, for our online shop, our Secondary Actors will need the ability to create an inventory, and our Off-Stage Actors will need the ability to monitor sales funnel activity through analytics.

To create a User Journey for a particular user group, we need to think about the journey from their perspective. One way to get ourselves into the right mindset is to create simple personas for people we think fit into this category.

 These don't need to be elaborate for this purpose; we're just creating a mindset shift for the group before we begin the next step. Also, our UX team may have already created personas. If they have, ask them to briefly introduce the relevant personas before creating the first user journey, then we can skip the following activity and jump to step 2.

The following activity shows how to create simple personas:

- **Activity**: Simple personas
- **What we'll need**: Index cards, sharpies, blu-tack, or wall-friendly tape
- **Timebox**: 10 minutes

Explain to the group that we're going to create simple personas to get us into the right mindset for creating a User Journey specific to people from a particular user group (whether it's Primary, Secondary, or Off-Stage Actors will depend on the user journey we're creating).

Share this simple template with them:

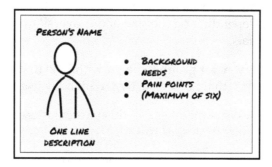

Share an example:

1. Ask each group member to create a persona for the particular user group.
2. Set the timer for 10 minutes and start the countdown.
3. When the time is up, ask for volunteers to share their persona with the group.
4. Post the results on the wall for everyone to see (either in a corner or on a separate wall from the one we're about to create the user journey on).

Step 2 – The first User Journey

Once we know who we're creating the User Story Map for, the next step is to create our first User Journey.

Many won't have done this type of activity before, so at the start it's worth doing an example run through before you start on the real User Journey. The example that Jeff Patton gives in his book User Story Mapping (O'Reilly, 2014) is **going to work each day**. It starts with the alarm clock going off and finishes with us at our place of work, ready to get started. In-between, we perform tasks such as hitting the snooze button, taking a shower, getting dressed, eating breakfast, running for the bus, and so on.

For this step, we'll begin with some silent brainstorming. Each team member should have a sharpie and post-it notes. Depending on the size of our overall group, we'll either work in small groups or as individuals.

We will focus on our Primary Actor group to begin with. The first journey will be our Primary Actor's most traveled, that is, the one they will likely use the most.

The aim is to keep it simple. We sometimes call this particular user journey the **Happy Path** because it goes without hiccups from start to end.

We explain to the group that this activity will be focused on a particular outcome that our user wants to achieve. In this instance, the result our user wants is to purchase some new shoes.

We start by describing this outcome to the group and write it as a statement on the whiteboard or similar so that everyone in the room can see it. Next, we ask the group to think about the individual steps that our user will need to take to achieve this outcome. Each task should be written down on its own post-it note. The steps should be ordered from left to right as a timeline.

For example, the following shows a simple User Journey for the customer outcome **purchase shoes via our online retail store**:

OPEN WEB BROWSER	BROWSE TO OUR ONLINE STORE	SEARCH FOR SHOE BRAND	FIND SHOE	SELECT SIZE + COLOUR	DECIDE TO PURCHASE STRAIGHT AWAY	ENTER DELIVERY ADDRESS	ENTER CREDIT CARD DETAILS	ORDER CONFIRMED

The list of **User Tasks** represents a customers complete end-to-end User Journey. It begins with our customer opening a web browser and navigating to our website. It ends when their order is confirmed:

1. Set the outcome with our group, for example: purchase shoes via our online store.
2. Set a timebox of 15 minutes.
3. Ask our team to work silently (unless in pairs or sub-groups) to create the User Journey task by task.

Once the timebox is up, ask everyone to stop working. We will then ask each person, pair, or sub-group to present their User Journey one at a time. Ideally, this will be by posting the User Journey onto a wall in the meeting room, or onto a large whiteboard. If neither of these is available, use the center of the table to lay out the timeline. Ask each person to place their timeline task by task from left to right.

When the first User Journey has been presented, ask the rest of our group to take turns to talk through theirs. Where a task is the same as, or very similar to, a task in the User Journey already presented, overlay the existing task. If the task completes a similar function but is an alternative way of accomplishing the task, place it on the timeline under the original task.

For example, the following diagram shows our User Journey example with two **alternative flow** tasks placed below the timeline of the main flow:

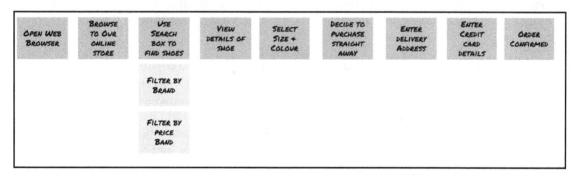

Filtering by brand or by price band are two alternative ways of finding shoes on our website, so we place both below the original to show they are variations of using the search facility.

Step 3 – Alternative paths, sub-tasks, details, and business rules

Each User Journey created during the individual/pair/sub-group brainstorming will contain different tasks to achieve the outcome, in the same way that we all have slightly different ways of getting to work in the morning.

The aim is to bring those various ideas together so that we create one User Story Map showing all possible alternatives.

The following diagram illustrates how we lay out the map:

OPEN WEB BROWSER	BROWSE TO OUR ONLINE STORE	SEARCH FOR SHOE BRAND	VIEW DETAILS OF SHOE	SELECT SIZE + COLOUR	DECIDE TO PURCHASE STRAIGHT AWAY	ENTER DELIVERY ADDRESS	ENTER CREDIT CARD DETAILS	ORDER CONFIRMED
		USE KEYWORD TO SEARCH FOR SHOES	VIEW PICTURES	SEE SIZING GUIDE	PUT IN SHOPPING CART	USE EXISTING DELIVERY ADDRESS	USE EXISTING CARD DETAILS	
		USE FILTER TO SEARCH OF SHOES		SEE WHAT DIFFERENT COLOURS LOOK LIKE	CONTINUE BROWSING	SIGN-IN TO CUSTOMER ACCOUNT		

It will involve a degree of de-duplication that is, removing tasks which are worded differently but perform the same task. It will also involve expanding the timeline from left to right as we merge multiple timelines, because some may be more descriptive than others. This just means more detail, and it's probably better to be more verbose at this stage than not.

We'll also begin to see tasks which have the same outcome but take different steps to get there. For instance, using the task **DECIDE TO PURCHASE STRAIGHT AWAY** as a reference point, we can see that the group thinks there are alternatives to just clicking on a **Buy now** button. Instead, our customer might decide to put an item in the shopping cart so they can purchase it later along with other items. They might decide the item isn't what they were after and decide to continue browsing. They might do both, put the item in the shopping cart, and then keep browsing.

At this stage, don't worry too much about the ordering of the alternative paths; just place them on the map so they sit below their similar/related tasks. At this stage, we should focus on creating a timeline which represents every single step our user takes to reach the outcome. It doesn't matter (yet) how they achieve it or that there are alternative ways of accomplishing it—we're just trying to create a complete picture.

Step 4 – Naming the activities

The final step is to look at the User Story Map from the perspective of the activities that our user is carrying out.

Look across the top line of the narrative and you'll notice that tasks can be grouped under a title which defines the activity being carried out by our user.

For example, take a look at the following four tasks in the timeline:

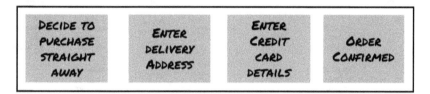

They all relate to a specific activity: **buying an item**. In this case, our user will **DECIDE TO PURCHASE STRAIGHT AWAY**, so they might click a button which says something like **Buy Now**. This is just one way that our user could purchase something from our website.

In future, we might implement a shopping cart, so they can purchase multiple items from us in one transaction; we might also implement an **Add to cart** function. If we name this activity **BUYING ITEMS**, when we talk about alternative paths for purchasing an item, we can frame the discussion around this activity.

We annotate the User Story Map so that it looks like the following:

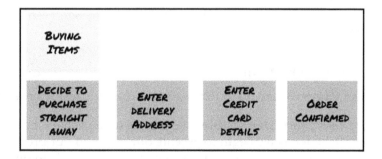

The **BUYING ITEMS** post-it is placed over the timeline above the task which starts that activity.

We can name the other activities in the same way, placing the activity's name over the first task in the sequence. The timeline would look like the following:

Each activity ends where the next begins. The last activity ends when the timeline completes. Some activities only have one task in the timeline from left to right; others have multiple tasks in the timeline, indicating that they are multi-stepped.

Naming the activities gives us the flexibility in the future to talk about the things our user does without prescribing the tasks specifically. This means we'll be less likely to prescribe solutions and can keep the team focused on the *why* instead of the *what*.

Each activity in our User Story Map will likely translate to a feature in our Product Backlog (features are large User Stories, also commonly referred to as Epics). Tasks and sub-tasks, with refinement, will translate to User Stories.

Leveraging the User Story Map

There are a couple of things we can do to make good use of our freshly created story map:

- **Make the User Story Map visible**: Making the map visible for all to see will help us strategize better as we begin to execute our plan and our product begins to evolve. The ideal way, assuming we're a co-located team, is to put our User Story Map on the wall. Or, if we don't have wall space, on a portable whiteboard. For instance, if we're already using a whiteboard for the Scrum Board, we could put our User Story Map on the back of that board.

- **Prioritize the User Story Map to create a roadmap**: The activities of our User Story Map translate to high-level features of a Product Roadmap. The tasks and sub-tasks from the story map will translate to User Stories on our Product Backlog.

To create our high-level roadmap and initial Product Backlog, we first have to prioritize the tasks in our User Story Map.

In `Chapter 3`, *Introducing Scrum to your Software Team*, we demonstrated a prioritization technique called MoSCoW, a word that we use to remind us of four prioritization categories: *must have, should have, could have,* and *won't have*. Remember that *won't have* is just for this release; it doesn't mean we *won't have* it at all. We can use the same technique here in prioritizing our User Story Map.

Another way to prioritize our User Story Map is to split the map into three releases. The first release will be our **Minimum Viable Product** (**MVP**).

The simplest way to achieve this is to mark out three lanes on the wall, whiteboard, or table (whichever we are using). We then prioritize the tasks by placing them in the appropriate release lane, as we demonstrate in the following diagram:

Impact Mapping

Impact Mapping is a collaborative approach to gathering and planning Agile requirements created by *Gojko Adzic,* see his book *Impact Mapping: Making a big impact with software products and projects.* In the following section, we'll create an Impact Map step by step using the example of our online retail store.

Activity – Creating an Impact Map

To carry out this activity, you will need a large whiteboard, whiteboard markers, and a whiteboard eraser.

As per User Story Mapping, having a selection of stakeholders and team members present will obtain a broader perspective.

Question 1 – Why are we doing this?

Here we define the business goal or one of the goals we're hoping to achieve for our next phase of product development. For instance, as the owner of an online store, we want to increase purchases.

The goal should be **Specific, Measurable, Attainable, Relevant, and Time-based** (**SMART**):

```
INCREASE
PURCHASES
FROM OUR
ONLINE STORE
```

It's also wise to determine how we're going to measure success—how will we know when we've reached our goal? The following format is suggested in the Impact Mapping book:

- **WHAT**: Increase purchases from our online store by 100% in the next three months
- **WHERE**: Revenue from purchases
- **CURRENT**: $250,000
- **MIN**: $375,000
- **MAX**: $500,000

Question 2 – Who will help us?

Here we're looking to discover who will help us achieve our business goal. We use the term *actors* to describe the people who interact with our system and we categorize them as Primary, Secondary, and Off-Stage Actors. This equates to first, second, and third-degree users of our service.

For example, a primary actor will be the person we're making our product for, in this instance, our shopper. A secondary actor is someone who interacts with the product to provide a service, for example, our marketing/advertising guru who ensures our retail store has a steady stream of shoppers. An off-stage actor is someone who interacts with our product indirectly, for example, by using analytics to determine where best to target the next phase of development:

Question 3 – How will they help us?

This is the way the actor will help us achieve this—for example, buying more items. In essence, this describes the outcomes that we believe will help us reach our goal:

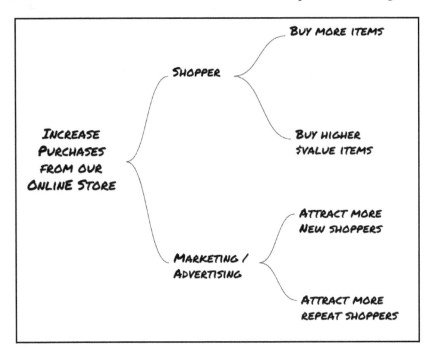

Question 4 – What will we do?

These are the features that we'll create or change to encourage our actors to help us achieve our outcome.

For example, we'll create a feature to inspire people to buy additional items by showing them what other people who purchased this item also bought.

In this step, we'll write down as many actions as we can think of, for each of the outcomes we identified in Step 3. The result should look a little like this:

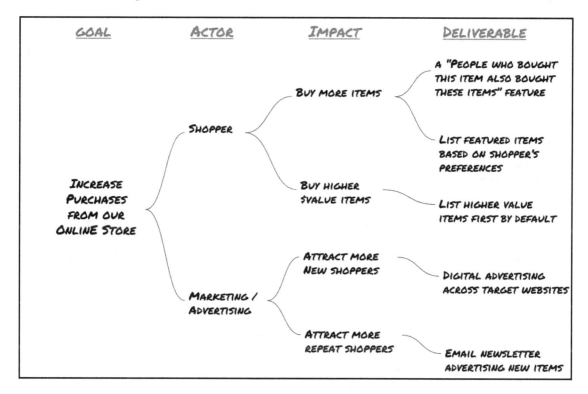

Once we've created all of our actions, we will need to determine which will deliver the highest value to the business soonest. So, the next step is to generate a consensus about the order in which we should carry out the changes. We can use a system called dot voting. Each person gets a set number of sticky dots (usually three votes) and votes on the ideas for action they think will increase purchases from our online store the most.

Leveraging an Impact Map

Once we've prioritized the **deliverables**, it's then easy to create the backlog and order the User Stories according to the priority we set in the Impact Map.

The template we use for writing User Stories is:

As an ACTOR I want ACTION, so I get VALUE.

On the Impact Map, this translates as:

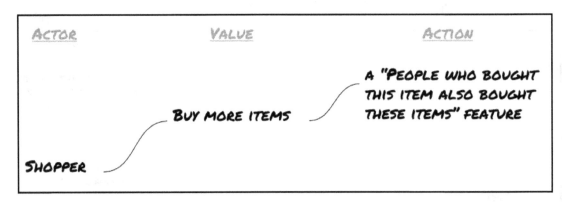

- As a **SHOPPER** I want the online retail store to have a **PEOPLE WHO BOUGHT THIS ITEM ALSO BOUGHT THESE ITEMS FEATURE** so I can **BUY MORE ITEMS**.
- As a **SHOPPER** I want to see a **LIST OF FEATURED ITEMS BASED ON MY PREFERENCES** so that I can **BUY MORE ITEMS**.
- As an **INVENTORY MANAGER**, I want to **LIST HIGHER VALUE FEATURE ITEMS FIRST** so that I can **SELL HIGHER VALUE ITEMS**.
- As **MARKETING/ADVERTISING STAFF MEMBER**, I want **DIGITAL ADVERTISING ACROSS TARGET WEBSITES** so I can **ATTRACT MORE NEW SHOPPERS**.
- As **MARKETING/ADVERTISING STAFF MEMBER**, I want an **EMAIL NEWSLETTER ADVERTISING THE LATEST STOCK ITEMS** so I can **ATTRACT MORE REPEAT SHOPPERS**.

Once we have a prioritized set of User Stories, it's relatively straightforward to create a release schedule based on the team's velocity (or estimated velocity).

We can also look at setting milestones for our measurements to check if we're on track. For instance, to meet our end-of-December deadline to increase the number of purchases by 100%, we should have raised sales revenue to $370,500 by mid-November.

As with the User Story Map, it makes sense to make the Impact Map part of our visible workspace.

Working collaboratively with the team to create a shared understanding

The two techniques we've described are ideally carried out in collaboration with a good representation of all stakeholders, including the business or customer and the technology team. The more members of the team and the wider group that we can involve, the better. Those involved in the User Story Map creation will not only contribute valuable ideas, but they will also come away with a shared understanding of what we're about to build.

Sometimes it's not possible to include our entire team in the creation of the User Story Map, just because of sheer numbers. Anything more than a maximum of 15 people in one session can be become difficult to facilitate in a way that isn't time-consuming and may result in people not being heard.

If this is the case, we should include as many representatives of our team as we can. Once the User Story Map has been created, it's crucial that we walk our remaining team through the map so that they have a good understanding of what we're hoping to achieve. This is another benefit of creating a User Story Map in such a visible way; we're also able to walk others through it.

The walkthrough will take time, but it is imperative that we get everyone on board with the approach we're taking. We want to avoid anyone making assumptions and taking a different route from the one we've mapped out.

Using Spikes to reduce business and technical unknowns

We carry out a Spike when we're about to embark on a new piece of work and are finding it hard to make decisions about direction in business terms, technical terms, or both.

Similar in concept to a hackathon, a Spike is an investigatory piece of work which should:

- Answer a single question
- Either be technical or customer-focused
- Reduce uncertainty and create a way forward

The key thing to note is that a Spike doesn't directly contribute to an increment in the working software. As a result, we don't estimate spikes, instead we timebox them. When the timebox is up, we determine if we've answered the question we set out to answer:

- If we have, the next step is to determine how this information will help move us forward. The usual outcome is to either create new User Stories or change existing ones.
- If we haven't, then we determine if we need more time. If we do, then we set a new timebox. If we don't, then maybe we've reached a dead end and we need a new line of inquiry. If so, it's time for us to regroup and decide what to do.

A Spike should seek to push through all of the layers of our technology stack, as each of these will inform any technical or user decisions that we make:

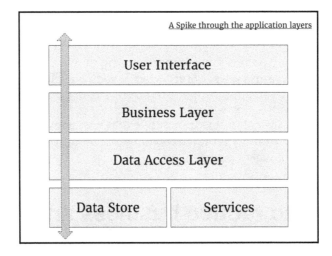

Be aware it's also a bad smell if our team use Spikes too often as there is a degree of the unknown in any User Story. A balance needs to be struck between moving forward and genuine uncertainty.

Also, any code produced during a Spike should be treated like any other prototype—rewritten to proper standards, likely from scratch.

Using Rolling Wave Planning for adaptive delivery

As per the Agile values, we should **adapt to change over following a plan**. Rolling Wave Planning approaches planning with the view that the near future is usually well defined, while the short-term future is less defined and the long-term future becomes more vague:

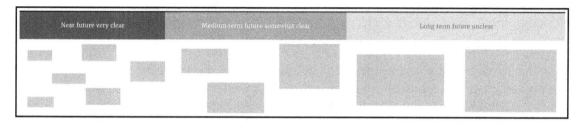

As we progress through the items on our roadmap, the feedback we gather as we begin to validate our ideas at each step will inform what we need to do in the future. With a Rolling Wave Plan, we should have regular checkpoints to incorporate new information and adjust our plan accordingly.

Scrum and other iterative techniques can be readily managed using Rolling Wave Planning by prioritizing the backlog and keeping the User Stories near the top, well defined and ready to go:

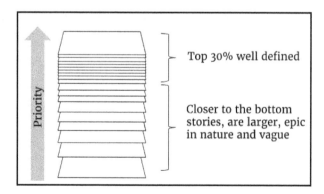

Summary

In this chapter, we've looked at how roadmaps play an essential part in creating alignment with our organization's purpose and strategic intent.

We discussed the Product Discovery phase, which we use to ascertain which direction our product is going to take.

We looked at two techniques for Product Discovery: User Story Mapping and Impact Mapping. These methods are both centered on user outcomes and help us determine how we'll solve the business problem with our customer in mind.

Next, we looked at why it's important to include the development team and stakeholders in the product discovery phase. Each group will have a valuable contribution regarding what we should build; one group represents the problem (business) domain and the other represents the solution (technical) domain. Most importantly, having both groups present will hopefully bring to the surface any assumptions and align them in terms of expectations.

We also looked at using a technique for discovery called a Spike, a sort of mini-hackathon that allows us to be better informed in our business and technical decision-making. Sometimes when we get stuck, the simplest thing is just to experiment and see what works.

In the final section, we introduced a continuous planning technique called Rolling Wave Planning. It fits well with Product Backlog management and allows us to make adjustments to our roadmap as we incrementally *build, measure, and learn.*

In the next chapter, we're going to look at how we can take our team performance from average to high-performing by understanding what makes great teams work well together.

11
Improving Our Team Dynamics to Increase Our Agility

Agile Software teams often work closely together and the communication lines between the team members are open and of high bandwidth. For team members new to Agile, they can often find this daunting because they aren't used to the level of scrutiny and transparency from their peers. If team members previously worked independently or in different teams, when they come together as a new team, they may find that their individual ways of working may not fit with the team norm.

There will often be a period where the team has to iron out their differences before they can start working harmoniously together. As discussed in Chapter 5, *Bootstrap Teams with Liftoffs*, liftoffs can help teams get off to a good start, but eventually, teams will begin to go through a "storming" phase with different degrees of conflict occurring as teams try to reach a consensus on how to work together.

The first part of this chapter looks at how to help the teams to navigate conflict so that they can move through the storming phase and start to normalize their working practices. Part of this normalization process is recognizing that the diversity among team members will ultimately result in more innovative and robust solutions. Teams that can navigate to this place will often move through a plateau of performance to much higher levels as they start to create new ways of working together and benefit from the subsequent systemic change.

Finally, we look at the similarities between technology teams and sports teams in the sense that just like sports teams, technology teams have to practice their game. To do this, we use team events such as *Hackathons* and *Innovation Days*, which allow teams to learn essential techniques such as rapid validation and end-to-end experimentation.

The following topics will be covered in this chapter:

- How to create high-performing teams
- The stages of team formation and how to manage them
- Learning and practicing
    - Hackathons
    - Innovation Days

How to create high-performing teams

There has been a fundamental shift in where the knowledge resides in an organization. Previously, it was in the domain of our management team to gather the requisite information on what needed to be done and then orchestrate the work from above.

Now, much of the work our software teams carry out requires improvisation and the use of judgment in situations that are often ambiguous. As we've already discussed, most of the problems we solve are complex and necessitate an empirical (scientific) approach to solving them. To do this successfully means they have to be good at gathering and wrangling vast amounts of information from initial ideas to specifications, UX design to test cases, code development to review feedback, and code quality metrics to production performance data.

Our experience of the sports teams that we follow or play in has a degree of influence on how we create high-performing teams. For example, in the game of rugby, each position on the field has a specialization and carries out a different job—forwards, wings, backs, fly-half, fullback, to name a few.

Despite their specializations, all of the players of a rugby team have to work in close collaboration to successfully win the game. Nonaka and Takeuchi observed something similar in successful product development teams; they called it *The Rugby Approach* in their paper, *The New New Product Development Game, HBR, 1986*.

They noted that when teams were comprised of a small number of people and the requisite specializations were given the autonomy to act on a clear purpose, they self-organized to solve the problem in ways much faster than any manager could have guided them.

Excellent communication is one significant aspect of a high-performing team. On the sports field, for example, communication often happens at a pace between players, it has to be clear and concise. In a sports situation, it has to happen face-to-face; it's a combination of body language, signals, and verbal information. Well-honed communication transforms an average team to a high-performing team. It requires practice and only occurs when team members know each other well; whether they are improvising or playing set pieces, team members need to be able to read the signs.

For a product development team, we also need clear communication to disseminate knowledge and understanding among our members. As with a sports team, this is a much higher bandwidth when face-to-face, as we're able to include other forms of communication to convey our message. For instance, by using hand gestures, or drawing on a whiteboard, or physically acting out a scenario, we're able to explain what we're saying more easily.

 This is why the Agile Manifesto advocates face-to-face as *the most efficient and effective method of conveying information to and within a development team*. Even with modern technology such as video conferencing and other tools for remote working, we still can't recreate the same effect as a group of people being in the room together.

The performance also increases between people who have formed strong relationships, that is, just like a sports team, they understand what each other is capable of and seek to play these strengths.

In this chapter, we'll look at some of the dynamics of Scrum teams and also look at ways in which we can change our game to perform better.

Collaboration is the key

As we discussed in `Chapter 8`, *Tightening Feedback Loops in the Software Development Life Cycle*, the sooner we can get feedback that we're heading in the right direction, the sooner we can build the right thing for our customer. This is how an Agile, adaptive planning approach speeds things up compared to traditional management styles.

There has been a dramatic shift in where the knowledge resides in organizations. Previously, it was held by the ones at the top, whose job was to oversee the *hands* of the organization perform an almost production-line-like series of repetitive tasks.

However, in a modern organization where the tasks carried out have become much more complex, knowledge is transferred to the specialists who now carry out these tasks. Large amounts of information are consumed by these specialists, in our case, in order to build useful software.

This is how the term *knowledge workers* was coined; the fact is that we have to become just as good at gathering information as we are at wrangling our newly gained knowledge. We have to collaborate closely in order to extract and manipulate this information in order to turn it into something useful.

Knowledge work and high-bandwidth communication

With great collaboration comes much communication. When we build a software product, a lot of information changes hands. To get things done rapidly, it needs to change hands both at a fast pace and accurately.

Any discussion, answering and asking questions, work coordination, and so, on will get resolved more quickly when it happens face-to-face.

Each of us has a combination of predominantly three different learning styles—**auditory**: learning via the spoken word, **visual:** learning by seeing, **kinesthetic**: learning by doing. When communicating with a group, it's good if we can engage all three learning styles, as this will increase the learning bandwidth, plus ensure we include people who might prefer one style over another.

So to keep knowledge transfer rapid, it is easiest to do with an interactive, in-person face-to-face interactive conversation, preferably with a whiteboard or some other form of visual communication so that we engage multiple senses at once.

To maintain a high level of knowledge transfer requires a fairly small group. When people around him were advocating for increasing communication, Amazon CEO Jeff Bezos' response was to say increasing communication is terrible and he introduced the two pizza rule. This meant that a team should be no bigger than can be fed by two pizzas. Anything over that size and information will start to get lost and the group will become nonproductive. High-bandwidth communication in small group trumps sitting in nonproductive meetings all day.

For example, compare the difference between a small birthday gatherings to a wedding. At the birthday, we invite a few close friends and family. The small group makes it possible to hold meaningful conversations with all of our guests, leaving us with the sense that we really shared the moment.

When we get married, it's a once in a lifetime event, we invite many guests. It's challenging for us to get around to all of them, our conversations are only fleeting, and the wedding can end with us feeling that we haven't had the opportunity to share our special day with everyone who came.

Next, we illustrate why communication gets so tricky once we move beyond a certain number of people.

Communication lines

5 team members results in 10 lines of communication, as shown in the following diagram:

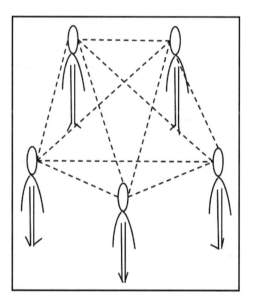

If we increase the team size to 10 team members, the number lines of communication jumps to 45, as shown here:

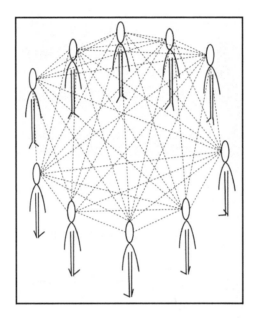

The formula is as follows:

$$\text{NUMBER OF COMMUNICATION LINES} = \frac{(N^2 - N)}{2}$$

$$N = \text{NUMBER IN TEAM}$$

So, 15 team members would have 105 communication lines to maintain, 20 team members would have 190, and so on.

Different teams will experience different results, but at 10 or more team members face-to-face communication becomes increasingly more difficult. The Daily Scrum will begin to take longer and longer. Our team will either seek to keep it short and curtail conversations or run the risk of people disengaging as the coordination conversation begins to blow out.

Either way, important information will be missed and not everyone will be aware of what everyone else is doing and the opportunities for strong collaboration will start to become fewer. When faced with situations like this, our team will often start to resort to lower bandwidth forms of communications, such as documents, wikis, and email. Ultimately, this will slow things down.

To avoid communication breakdowns, Scrum advocates small cross-functional teams of five to nine. It happens to be around family unit size, which is where teams operate best when maintaining close connection and communication.

A small team means that each team member can hold a good mental model of what each other is up to, with a lessened cognitive load. Less load gives us the capacity to collaborate more closely. Being able to maintain high-bandwidth communication lines is what gives a Scrum team its speed advantage.

One final note, Robin Dunbar proposed that the maximum number of stable relationships that can be maintained by one person is 150. This figure is commonly referred to as Dunbar's number. This is worth bearing in mind as the number of teams we have working on a particular product start to scale.

Taking the median size of a Scrum team as seven, and then there would be an approximate maximum of 21 teams in the group before coordination between these teams gets strained, and we will need to find a way of further dividing the work.

Psychological safety – what it is and how to create it

Human evolution has led us to develop survival mechanisms that allow us to move fast in order to get out of life-threatening situations. A potential threat triggers a number of physiological changes as our brain starts to prepare us for action by sending signals that put our body in a state of heightened awareness and response.

In this state, the redirection and reallocation of our body's resources, including within the brain itself, means that, among other things, our capacity for reasoned thinking is compromised. This survival mode is widely known as the **fight-or-flight response**.

Besides diminishing our ability for reasoned thinking, the heightened state of awareness suppresses our immune systems and causes our digestive system activity to minimize. This means, if we are in the mode for sustained periods, we are more likely to get sick or become exhausted.

Threats and bullying, typical in pressure-driven workplace cultures, will result in our survival instincts being activated. There is also evidence that in this state we're more biased in our judgment of others' behavior and more likely to judge it with negative intent. This further compounds the problem and will often end up in team members taking defensive positions.

For example, if our team's Product Owner berates the team for always asking questions and is openly frustrated with their lack of progress, the team will stop asking questions because it no longer feels safe to do so. Our team feels shut down and to protect itself from the open hostility, will just get on with the work as requested.

However, down the line, this can lead to further problems if our Product Owner then shows further frustration toward our team when they don't deliver the right thing. For our team, it's a vicious circle and will likely lead to further protectionism, resulting in increasingly less communication and collaboration.

This causes problems for knowledge workers, who in order to be successful in our work, need to gather, interpret, and convert large amounts of information into useful output, in our case, software. It often requires our team to interact with other teams or people both inside and outside of our organization in a cooperative fashion. The more complex the problem, the more likely there is a need for this.

Research work carried out by Amy Edmondsen, Harvard University, shows that a team's learning ability is affected by a team's perception of how psychologically safe it feels to be open and honest.

As she shows in the following diagram, if we push to increase our team's motivation and accountability without them feeling psychologically safe to do so, we push our team into the **Anxiety zone**:

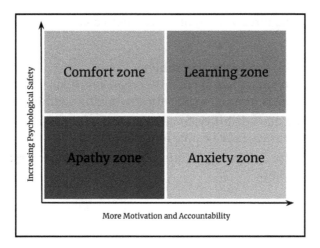

Here, they will be motivated to get things done, but in their state of anxiety will lose the ability to think strategically, often taking shortcuts or wrong turns and increasing the likelihood of rework.

If we increase psychological safety but don't give our team the drive, they will sit in the **Comfort zone**, happy until their lack of achievement begins to frustrate them.

If we do neither, then they sit in the **Apathy zone**, unable to move forward and not caring about it. It will all feel like somebody else's fault anyway.

However, if we increase both psychological safety and motivation, our team will move into the **Learning zone**, where they will begin to take full accountability and make strategically important contributions to the organization.

 Several years of research at Google, under the code name *Project Aristotle*, looked into what made the perfect high-performing team. The research team spent several years correlating data across 180 of their teams in an effort to discover a pattern that put certain teams ahead of others. They looked at factors such as team diversity, gender balance, and interpersonal relationships, but without success. It wasn't until lead researcher Julia Rozovsky came across research on psychological safety that a pattern began to emerge. They discovered that factors such as purpose, dependability, structure, and clarity were also important, but without feeling psychologically safe to do so, a team wouldn't thrive.

Amy Edmondson suggests three ways that we can help create psychological safety within our organizations:

1. **Frame the work as a learning problem**: Present the work to the team as problems that need to be solved, rather than solutions that need to be implemented. This promotes collective ownership within the team.
2. **Acknowledge our fallibility**: State that we don't have all the answers, but by working together we may be able to find them.
3. **Model curiosity**: Ask plenty of questions and demonstrate to our team it's ok for them to do the same.

Further reading

This first link is to Amy Edmondson's original research paper on the subject of psychological safety:

- *Psychological Safety and Learning Behavior in Work Teams*, Amy Edmondson, Administrative Science Quarterly, Vol 44, Issue 2, pp. 350 - 383, First Published June 1, 1999, https://doi.org/10.2307/2666999

This is the *New York Times* report on Project Aristotle, the project that Google ran to find out what made some of its teams more successful than others:

- https://www.nytimes.com/2016/02/28/magazine/what-google-learned-from-its-quest-to-build-the-perfect-team.html

This article from *Harvard Business Review* gives important pointers on how to create a psychologically safe environment for our teams:

- https://hbr.org/2017/08/high-performing-teams-need-psychological-safety-heres-how-to-create-it

The stages of team formation

In 1965, Bruce Tuckman published a paper *Developmental Sequence in Small Groups* in the *Psychological Bulletin, Volume 63, Number 6, Pages 384-99.*

In it, he described four stages of group development:

1. **Forming**: The *getting to know you* phase, where our team finds out more about each other and about their mission
2. **Storming**: A phase of conflict during which our team challenges assumptions about how we are going to work together
3. **Norming**: Differences are ironed out, and a consensus is reached, and then the team begins to work as one
4. **Performing**: Team practice and process improvements along with a better understanding of how the problem will be solved; all work together to create a profound shift in the team dynamic and its likelihood of success

The following diagram shows the stages of team development represented visually:

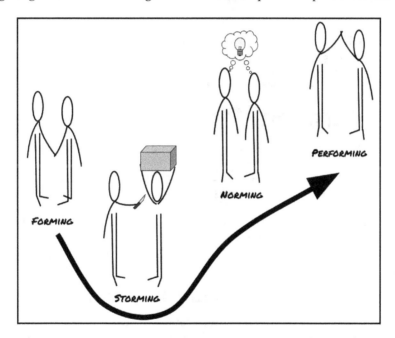

- **Adjourning**: Tuckman later added a fifth stage, adjourning; this reflects the period a team transitions during its disbandment. Sometimes also known as mourning, depending on how close-knit the group has become and how invested they were in their current workstream.

The important aspect of team development to understand is, regardless of how experienced individual members are any team that is newly formed or has approximately 50% of its membership changed will go through these stages to one degree or another.

In the following sections, we'll look at each stage, how this relates to our team, what we might encounter, and what we can do to help them progress to the next phase of development.

Remember, these are more of a topic for conversation with our team to help them understand what is happening and to provide some useful activities that will hopefully help them engage proactively with each other.

Don't use Tuckman's model to try to put our team into a box, it won't help them progress. Instead, accept that they may be in multiple boxes at once. Look for signs and symptoms and facilitate the conversation.

Sometimes a team will take big leaps forward, for example, they may bypass the storming stage entirely. Sometimes they may take one step forward and two steps backward.

Stage 1 – forming

The **forming** stage is the getting-to-know-you phase of team development.

There will be a high degree of relationship building during this stage, and our team will also start to get familiar with their team mission.

For some, there will be excitement; for others, there will be a sense of trepidation. Either way, expect there to be a lot of questions.

Helping our team process this phase

The key activities in the forming phase center around the team liftoff. This will help each team member understand the team process, the team mission, and how each individual will contribute to the successful outcome of that mission.

In `Chapter 5`, *Bootstrap Teams with Liftoffs*, we looked at how to give our team a structured approach to follow during their formation so that they can easily identify:

1. Their team mission and objectives
2. How they will work together to achieve that mission
3. How they will leverage their strengths for a successful outcome

The key outcomes of team liftoff is a team working agreement, which helps the team understand the boundaries they will work within, also known as the team container.

Relationship-building games

During the forming stage, team members will often work as individuals and be very task focused. To move beyond this stage, they will need to start to form interpersonal relationships and start to work together. A good way to seed this is with some team building, here are some suggested activities:

- **Journey lines**: With an A3 sheet of paper and some pens, each team member draws their journey from the point they think is most relevant (when they were born/left school/left university) to the point that they arrived in this room. Timebox the drawing for 15 minutes, and then ask each team member to present their journey line one-by-one. Allow each team member 5 minutes to present and 2 minutes for questions.

- **Highs or lows**: Each participant shares something that was a high and something that was a low, either in their career or their life in general (this will depend on your organization and how comfortable individuals are with sharing personal information).

- **"I can tell you about..."**: Take it in turns to go around each team member, when it's their turn, ask them to list subjects they can tell the team about by starting with the phrase "I can tell you about..." For instance, "I can tell you about football, I can tell you about Funko Pops, I can tell you about my little baby boy," and so on. When a team member, any team member, hears a subject they want to hear about, they say, "Stop, tell me about..." For example, I'd be interested to hear about Funko Pops, so I'd say, "Stop, tell me about Funko Pops." Timebox the telling for 2 minutes. Then move to the next team member.

- **Improvisation games**: I once heard two improvisation comedians talking on a local radio show about how they worked on stage. They said the number one rule in improvisational comedy was the *Yes and* rule. For example, when one comedian leads by saying something like "I'm a Tyrannosaurus Rex, hear me roar!" the other might say, "Yes and... I'm a paleontologist who's time traveling so I can record that roar." The "Yes and..." rule is simple and means two key things take place; the first is we need to listen (active listening); the second is the dialogue is always built upon, nothing is ever taken away. This creates a supportive approach for you and your fellow comedians from which you can hopefully create great comedy. This translates to our team environment because so much of the work we do has degrees of ambiguity and requires a range of perspectives from our team to get a good outcome. Improvisation techniques are important during the periods of negotiation between team members and helps us create a win-win situation; teams will create kickass solutions and team members will feel heard, understood, and more cohesive as a team. Management 3.0 offers a game that will help us learn to improvise: `https://management30.com/product/improv-cards/`.
- **The marshmallow challenge**: Each team has 18 minutes to build the tallest free-standing structure they can with just 20 sticks of spaghetti, one yard/meter of tape, one yard/meter of string, and one *marshmallow*. The crunch is that the *marshmallow* needs to be on the top. This is best done with multiple teams for a little bit of spirited competition. For more information, follow this link: `https://www.tomwujec.com/design-projects/marshmallow-challenge/`.
- **Online video games**: Games such as *Keep Talking and Nobody Explodes* is a fun team building game, where a team member has to defuse a ticking virtual bomb while teammates give them clues on how to defuse it. The game is available on Valve Corporation's Steam platform.

Moving constellations is one icebreaker for team building that allows our team to understand each other's opinions on a range of subjects. So let's start:

Activity: Moving constellations

What you will need: An open/cleared space. An object that you can put in the center of the room (such as a Frisbee, a soft drink can, or a hacky sack):

1. Show the object to the team and place it in the center of the room.
2. Ask our team to stand scattered around it.

3. Explain to them that you will be reading some statements. Once the statement has been read, they then move closer to or further away from the item in the center of the room relative to how true the statement is for them. For example, if they very much agree with the statement they move to stand close to the object in the center. If they very much disagree, they move to the outside of the circle. If they're somewhere in the middle, they stand neither at the outside or close to the object in the center, but somewhere in between.

4. Once the statement has been read, and everyone has moved, have our team look around and see where their teammates are.

5. When everyone has had the opportunity to look around, read the next statement.

6. The final stage, once everyone is comfortable with the exercise, is to have our team sit down and write statements that they would like to gather the team's feelings on. Timebox the statement writing; 3-5 minutes should be plenty. Gather up the statements from the team and continue with the exercise.

The following diagram shows our team's response to one of the statements:

Two of the teammates are standing relatively close to the can in the center and obviously agree with the statement. Three are standing in the corners of the room; they don't agree with the statement. One is standing somewhere in between and is more neutral.

As an addition to the preceding set of rules, after we've read a statement and our team has moved to their new positions, we could ask them to tell us why they chose that particular location. This will add clarity to the conversation if it's needed.

Stage 2 – storming

The second stage of team formation is the **storming** phase. The honeymoon period of team formation is over at this point; during the initial excitement of forming, the teams have got to know each other and the business problem they were being asked to solve and at this point, they are in full swing of trying to deliver.

It's at this stage that team members might start to show visible frustration around both progress and process, either directed at the other team members or the leadership group.

Individual team members may find that assumptions they made on how our team might work together or their understanding of the team mission start to become challenged. Assumptions have the habit of becoming expectations unless identified and handled. When these expectations are out of alignment with others, tension will start to become tangible.

For example, acclimatizing to a new way of delivering software isn't easy and will make our team feel unproductive at first. The cause of tension is most likely differences in opinion in how to do this Agile "thing."

This will feel uncomfortable for our team and may result in team members trying to resort to doing things in the way they did previously. This will cause conflict with the ones who are trying to adapt to the new way of working.

We can see this as all part of a team's formation process. In most cases, our team will gel, and we'll move through it. Unfortunately, sometimes a team gets stuck.

If this happens for too long, the conflict will cause a toxic atmosphere and people will leave because they feel unable to do their jobs. The only avenues at that point are somewhat radical and time consuming for all involved. However, because we know this stage for a team will be coming, we can prepare for it.

Helping our team process this phase

The coaching style during this phase will start to be less directive and more facilitative in nature. The team will start to question both its process and progress. During this time, our support should focus on helping our team understand its mission more clearly. In particular, they will need support in breaking down work to fit an incremental approach.

Facilitate any conversations that start to go beyond the bounds of acceptable behavior. Encourage the team to be respectful of each other and ask them to understand that their frustration is likely with either the mission or the process, not each other.

Coach – diversity is a good thing

We are all unique human beings, it would be crazy to think that we all think or do the same. This is a good thing, a diversity of opinion is what allows a team to cover all aspects of a problem from different perspectives and build more robust solutions.

Differing, sometimes conflicting opinions, are a fact of life, and they are not necessarily a bad thing. Instead, there is an opportunity for our team to bring together their understanding of different domains and disciplines. Ultimately, this creates better solutions.

However, diverse backgrounds will cause problems in team alignment; team members will struggle to align if they don't share similar experiences. The more diverse our team members' backgrounds are, the less likely they will be able to collaborate and the more likely they will fall into conflict.

To foster an environment where diversity of opinion is represented, we have to provide a way for our team to better understand each other's styles and to navigate conflict when it occurs.

Many tools can help our team understand our different personality or communication styles. These tools help us understand our differences as well as our similarities and give us insight into how we might go beyond any initial clash of styles so that we might work well together.

The DiSC personality assessment test is one such tool to help us understand our personality type and will get us some of the way toward fostering better collaboration among the team.

The other part of team collaboration, navigating conflict, involves learning how to have powerful conversations. Let's look at that in a bit more detail in the upcoming section.

Coach – conflict happens, how to navigate it

Our teams work in high-pressure situations; conflict will occur from time-to-time, it's only natural. Our teams need to have tools that will help them deal with it when the time arises.

To start, we need to take the right view of conflict:

- Take a human system's perspective, that is, it's about the process, not the person; to help this thinking, we need to view it from the perspective of the team container, not from the personal perspective of the individuals
- See conflict as a positive change urge—an opportunity, not a problem to be managed
- Consider it to be a manifestation of the system's diversity and its intelligence
- Self-organization happens when we hear all perspectives and incorporate aspects of some or all of them into our approach

What's the benefit?

- Constructive conflict will often result in systemic change
- It creates win-win solutions
- It can significantly increase performance

How do we integrate this?

- Educate about conflict and how to keep it constructive
- Establish conflict protocols to resolve issues before they get toxic

Positivity and successful relationships

There has been plenty of research carried out on how positivity affects teamwork. Since the 1970s Dr John M. Gottman (https://www.gottman.com/about/research/couples/) has been studying one of the smallest, most ubiquitous of teams - married couples. In a series of interviews, he tested each couple by asking them to fix an area of conflict in their relationship within 15 minutes. He then observed the couple's interactions.

His critical observation was that those who were able to resolve their conflict had a high degree of positivity in their conversation. He went on to predict, with a high degree of accuracy, which couples would stand the test of time and which would not.

He found that relationships that were likely to survive longer had between a 2:1 to 5:1 ratio of positive to negative comments when they conversed with each other.

Losada and Heaphy, in their 2004 paper (*The Role of Positivity and Connectivity in the Performance of Business Teams*: A Nonlinear Dynamics Model, Marcial Losada, Emily Heaphy, American Behavioral Scientist, Vol 47, Issue 6, pp. 740 - 765) extend both Gottman's and Losada's earlier research. They studied positivity and how it affected team dynamics at various companies and organizations.

Their work involved looking at teams, judging their effectiveness on financial performance, customer satisfaction ratings, and 360-degree feedback ratings of the team members.

Their study showed that similarly to Gottman's research on human relationships, the positivity ratio affected teams in the following way:

- High-performing teams had a 5.6:1 ratio positive to negative comments, that is, for every negative comment they made five positive comments
- Medium-performing teams had a 1.9:1 ratio positive to negative comments
- Low-performing teams had a ratio of 0.36:1 positive to negative comments in their conversation, that is, for every positive comment, they made two to three negative comments:

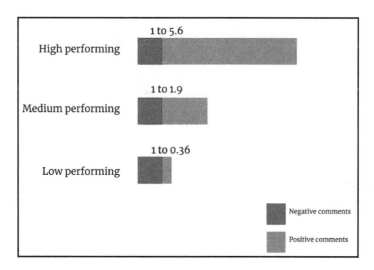

One key aspect of positivity is the broaden-and-build theory put forward by Barbara L. Fredrickson. Her paper - Fredrickson, B. L. (2001). The Role of Positive Emotions in Positive Psychology: The Broaden-and-Build Theory of Positive Emotions. The American Psychologist, 56(3), 218–226 - supports the idea that human behavior can be more flexible and creative when framed with positive emotions.

Extensive research work carried out by Fredrickson shows that individuals are more able to learn new skills and be open to new ideas when we're in a positive state of mind. This only further supports the concept of psychological safety (see the section on psychological safety earlier in this chapter) being key to the collaborative and creative teamwork needed to solve complex problems.

In his book, *7 Habits of Highly Effective People,* Dr. Stephen R. Covey suggests our relationships operate like transactions in a bank account. In this instance, it is an **Emotional Bank Account.** Instead of crediting or debiting cash from our balance, we're making emotional deposits and withdrawals.

Here are some examples of deposits and withdrawals:

EMOTIONAL BANK ACCOUNTS

DEPOSITS	WITHDRAWALS
• APPRECIATIONS	• BLAMING
• ACKNOWLEDGEMENTS	• DEFENSIVENESS
• MORE ENQUIRY, LESS ADVOCACY	• STONEWALLING
	• CONTEMPT
	• EXCESSIVE ADVOCACY

How do we integrate this? We'll need to keep in mind the following:

- What is our team's positive/negative ratio? How do they interact with each other, are they emotionally withdrawing from the conversation or are they constructive in their interactions?
- When are your teams engaged in a conflict which is toxic? If the team is falling into destructive behavior, what is the pattern? Can we help them identify it so they can avoid it when we aren't around?
- Get curious, ask open/neutral questions, listen to the other person's perspective and integrate it into our understanding. This will ultimately create better solutions.
- Encourage our team to use the *yes and* rule of improvisational comedy. See the suggested activities in the previous section *Forming*.

Activity – process the conflict

When conflict occurs, work out what the change urge is and process it.

The following are the tools we can use to do this:

- Group decision making
- Focus on the task, not the person—conflict dynamics
- Conflict protocol agreements
- Practice giving feedback

Group decision making

Some people talk to think, while the others think to talk. If we don't provide for these two different scenarios, we may lose good ideas to conformity bias.

Group decision making makes space for the minority voice and the people who don't speak often. For example, a common approach during Sprint Retrospectives is to use silent brainstorming. Silent brainstorming is where we ask team members to work as individuals initially, for example, to write their ideas down on post-it notes first. We wait until everyone is finished transcribing their ideas before we share them with the group.

Silent brainstorming enables us to hear all the voices in the room without individuals being swayed by the person who speaks the first, the person with the most influence, or by the group in general. If all the opinions are voiced and considered, then we're more likely to reach a place of consent without anyone in our team feeling sidelined.

 We often aim for consent in an Agile team rather than consensus. Consent is defined as *giving permission to do something*. It doesn't mean that we each fully agree, but we are prepared to work with the group toward the aims of the decision. Consensus, on the other hand, means that all members of the group have to agree this is the right thing to do. If we have to wait for consensus, then there will likely be much debate. A good way to shortcut this is to gain consent to conduct an experiment to find out whether or not an idea is worth pursuing. If the experiment is a success, we'll have evidence to support our idea, if it's a failure, we'll drop it. Either way, everybody will be happy with the outcome.

Here are some example group decision-making practices that can be used by our team:

Fist to five	We often want to gauge how our team feels on a scale rating from strongly agree to strongly disagree. Fist to Five allows us to do this, with team members being asked to rate how they feel, with their fist equal to zero (strongly disagree) and their open hand equal to five (strongly agree). If we get all fives and fours, we're OK to proceed with the idea. If we get zeros and ones, we should not proceed. Anything in between we should discuss as a group, after which if we feel the mood has shifted, we can try a re-vote. If the group sentiment still hasn't shifted, we should put the idea on the backburner or find an alternative.
Roman voting	Thumb up = yes Thumb down = no Thumb to the side = neutral/unsure
Round robin	Everyone takes a turn to speak. The one rule of this approach is that we decide who speaks first, not just the people who always speak.

Coach – focus on the task, not the person

Conflict often falls into one of two categories:

- **Cognitive**: This involves conflicts aimed at tasks, issues, ideas, principles, or processes. This impacts our team's boundaries and the rules we operate by. We can fix these types of conflict by adjusting our team's working agreement.
- **Effective**: This involves conflicts aimed at people, emotions, or values. It will have a direct impact on our trust and respect for each other. These types of conflict are not so easily fixed.

The problem is that while task-related conflicts will resolve more easily, with little to no damage done to our interpersonal relationships, conflicts often spill into both areas at once. If this causes a breakdown in trust within the team, we'll effectively have team members in either open conflict or simply not talking to each other. Broken trust can be extremely hard to repair.

If we're to resolve conflict without causing damage to our team's trust, we need to keep our minds focused on the cognitive aspects of the problem we're trying to solve. The first step to achieving this is to **assume** that everyone on our team has **positive intent**. After all, we all want the same outcome, a productive and successful team.

Coach – conflict protocols

Making our team aware that conflict is likely to arise will enable them to process it more easily. Discussing different strategies to managing conflict will give them tools to fall back on when things get a bit sticky between team members.

We should look to form an agreement on which strategies to use when we're calm and cool so that we can handle things when we're not. To set up the agreement we'll need:

- The consent of the team
- The leader to take the facilitator/coach role in holding the team to their agreements

The following are examples of conflict protocols:

- Don't triangulate: a polite way of saying don't talk about someone behind their back
- Address it or drop it within 24 hours
- Let go of stories
- Be candid and straightforward
- Depersonalize—treat feedback as a team issue, it's not personal, the whole team is responsible

Remember, conflict is usually caused by the system and the pressures within it. If we take this perspective, it allows us to get to the root cause of the problem much more quickly. If a team member isn't performing well for instance, is it the team member's fault? Likely not, people aren't inherently lazy. Getting curious without directly challenging someone personally will help defuse the situation before it comes to a head. In the following section we'll look at how to give constructive feedback.

Coach – giving feedback

Being able to give and receive feedback well is a fundamental first step to solving some of the problems of the Storming phase. This will allow the team to share any potential issues before things boil over.

In the Conflict Dynamics model of the world, we can see that expressing emotions is vital to having an active, constructive conversation. One approach to feedback that incorporates the expression of feelings is described by Kristen Hadeed, in her book *Permission to Screw Up*, and is called the FBI.

FBI is an acronym, which stands for **Feelings Behaviors Impacts**. With an FBI, we construct feedback in the following form:

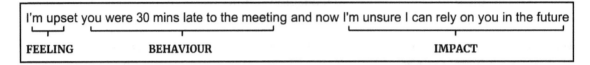

This is a simple way of giving direct feedback that enables the person giving the feedback to express how they feel, explain the behavior that caused the feeling and the impact that the behavior had.

The person who you're giving the feedback to will be able to understand why you might be feeling that way. If you're upset, it will provide them with an opportunity to apologize (if necessary), to explain why and it will hopefully lead to a resolution to prevent it from happening again.

Constructive feedback is an essential aspect of helping us all improve but is not something we often practice and are therefore not comfortable with doing. When we get comfortable with both receiving and giving feedback it opens up opportunities for performance improvements that will be rewarding for all involved.

Stage 3 – norming

At the **norming** stage, the team has developed a clearer understanding of how to operate. They begin to make progress and are now more comfortable with their process.

Individual team members will make an active effort to resolve any misunderstandings of how they work together. There will be more focus on the task of the team mission. Teams that reach this stage will have an increased acceptance of each other, recognizing the diversity of opinion among the group as being a strength.

Trust and respect will be increasingly evident. Team members will be much more comfortable in sharing their ideas. They will listen to understand each others' perspectives. They will also welcome both receiving and giving feedback.

Helping our team process this phase

During this stage, the goal of the leader will be to help the team fine-tune its processes. It is often the most exciting phase for an Agile Coach or Scrum Master because at this point the team will be open to ideas on how they can improve their approach.

Activity – experiments in process

One of the simplest ways for our team to change up how they work is to experiment. This will most likely come from a team improvement action created at the Sprint Retrospective, or from a suggestion made by a team member at a Daily Scrum. Either way, a champion from within the team will usually come forward to run the experiment and present their idea for change.

One easy way to fit this into our team's everyday flow is to ask the champion to select a candidate story that is well suited to implementing this change. For example, if the team has chosen to implement **Behavior-Driven Development (BDD)**, then the BDD champion(s) would work with the rest of us to select a candidate story. When the story is pulled into the *to-do* column, the champion, with assistance if necessary, would work this story to completion using BDD. Estimate the story bearing in mind that the BDD framework will need to be set up.

Before working on the candidate story, the team should work together to set up the experiment with a hypothesis. We described a hypothesis template in the *Hypothesis-Driven Development (HDD)* section in `Chapter 9`, *Seeking Value – How to Deliver Better Software Sooner*.

Measuring the experiment's success is key to whether the team will carry the improvement forward into their everyday work, or at the very least expand it into other areas to see if it works in the broader setting.

Activity – improve the team's ability to self-assess

Over and above the team's usual Sprint Review and Retrospective, they will start to look for feedback about how they are performing in their environment.

Individuals, at this phase of the team formation, will feel comfortable about asking for direct feedback from their fellow team members.

The 360 Hotseat Review is an extension of the 360 Review format, but instead of getting feedback anonymously, our team members gain direct feedback from each other. It takes the following format:

Activity: 360 Hotseat Review

What you will need: Some privacy in a space big enough for your team. A chair for each team member.

Arrange the chairs in a format similar to the one shown in the following diagram:

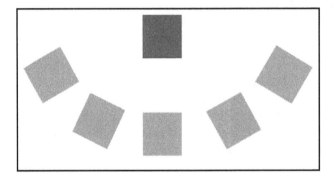

Follow these steps to facilitate the session:

1. Explain that each person will take it in turns to sit in the hot seat.
2. The team members sitting in the circle will make statements that answer one of the following questions:
    - What is one thing the person sitting in the hot seat does that improves the outcome for the team?
    - What is one thing the person sitting in the hot seat could do that would improve the outcome for the team?
3. The person in the hot seat can only answer with one of the following statements: "you're welcome" or "thank you."
4. Ask for a volunteer to take the hotseat.
5. Timebox feedback to 5 minutes.
6. Once the timebox is up, the team member leaves the hotseat.
7. As for the next hot seat volunteer, repeat until everyone (including you) has taken a turn.

It will be initially unnerving for any team who hasn't tried this form of feedback before. As the facilitator, perhaps take the hotseat first to demonstrate by example, this will hopefully help alleviate any fears.

Stage 4 – performing

There is a much greater sense of satisfaction among the team at this stage as they start to make significant progress on their mission. They feel like they understand each other's abilities and the process that they all follow. They will feel comfortable in making profound changes to the way they work, suggesting the introduction of new approaches for the team to experiment with.

As we'll discuss in `Chapter 12`, *Baking Quality into Our Software Delivery*, the boundaries between roles will start to blur and the hand-offs between team members are minimized by close collaboration such as pair and mob programming. Our team will start to exhibit the hallmarks of skill cross-pollination, where they will be able to pick up elements of each others' specializations. Team members will know what each other is capable of and will play to these strengths. A feeling of invincibility will start to develop among our team as their confidence in their team's ability grows.

Helping our team process this phase

Coaches should transfer ownership of the process to the team and provide them with the support they need to make changes as our team sees fit. Help them understand that the meetings such as the Daily Scrum are their meetings, ideas for making them more effective should now come from within the group. As coaches, we're far less hands-on and will only provide our team with options if they need them.

By this point, our team will be familiar with the concept of hypothesis-driven approaches (experimenting) in order to change up their working environment. Coach the team to continuously analyze and improve how they carry out their work. The Sprint Retrospective is an ideal forum to identify areas that need attention.

Activity – 360 team review

A similar concept to the individuals in our team inviting 360 feedback from other team members. In this version, our team seeks input from a broader selection of the stakeholders and the teams with which it interacts.

Feedback can be sought at multiple levels and from a variety of stakeholders in the team's environment:

1. Broaden the input received at the Sprint Review by inviting more widely from the broader group. Spread the reach across silos, include business stakeholders and other teams.
2. Periodically survey the primary/secondary/tertiary users of our product.
3. Similarly, survey key user groups each time we deliver a new feature or significant enhancement. Get direct feedback to determine the success of the feature.

Teams can create online surveys, for example, using Google Forms or similar. One way to do this would be to run a workshop with the team with the following format:

1. Review the team mission
2. Determine who are the stakeholders in this mission
3. Split the team into at least two groups
4. As them to create a Google Survey that we could send out regularly to our stakeholders to determine if we're on a mission and they're happy
5. Each group presents their survey back to the rest of the team for feedback

Stage 5 – adjourning/mourning

Whether you're running long-lived product teams or running projects, all good things do eventually come to an end. And just like any form of ending, there will be a period of grief for at least some of our team members, especially if the team has lasted for a long time.

Team members will feel conflicted about both their sense of success and sense of loss, around both the work they've been doing and the relationships they've formed. It's important that we pay attention to how we close the chapter on what may be for some, months or years of teamwork and at the same time show them the opportunity as we open the new chapter.

This will allow individual team members to move on, will reduce the amount of time they spend grieving, and enable them to remain productive during the transition phase into their new team.

Helping our team process this phase

There are a number of things the team will need to do during this period. The following diagram shows some possible stages with example activities for each:

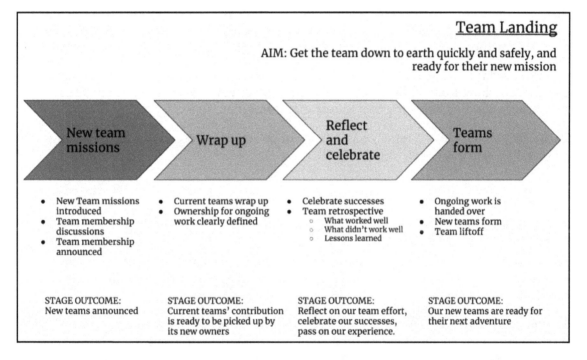

We should first let our team know that change is on the horizon. If we already know where they will be moving on to, we can prepare them by involving them in the new team missions and membership discussions.

Next, our team will need to wrap up their current work, so it's ready to be handed over to its new owners.

We should take time to reflect and celebrate the team successes. We also need to record our learnings so that we may pass on the benefit of our experience to improve both ourselves and others. One recommended way to do this is in the form of a retrospective.

Depending on how long the team has been formed and working on its current piece of work, this could potentially be quite involved. The longer the engagement, the more time that will be needed.

One of the most significant challenges with any retrospective is remembering what happened, particularly over such a length of time as two years. Even in a two-week iteration retrospective, people often say things like, "I can't even remember what happened yesterday, let alone last week."

When setting up the retrospective, we need to start prompting team members' memories so that when they come to the retrospective, they can recount their collective experience. The simplest way to do this is to send out invites to the retrospective early enough that it will trigger some thought.

I've also used tricks like asking the team to bring a souvenir from their time together. It could be anything from a printed piece of code to a desk ornament, anything that has significance and that holds/triggers a meaningful story.

Here's the full outline of a retrospective I ran for one team at the end of a long-running project: *Project now departing at Gate 12*: `https://making.stuff.co.nz/project-now-departing-gate-12/`.

Learning by practicing

As mentioned in the introduction to this chapter, there are some similarities between product teams and sports teams in the sense that just like sports teams, product teams have to practice their game.

To do this, we can use team events such as Hackathons and Innovation Days. They will provide an environment for exploration while also allowing our teams to learn essential techniques such as rapid validation and end-to-end experimentation, all while honing our information sharing and collaboration skills.

Innovation Days are set up in a similar way to Hackathons, in that they are a set time away from the current teamwork. Hackathons usually focus on exploring different uses of a specific technology, while Innovation Days focus on a particular problem solved by any technology.

We'll look at both in a little more detail in the remainder of this section.

Hackathons

A Hackathon is an informal gathering of people with a related interest in the goal of creating usable software. A Hackathon will usually have a theme, of which some examples include:

- A specific item of technology such as an API or a programming language or framework.
- A specific subject matter, for example, open government.
- Sometimes it's about the demographics of the programmers. Personally, I like the *grey-haired C programmers'* Hackathons the best.
- Or it may just be about a group of developers getting together to share ideas and show each other some cool stuff.

As well as a theme, Hackathons will usually have categories and there are usually prizes for the entry judged best in each category. For example, here are a few of the categories for a recent open government Hackathon in New Zealand called *GovHack NZ* 2017:

- Re:Invention (International)
- Tourism Hack
- Geospatial (Location) Hack
- Most innovative hack using Stats NZ data
- Data Journalism
- Making Donations Easy
- Search and Rescue Comms
- Sustainable New Zealand

So yes, you will need a judging panel. If you're doing an internal Hackathon, you can ask for ideas for categories from around your organization. You can then ask those who suggest a category that is used if they could be on the judging panel for that category.

The number of days dedicated to a Hackathon really depends on what you're trying to achieve. For public Hackathons, they usually require a single day or an entire weekend. It's an opportunity for teams to learn how to work together.

Innovation Days

Innovation days were first popularized by Atlassian with their 24-hour events known as 'FedEx Days'. Small, cross-functional teams form around solving a particular business problem. At the end of the time period, each team demonstrates their solution in the form of a working prototype. Prizes for the most successful are awarded, usually across a range of categories.

What can we gain from running an innovation day? It demonstrates to our team that problems can be solved in a surprisingly short period of time, and although it may not result in completely polished solutions, simply working closely with members of our stakeholder group means that we're likely to get something that they want/need sooner.

It is something they should be doing in their day-to-day work, but because an innovation day is a more "fun" environment, they are more likely to experiment with their approach. This is mainly down to the time-driven, sometimes competitive nature of these events.

While we mentioned earlier in this chapter that competition among teams and setting arbitrary dates can be counterproductive to collaborative, information sharing cultures. In this more playful environment, time pressure and an inter-team competition may spark a different type of creative thinking.

The business will often work closely with our team so that we can get ideas to innovate on. Here are a few options for how this can be set up:

- A more substantial problem with everyone working to contribute to the overall solution, either as a single team or as a group of teams
- A smaller problem with each team providing a different solution to solving it
- A mix of individuals and teams working on a single problem

Running a hackathon or innovation day

When organizing an innovation day/Hackathon, it's worth planning ahead. Communicate often and early that we intend to run an innovation day and give the specific dates and timings, repeatedly.

This should probably start at least several months before the intended date. Put it on everyone's calendar far enough ahead of time so that everyone is guaranteed to be available. An example format with the suggested timings is as follows:

1. Hold a 2-hour liftoff session, approximately 2 weeks in advance of the innovation day. Treat this like a mini-team liftoff session, with a mission briefing and working agreements (the rules that we'll operate under). People will need to find teammates and start thinking of ideas to work on; this event should trigger those thought processes.

2. If you're awarding prizes, make sure you've organized them.

3. Hold another session just before the team starts work on their innovation project. There will be a bunch of small teams and maybe even some people who have chosen to work as individuals. Give each group/individual a small timebox to present the idea that they will be working on. From this point onward, everyone commits to demoing the results in the event showcase at the event finale.

4. Make sure you have a clear start and end of the event. For example, from 10 a.m. Monday until 10 a.m. Wednesday. Some people like to kick off on the first day with a morning breakfast, others choose to wait until 12 p.m. The midday timing is especially good for 24-hour events, as it allows people to get some shuteye in their normal sleep cycle.

5. Circulate among the teams during the event to check in with them. Make sure enough drinks and snacks are available. Make sure they have the things they need.

6. At the showcase, stick to the timebox for each demonstration and allow time for a Q&A.

7. If you're awarding prizes, have a small break after the showcase to collate the judges' scoring and feedback. Reconvene everyone and hold a separate prize giving.

Google's 20% time and other alternatives

Many companies have their version of an Innovation Day or Hackathon. Atlassian calls them **FedEx Days** because it sets a timebox of 24 hours; an idea spawned from a FedEx ad campaign with the slogan, *When it Absolutely, Positively has to be there overnight*. Some companies, Google most famously, also have the concept of setting aside time for employees to work on their own projects; at Google, this is called *20% Time*.

Google claims that some of their most famous products, such as Gmail and Adsense, came from their employees' *20% Time*. Experience shows though that it is quite difficult to maintain a dedicated *20% Time* when teams usually have so much else going on in their current assignments. As we will see later in Chapter 13, *The Ultimate Software Team Member*, maintaining enough time for individual professional development training requires team members to have a few tricks up their sleeves to make space away from their regular teamwork.

Summary

In this chapter, we looked at how the shift in where knowledge resides in an organization and how the necessary specialist skills to process that information now lie at the team level.

It has meant a shift in our team dynamics due to the complexity of the problems that software teams solve. We can no longer afford to work as the individual cogs in a machine; collaboration and communication are fundamental to a team's high performance.

Much of the work our software teams carry out requires improvisation and the use of judgment in situations that are often ambiguous. The problems we work on are complex, often requiring novel solutions and an empirical (scientific) approach to solving them.

The role of our job as leaders is to be agents of this change and to provide support and a high-enough level of comfort to the team so that they are more able to assimilate all of the new stuff they are learning. Remember that positivity, trust, respect, and psychological safety are paramount to creating innovative solutions.

In the next chapter, we'll look at how we bake quality into our product from the outset. Particularly relevant to the discussion in this section, we'll see how Mob Programming can bring our team together more quickly regarding interpersonal relationships and working agreements.

12
Baking Quality into Our Software Delivery

As teams begin to tighten their feedback loops, handovers between tester, developer, Product Owner, and UXer will start to blur. Using the metaphor of rugby, as Nonaka and Takeuchi did in their paper *The New New Product Development Game,* the ball will begin to be passed very rapidly between team members and the distinction between who is testing, who is building, and who is designing will be very hard to make.

Also, as the teams start to get much better at breaking down their work into small, similarly sized discrete chunks of value, certain aspects of their work such as estimating will begin to become less necessary.

Finally, because the team members are working so closely, aspects of their work, such as quality, will improve considerably.

In this chapter, we look at several popular approaches that teams take to improve their performance.

The following are the topics that we will cover in this chapter:

- Cross-pollination of skills in cross-functional teams
- Mob programming
- No more bugs
- No more estimates

Cross-pollination of skills

Cross-pollination of skills happens as our team starts to hone its techniques for collaboration. Communication between team members will begin to get so tight that it will be difficult to see where the handovers between different roles are taking place.

Where before we saw clear boundaries between user experience, software engineer, test engineer, agile coach, and Product Owner, we will start to see the edges begin to blur. As collaboration improves, handovers will become redundant as the knowledge transfer between team members becomes seamless.

Unless we've worked on Agile teams before, few of us will have experienced this; a phased process such as Waterfall often keeps the roles separate. So, how does this start? For most teams, it begins as we learn more about each other's roles as we start to work together. In the team Liftoff, we explicitly discuss our roles and what each of us brings to help the team complete our mission. In Sprint Planning during estimation and task breakdown, we consider how we will each contribute to doing the work. And in the Daily Scrum, we discuss how we will coordinate with each other to get the job done.

For instance, consider the scenario shown on the Kanban board below, where work progresses so far before it gets stuck in a particular column: in the **Code Review** column or the **Test** column. These logjams where work accumulates often happen at a handover point between team members:

To-do	UX / Design	Code	Unit Test	Code Review	Test	Merge	Deploy Staging	UAT	Deploy Prod	Confirm	Done
Work item		Work item	Work item	Work item	Work item		Work item				Work item
Work item					Work item		Work item				Work item
Work item					Work item						
Work item					Work item						
Work item					Work item						

Work is accumulating because the team member is waiting for a tester to do some specialist testing work. Logjams in our workflow can happen temporarily because team members with specialist skills are away, or because they are just too busy, or because we don't quite have the right balance in our workflow.

When this happens, when we see a problem with our workflow, we need to debug it just like we would if it were code; our aim should be to get these valuable software features into the hands of our customer as soon as possible.

Probably the first thing to do is for the team to swarm on the logjam of work and release as much of that value as possible. Swarming is awkward at first because team members who don't usually do a code review or testing will need to learn how to do it and team members with those skills will need to coach the others.

We can help the transfer of specialist knowledge by being selective about our pairs when pair programming in these situations, for example, pairing a developer with a tester; having team members that are more cross-functional will only increase the team's resilience in the long term.

The next thing to do, once we've unblocked the logjam, is to consider how we can prevent it from happening again; any accumulation of unfinished work in one part of our system is a potential symptom of a broader problem. For example, if work is accumulating in the **Test** column, what is the reason? The reasons are listed as follows:

1. Is it because there are more programmers than testers and the testers can't keep up?
2. Is it because testing is usually approximately 70% of the work in developing software, regardless of whether you automate your tests?
3. Is it because the programmers are producing code of too low quality and much rework is required?
4. Perhaps the programmers aren't automating the tests, expecting the testers to do so. This approach tends to generate a significant amount of rework, as the testers will often test the specifications, not what the programmers have written.

Whatever the problem is, if the programmers and the testers don't work together to solve the problem, it will continue.

Managing **Work In Progress** (**WIP**) limits, and actively breaking down work items into bitesize chunks of discrete value, is the most straightforward approach to increasing workflow.

However, even with this approach to increasing workflow, our team will soon notice, if they still have an element of phased delivery, that the handovers, although smaller, will still cause issues.

Handovers bleed information in the transfer process, anywhere up to 50% of the knowledge will be lost. If our team works together to solve the problems in the transfer of knowledge, we will gradually get to know more about what each other's role entails. We'll even take on some of the responsibility for different functions, and the cross-pollination of skills will begin.

Test automation is essential to any Agile team's productivity. Code review is another gate where we could benefit from automation as well. Employing tools such as SonarQube will go a long way to help our team build the code right the first time. If we are to implement either of these, our group first needs to set their standard around testing and code reviewing standards. To do this, they'll need to work with the specialists in our team who understand how to do that.

Once we've implemented automation strategies around testing and code review, it isn't to say that we should do away with an explicit testing or code review stage. There are still many benefits from an *eyes and hands-on* approach.

However, the more we can automate, the more quickly we'll get feedback on these hygiene factors. We don't make our jobs redundant by automating; it makes our jobs more stimulating because it allows us to move up our practice to the next level, whether it is testing, writing code, code review, or something else.

Boundaries will also start to blur as we begin to automate our process; test automation (TDD and BDD) blurs the lines between software design, programming, and testing. Continuous Integration/Deployment will blur the lines between software development and operations. In both of these scenarios, if we're lucky enough to have specialists in these fields (test automation and DevOps), they will likely act as coaches as they both help the team create our frameworks and pipelines as well as transferring their knowledge in automation practices.

Cross-pollination of skills is essential if our team is to reduce the time it takes to deliver and skill cross-pollination will give our team the confidence to act knowing that they're covering each other's backs.

Mob programming

We've all had those moments when we need a group assessment of a problem to find a solution. As the saying goes, two minds are better than one. In the case of mob programming, it's *all the minds of the team are better than one.*

When a team at Hunter Industries faced some significant enhancements on one of their systems, their lead, Woody Zuill, suggested that they assess the state of the code as a group. He figured that diving into a large code base was going to be challenging, and if done individually, would likely result in not everyone seeing the same thing or being on the same page at the end of it.

He booked out a meeting room for the whole team, and they meticulously studied the code together, calling and pointing things out as they spotted them. The team who had spent some of their time in the past few months improving their skills, learning together through Coding Dojos, quickly found a problem in the code and started to refactor it.

After a couple of days, he fully expected them to stop, but they didn't, they kept booking meeting rooms and kept working together as a team. Eventually, when Woody realized the team was going to continue working this way, they reconfigured their workspace for mob programming.

Why does mob programming work?

Swarming on a problem is typical for teams, especially when there is a high degree of complexity or a high degree of uncertainty on how to proceed. Or perhaps there is just a significant amount of excess work in progress, creating a logjam on our board, and our team rallies to help each other.

Mobbing is the same, except the swarm continues until the user story is done and delivered into our customer's hands.

Just as Kent Beck turned up the dial to 10 for code review and created pair programming, mobbing is the dial turned up to 10 for collaborative cross-functional teamwork. With a mob, we can include other specialists such as testers, user experience, the Product Owner, or other **subject matter experts (SMEs)**. When in a mob arrangement, communication feedback loops close incredibly quickly.

But how can our team be productive when they are all working on one work item at a time, at one computer? Woody Zuill says this is the question that he gets asked the most about the Hunter Industries mobs. However, he realized that this probably wasn't the right question to ask. Instead, he reframed it and asked, "What are the things that destroy productivity?"

Here are some of the things that he listed with my interpretations:

- **Communication problems**: There are no handovers in a mob, we have all of the people present to carry out the job. If we need information/feedback from outside the mob, we can delegate responsibility to one of the team members to get this, while the others continue to work.
- **Decision-making problems**: A mob will reduce the chain of command as our Product Owner often works with us directly. Any decisions can be made then and there.
- **Doing more than barely sufficient**: When we work in isolation from feedback, or our feedback cycles are too long, we tend to make assumptions and end up doing more than is necessary; we over produce. To avoid breaking the Agile principle: *Simplicity—the art of maximizing the amount of work not done—is essential*, takes discipline; the mob will provide that.

- **Technical debt**: When working individually, we often create technical debt, sometimes without realizing, sometimes deliberately in the spirit of getting things done. As with simplicity, discipline is hard when we're moving fast—as Blaise Pascall, the 17th Century mathematician remarked: *I have made this longer than usual because I have not had time to make it shorter.*
  A mob of programmers is more likely to maintain a no *broken windows* policy to keep the code cleaner and more succinct. The mob makes it easier to get it right the first time as we're more likely to take the opportunity to refactor.
- **Thrashing**: In a computer system thrashing occurs when the CPU is under load, trying to service many requests. System memory starts to become limited as the CPU swaps between tasks in an effort to get as many things done as possible. In this state the CPU begins to slow down as it starts to intensively manage its limited resources. This is a similar situation for a team when it has too much work to-do. A team starts to thrash when its members start to multi-task in an effort to get the work done. The mob helps avoid team thrashing by minimizing the tasks being carried out, focusing the team's effort on one task at a time. If an individual does get distracted by something deemed urgent from outside of the mob, the mob is able to continue until the team member returns.
- **Politics**: This impacts us when different business groups aren't aligned, often pushing and pulling us in different directions via the use of shoulder tapping to coerce individual team members to do their bidding. The group nature of a mob makes it harder for individuals with an agenda to interrupt and distract us, making us more resilient to political overtones.
- **Meetings**: All meetings become *doings* or workshops, meaning that our team is never distracted from its work.

Talking about Woody's first point, communication problems, as we mentioned in the previous section, handovers between different team members can cause a significant delay in our process. There are two main reasons for this:

- **Availability**: It's likely that handovers won't transition smoothly as team members are likely working on other pieces of work. We'll need to wait until they become available.
- **Information transfer takes time**: As we've already discussed, handovers can lose anywhere up to 50% of the information gathered by the person in the preceding step. Many information transfers result in much signal loss and therefore much relearning.

Lean thinking advocates a single-piece flow, which leads us to minimize the waste of waiting and handovers. Instead of optimizing a single part of the system to maximize local efficiency, we streamline the flow of individual work items across our board.

Mobbing is one approach to software development, which optimizes for flow. So, we don't have to deal with the logjams we sometimes get on our board, as we have on the board example shown here:

To-do	UX / Design	Code	Unit Test	Code Review	Test	Merge	Deploy Staging	UAT	Deploy Prod	Confirm	Done
Work item		Work item		Work item	Work item		Work item				Work item
Work item				Work item	Work item		Work item				Work item
Work item				Work item							
Work item				Work item							
Work item				Work item							

We optimize the flow across the board from end-to-end as we discussed when we considered the system as a whole in Chapter 8, *Tightening Feedback Loops in the Software Development Life Cycle.*

This thinking may seem counter-intuitive regarding speeding things up, but in fact, we achieve the opposite, especially when we start to measure the overall end-to-end delivery into our customers' hands, and not just the time it takes to write the code.

With the mob programmers I've worked with, we've observed that a mob is more likely to build more maintainable code with fewer to no bugs coming back to bite us and interrupt essential new feature work.

Overall, the finished product will likely be more robust, so if and when it does fail, it fails within tolerances that are more easily recoverable and with less likelihood of seriously inconveniencing our users. Building resilience in means that in the short term we may take longer to write code, but in the long term, the system is more likely to do what it says it would do on the tin.

One other aspect of mob programming that is important to consider is that this is the team. In Chapter 11, *Improving Our Team Dynamics to Increase Our Agility*, we discussed how communication and collaboration between specialists were similar to that of a sports team. However, some of the thinking behind good sports team management doesn't always translate well into product development.

For example, one competitive aspect of a sports team is in the selection process where team members vie for their place in the team. This allows the team manager to field the best players and creates a healthy competition (hopefully) within the team as each player seeks their place in the A-team.

In product development, we don't have the luxury of having a selection process, as in the A-team/B-team approach where players vie for a spot in the A-team. In fact, we rarely have the opportunity to pick and field alternative players from the bench as it's unlikely that we have substitutes in the first place, such are the pressures of product development in the modern age.

Even when we do have a pool of talent to choose from, as we all know just adding additional people to a team in the middle of solving a complex problem won't speed up things overnight. In fact, it will likely slow things down until that person becomes embedded in the team; not just forming relationships, but also developing an understanding of how the team works and the problem that it is solving. This has been well documented since Fred Brookes highlighted it in his book *The Mythical Man-Month*.

Mobbing allows our team to operate at a sustainable pace, and when people are injured, or not up to their game, the team can continue without affecting the work.

How does mob programming work?

Different examples of mob environments exist, for example, Hunter Industries uses an open office environment, where each mob has its own area with desks facing several large hi-res screens, surrounded by whiteboards.

There is one computer with one keyboard, the team member who sits at the keyboard is known as the driver. The other members of the team are known as the navigators. There is room for others to sit at the desk, including the team coach.

For the mob to switch out drivers quickly, it's probably wise to be familiar with one IDE and set of tools. Although it's not impossible to have more than one IDE set up on a computer, there are benefits from everyone in the team using the same environment, knowledge sharing, for example. Reaching a consensus shouldn't be hard and the benefits of agreeing on one environment outweigh the potential pitfalls of many different setups.

Around the outside of their space, there are desks where team members can go to work if they are focussed on something else and don't want to work directly with the mob. In this way, they can still hear what the mob is up to without actively engaging.

Of course, if people don't feel useful or dislike what they are contributing, they are allowed to leave the mob environment and take a break.

It's a good idea to discuss beforehand how the team will work as a mob. Here is one team's working agreement for mob programming:

Mob etiquette:

- Core mob size: 3 to 4
- Need some way of letting people go and do their thing and then bring them up to speed when they rejoin.
- Define breakpoints, so we can have lunch, check emails, and perform admin tasks.
- Need to accommodate other work tasks, such as helping someone else.
- If we leave the Mob, we need to communicate what's going on, not a permission slip but a courtesy.
- If we need to do something that isn't mob work, maybe step away from the mob. (It isn't fair to the rest of the mob if we're distracting them.)

Ergonomics

Whatever our setup, whether it is by individual working, pairing, or mobbing, we have to work in a way that is sustainable over a long period of time. This means that our mobbing workstation needs to be set up with ergonomics in mind.

Here's an example of one of our collaborative spaces:

Photo credit: Raf Gemmail

Here's another:

Photo credit: Raf Gemmail

The following is what we've learned through our experiences with Mob programming:

- The ability to either comfortably sit or stand while navigating requires the monitor or projector to be set to an agreeable height.
- Comfortable ergonomic seating is required.
- The single keyboard and mouse for the driver only works if you can agree on conventions. For example, we may need more than one keyboard if some prefer a Dvorak to a Qwerty key layout. Try to make the setup as easily configurable as possible and provide options such as a touchpad or trackball as well as a mouse.
- A large screen with a decent resolution, or a projector.

No more bugs

Back in Chapter 8, *Tightening Feedback Loops in the Software Development Life Cycle*, we discussed how we tighten feedback loops from a variety of sources for us to ascertain two things:

- Are we building the right thing?
- Are we building the thing right?

Bug reports are a form of feedback that we should welcome, as they are the most straightforward problem detection system we could ask for. They cover many facets of our software, from a user requirement not being quite right to a broken API connection, from the user experience not being satisfactory to performance being suboptimal.

Some teams try to argue that a bug isn't, in fact, a bug. For example, they may say it's a case of the business requirement being wrong. Perhaps the user didn't know what they wanted. This is old-school contract thinking, which gets litigious because of the upfront promises we've made.

Collaborative thinking would lead us to a more service-oriented mindset, where we would want to delight our customer. Therefore, don't get into semantic wars over what a bug is or isn't; remember everyone is right to a certain degree. Embrace it as good feedback and collaborate to fix the problem.

From a lean perspective, bugs result in one of the biggest wastes we have in the software industry because they slow us down in two ways:

1. The time taken to rework our software due to building the wrong thing.
2. The time taken trying to write code on top of software that was built the wrong way.

When we get a bug report, for us to have a chance of preventing this kind of bug from happening again, we have to understand the reason it occurred in the first place and fix the underlying problem.

To do this, we need to triage the bug and perform some root-cause analysis. The quickest method is the 5-Whys, a more in-depth approach is the Ishikawa diagram (we showed an example 5-Whys in Chapter 8, *Tightening Feedback Loops in the Software Development Life Cycle*).

When we use root-cause analysis, we might be surprised to determine that there are some common root causes of bugs. These can be roughly categorized as follows:

- Those caused by the way we write code and design our software
- Those caused by our understanding of the problem
- Those caused by the nature of the problem changing

For the first two points, we can put strategies in place that can bring these directly into our control. For the last point, we can mitigate the problem, primarily by being able to respond quickly to the change. We can also put strategies in place that will build in resilience, so for example, if a change is made to a third-party API, our service won't be impacted or will degrade gracefully.

Bugs caused by the way we write code and design our software

The first two are problems related to our computer system. We can fix these by paying attention to how we create software, both in the coding and design.

As Arlo Belshee points out in his talks on #BugsZero, the likely cause of a bug isn't always what we might think; he lists the causes in the following order:

- **Readability of code**: Not paying care and attention, bad use of whitespace, poor naming, and long methods all contribute to the lack of readability
- **Context dependence**: When code is dependent on the context it is running in and we introduce design flaws such as tight coupling, we make it overly complex and hard to test

The complexity of computer systems can mask the root cause of the bug, especially where multiple different pieces interact, with varying degrees of coupling. Of course, we try to prevent bugs by using a variety of quality assurance techniques. These traditionally involve testing after the code is written, but test-after strategies have little to no impact on how we design software.

Another bad smell when automating our tests is that we find our code hard to test; having untestable code is a reliable indicator that the code is not straightforward. To overcome this, rather than refactor the code, teams will use complicated and fragile testing strategies, such as the ones driven by the UI (Selenium, for example) or too many mocks.

Instead, if we're serious about reducing bugs, we have to get serious about making our code more readable and also reducing code complexity. This requires strategies, including clean coding standards, TDD and refactoring, emergent architecture, trunk-based development and continuous integration, and so on.

This has caused a shift to the left as we discussed in Chapter 8, *Tightening Feedback Loops in the Software Development Life Cycle* for these activities. We don't just flip straight to writing code. Instead, we consider and incrementally implement strategies for their automation. Plus, if we're serious about continuous integration, we will learn how to avoid long-lived feature branches by becoming more trunk-based in our code committing strategy.

Test-Driven Development (TDD) helps fix an important aspect of this problem because code designed with TDD is often much more atomic and simple in nature. From this perspective, we can see that the *test-before* nature of TDD isn't really a testing strategy; instead, it's a design strategy which uses a test harness to make refactoring our code safer and more effective.

To reduce code complexity with a *test-after* testing strategy then we first need to be serious about good design principles and refactoring. Test strategies in themselves are not preventative; as the saying goes, testing only proves the presence of bugs, not the absence of them.

As a baseline to all of the above, we have to write clean code proactively; all Agile teams should be familiar with Robert *Uncle Bob* Martin's book *Clean Code*. The boy scout rule that each time we touch the code, we leave it in a better state than when we found it, is imperative if we're to remain light and nimble without the burden of technical debt.

If we're not in a greenfield, entirely new development space, that is, we have some legacy code, we can also employ tools to tell us where cyclomatic complexity exists. Cyclomatic complexity indicates which code is most used and will, therefore, help us target areas for refactoring which will be most fruitful.

However, the greatest contribution we can make to preventing bugs is to write all code from that point onwards with the understanding that we have to write clean, simple, and readable code.

Bugs caused by our understanding of the problem

This category is human-system related, a category which we can roughly define as *us not understanding the problem* and includes:

- Miscommunication and mis-understanding
- Lack of knowledge
- Making assumptions without validating them
- Not knowing what we want until we see it

One mindset shift that might help with this is to consider everything we do to the point where we deliver our software as design; this includes writing the code. This thinking will help us understand that in each step toward delivery we should be asking "Are we building the right thing?"

As we discussed back in `Chapter 1`, *The Software Industry and the Agile Manifesto* complex problems tend to hide details that we don't uncover until we start building, delivering, and using our software. These details often don't make themselves visible until we start to tease them out and are what NASA referred to as *unknown unknowns*.

We can fix these by paying attention to the human aspects of software delivery, for example, having our Product Owner co-located with us will significantly improve our feedback loops and decision-making process.

 One step better: we could consider going to co-locate within our user's environment. Sitting in our customer's space will teach us much about how our software will be used; it's incredible the amount of information we can absorb just hearing and seeing what they do at first-hand.

Here are some other techniques we can use to get a better understanding of what our customer needs:

- **User Experience:** Techniques that help us uncover what our user wants or needs include user story mapping and impact mapping (both discussed in `Chapter 10`, *Using Product Roadmaps to Guide Software Delivery*). Both of these techniques are designed to form high-level objectives plus an initial breakdown of features. From there, our user experience specialists can help tease out further details by creating various forms of prototypes, from paper-based mockups through to actual screens that have limited, but real-life interaction capabilities.

- **Behavior-Driven Development (BDD)**: The great thing about BDD is the way that it encourages us to work collaboratively with our customer to determine the requirements for our software. We use scenarios as a way to tease out acceptance criteria for User Stories.

The following is an example of a simple autoplay feature on a video player, which automatically plays a video unless our user is on a touch device:

```
GIVEN that a user is viewing a page which has a video
WHEN they hover over the video
THEN the video should start playing after 5 seconds
AND the video frame should include a countdown

GIVEN that the user has hovered over the video
WHEN the video countdown has started
THEN play and pause buttons should show

GIVEN that a user is viewing a page with a video on a touch device
WHEN the user swipes vertically on the player
THEN the video should not play

GIVEN that a user is viewing a page with a video on a touch device
WHEN the user taps on the player
THEN the video should play
```

The scenarios are written in familiar language as we need to formulate scenarios in a way that everyone on our team can understand them; non-technical people shouldn't be an afterthought, they should be the main focus.

We then take these scenarios and automate tests around them, and because these scenarios represent our acceptance criteria, this means the tests we build represent our acceptance tests.

One common way of breaking a large user story down into something more manageable is to split it up based on its acceptance criteria. This should become easier with BDD because we're rewriting the acceptance criteria as scenarios, which gives us a common language and verbose format. Using the preceding scenarios as an example, we could split out two different User Stories. One implements video player autoplay for devices using a pointing device and one implements the video player, without autoplay, on touchscreen devices.

This automation represents a significant step in **shifting left** (that phrase again, which means doing it early and often in the life cycle) because **user acceptance testing** (**UAT**) is usually left until the end of the process. Writing acceptance tests with our Product Owner before we implement the code to fulfill them means that we are much more likely to build the right thing without over-elaborating. Hopefully, this helps us adhere to the Agile principle—*Simplicity- the art of maximizing the amount of work not done - is essential.*

Of course, sometimes people just don't know what they want until they see it or use it. While all of the preceding techniques mitigate this happening, we should still expect a degree of rework after our customer finally gets to use our software. This is why incremental delivery of **working software** is key to ironing out bugs.

Each of the preceding suggestions is a way for us to take our understanding one step closer to the real thing. It's important that just like our software we incorporate these techniques into our incremental delivery adopting the Goldilocks approach of not too much, not too little, but just the right amount of work to take us forward.

Bugs caused by the nature of the problem changing

Then, of course, there are bugs when things just go out of date. For example, legislation changes for sales tax, a third-party API or library becomes defunct, a third-party service such as a Content Distribution Network is impacted, or people's tastes change to prefer touch/verbal interaction as technology advances.

These may seem like the group of bugs that are least in our control. Dependence on a third party always causes issues that can involve a degree of disconnection and stretch the time these bugs take to resolve.

To some degree, third-party integration issues, such as deprecated methods, should be handled by notifications from the third party. However, I've known many instances where this hasn't happened.

The key thing to mitigate the change around the boundaries of the system is to build a degree of resilience, sometimes known as graceful degradation of service, and to automate tests which look specifically for any change, for example, by automating notifications to flag a problem when integration with third-party software changes.

Netflix famously employs a **Chaos Monkey** to help it build resilience into its service. The Chaos Monkey is responsible for disrupting the Netflix service by impacting various parts of its infrastructure so that they can see how the rest of the system will respond. This is all done in the live system, creating a culture of being able to deal easily with worst-case scenarios.

To do this, we have to run integration tests against the live third-party system. In some cases, this can be expensive to perform continuously for tests that we run in our development environment. I'm thinking both in terms of the time it takes to run, but also regarding cost—banks, for example, often have to pay per transaction.

In this instance, it's best to adopt a phased approach to integration testing by *simulating* the integration tests you run regularly with the third party. The trick with this approach is to *re-record* the transaction simulation against the live system when changes in the interface are noticed.

In a phased approach, where we're trying to keep costs of running tests down, we can adopt the strategy that only the last set of tests in our CI/CD pipeline is run against the actual live system. If a change is noticed, we send a notification and stop the deployment.

Refactoring our environment

In his #BugsZero conference talk, Arlo also points out that there are a number of behaviors, which can make all of the preceding worse—distraction, busyness, and, perhaps the worst, accepting errors as the norm.

All of these require us to think from the Lean perspective and view the system as a whole.

For example, limiting work in progress is our primary weapon in avoiding busyness and distraction. It seems counter-intuitive, but when we context-switch we have to put down one problem and its associated mental model and pick up another.

This additional cognitive load means that we lose around 30% of our time to these mental model switches. Therefore, trying to work on multiple things at once (multitasking) just causes both things to drag out further than they would have if we'd have worked on them sequentially. This results in putting us under more pressure to deliver. This is why multi-tasking doesn't work well when switching between **complex** tasks, it just leads to us mess up multiple things at once.

In addition to limiting work in progress, we have to become rigorous at work prioritization. Back in Chapter 10, *Using Product Roadmaps to Guide Software Delivery* we look at one approach called **Weighted Shortest Job First (WSJF)**. In essence, this economic approach is how we deliver the largest amount of value in the shortest time possible. Delivering value is what builds trust with our business and when they see us doing the work that is most valuable, it avoids them interrupting us with other work.

The final category *accepting bugs as the norm* is perhaps the most powerful from the team's perspective. As we discussed earlier, we should see bugs as valuable feedback that we haven't got things right. If we triage each bug by performing some root-cause analysis, it will help us fix both the bug and the failing in the system that allowed us to create the bug in the first place.

Remember, to be successful with this amount of rigor we have to adopt a no-blame culture. We avoid blaming the individual we might think is responsible; instead, we look to fix the system and create an environment where bugs can no longer be created so easily.

Everybody is human and forgets to do things sometimes, and so, if the bug was caused because an individual forgot to run tests when they checked in code, then automate the running of tests each time the code is committed. The team has to take responsibility as a whole to fix errors.

No more estimates

A common theme throughout this book has been a focus on building software in small manageable chunks so that we can deliver incrementally and gather feedback as we go. We discussed adaptive planning and how this compares to traditional project predictive planning back in Chapter 1, *The Software Industry and the Agile Manifesto*. In particular, we talked about estimates in the software industry and how difficult they were to get right when used to predictively plan large pieces of work.

The Standish Group's Chaos report is an annual report which looks at the state of the software industry. In 2015, it looked at over 50,000 software projects worldwide and assessed them based on their ability to deliver on time, to budget, and to obtain a satisfactory outcome. Based on this criteria, only 29% of projects were successful. Of the rest, the ones that failed outright made up to 19% of the total. Those that were challenged, that is, the final product was compromised somehow, comprised the remaining 52%.

One key aspect of the 2015 report was that the Standish Group used their new metrics for measuring a *satisfactory outcome*. Previously, they'd only measured on target, meaning the percentage of requirements delivered. In 2014, they re-coded their database to include measurements for **satisfied** (very high to very low), **value** (very high to very low) and on **strategic corporate goal** (precise to distant).

This is a major shift in our industry. As the saying goes, w*hat gets measured, gets improved*. In other words, if we measure value, we get value. And up until this point, our industry has had a very poor reputation for value return on investment. As Angel Medinilla points out in his excellent book, *Agile Management: Leadership in an Agile Environment*, this is sometimes as low as 50 or 60 cents per dollar spent.

In Chapter 9, *Seeking Value – How to Deliver Better Software Sooner*, we talked about focusing on value as a more important metric for measuring a user story's successful outcome. So delivering on value is far more important than delivering on time and budget. Think about it; if we deliver on value, then we must have delivered on time and budget, otherwise, all value would have been destroyed by the lack of the latter.

So, when we accept that we're bad at estimating and that value is a better measurement than budget or date, if we combine these two things, our view of how we focus on getting predictability in delivering our work will start to shift.

If we want to increase our likelihood of a predictable outcome, we first need to focus on aspects of delivery that include stability, frequency, and cadence; all of these contribute to reducing variability. If we focus on these, then because we have more predictable outcomes, we will naturally get better timelines.

If we combine this with a focus on value creation, adopt lean software development principles to maximize the value delivered, and the value we create continues to offset the cost of creating it, then the need for estimates will start to become a moot point.

Combining lean thinking with incremental delivery means we begin to focus on the flow of work, and as discussed in *Introducing some Lean thinking to improve flow* in Chapter 8, *Tightening Feedback Loops in the Software Development Life Cycle*, focusing on flow means we focus on the following two aspects of delivery:

1. How long a piece of work takes to go from *to-do* to *done*. Also known as the *cycle time*.
2. Breaking down work into small discrete chunks so that we can deliver value, which either adds directly to our customer's business value, or to our understanding of how best to solve the business problem.

Our aim with this is to focus on small batches of work and foster collaboration for end-to-end delivery. Once we can do that, and we have some completed work that we can use as a benchmark, we can even start to forecast how long it will take us to complete other parts of our work. For example, if we complete 5 User Stories in 2 weeks, and we have a further 10 similar User Stories to complete, we can forecast it will take us another 4 weeks.

However, several things make forecasting difficult *with or without estimates*:

- If we're working in the same area of our system, we can compare User Stories that we haven't done with User Stories that we have done. If our area of work changes, then it will no longer be possible to compare like this. Instead, we'll have to wait until some aspect of that work has been completed before we can start forecasting the remaining stories.
- Our backlog isn't all equal, some stories have been refined and broken down, some haven't. We will be able to compare the stories that have been broken down to stories that we've already completed. This will lead to a more accurate forecast but only for those stories.

The aim of the No Estimates movement is as follows:

- Focus on value, both delivering and measuring it.
- Make delivery more predictable by focusing on reducing waste (including bugs).
- Understand that there are better options than estimates.

Imagine if we could shift our entire focus to value creation and measure our value return on investment rather than how long it took to build something. This is when our team/organization will become a true learning system.

Summary

Sometimes it takes another person to connect the dots for you, and it wasn't until I saw Arlo Belshee deliver his #BugsZero talk at Agile Singapore 2016 that something changed. Up until that point, making bugs an avoidable occurrence was a light with a dimmer switch at about 50%; now it was fully on.

For a number of years, up until that point, I'd worked on teams that had very few bugs in their production environment, few enough per year to be countable on one hand. To get to this point, we had to adopt behavior driven development and worked closely with our customer. We used Continuous Integration and Delivery and avoided long-running feature branches like a very contagious disease.

Previously, we had identified a great deal of technical debt in our system, but by using a Technical Debt Heatmap, we had made it visible. We had then managed to slash out technical debt by regularly tackling it every Sprint, either as part of user story when making changes in that area or by deliberately going on time-boxed bug hunting missions.

It wasn't until we started pair-programming in earnest that things really began to change for us. With the two minds are better than one philosophy, we began to smash it out of the park. Pair-programming isn't a compromise regarding productivity. And it certainly doesn't reflect a programmer's ability to do their job. Pairing is powerful; it shortens feedback loops, makes solving complex problems universally easier, creates a disciplined approach, and produces code that is more likely to be simple and bug-free.

We didn't just pair with other programmers, we also paired with our Product Owner and/or subject matter experts. Having our Product Owner co-located with us significantly improved our feedback loops and decision-making process. If we can't get our Product Owner to co-locate with us, we should consider going to co-locate with our Product Owner. It's amazing what we can learn by osmosis when sitting in our customer's space.

Once we'd become well-practiced at pairing and understood its benefits well, taking the next step to mob programming seemed more logical than anything. We naturally fell to working this way on a number of occasions.

The long-term effect of this level of quality is significant for any software application, making bugs a thing of the past allows us to focus on new features and enhancements. Plus, getting there isn't as hard as we think it might be, it just requires a mindset shift to realize that bug reports are feedback telling us something isn't right. If we incorporate that feedback, analyze its root cause and action ideas to stop these types of bugs from occurring, we will lessen the chances of this pattern repeating. As we continuously improve our approach, we will start to throttle the number of bugs that we receive to zero.

In the next chapter, we'll look at a different form of continuous improvement; how we can become the best Agile team member that we can be.

13
The Ultimate Software Team Member

In the past few years, there have been some positive shifts in how software developers interact with their customers.

Anthropologically, we're an interesting bunch. Many years ago, our work was viewed as backroom; we had little or no contact with the people that were using our software. We saw computers as something like mythical beasts and computer programmers as their keepers.

Now, in just the same way that technology has proliferated into everyday life, so too have software developers. Where before we'd use go-betweens such as project managers and business analysts, software developers now have direct contact with the people who use our software. In fact, in this past decade, we've begun to see a shift from having separate IT departments to the increasing integration of our business and technology groups. This transition has meant that we have learned new skills; for example, we now know how to listen to people, understand their wants, and turn them into needs. Skills that we used to call soft skills are now genuine skills that every software developer needs to have.

At the same time, technology is moving fast, really fast. Software developers have a hard time keeping up. The reality for us is that we have to learn quickly, and we've become very good at acquiring knowledge rapidly and often on the job.

This chapter looks at what makes software developers tick, what motivates us to get out of bed in the morning and go to work. We'll also look at the way we've adapted to a rapid learning environment.

Finally, we'll look at practical techniques for fostering learning in software developers, so it becomes an innate part of what they do.

The following are the topics we will cover in this chapter:

- The power of motivation
- The entrepreneurial developer
- The team player
- The growth mindset
- Fostering a learning habit

The power of motivation

I had a conversation with a developer not so long ago; I asked her why they did what they did. She responded that nothing drove her to be a software developer other than the money in fact, she would sooner do another type of job if it paid as well.

What she said preyed on my mind. To be truthful, this made me a little sad. I was sad that a person who'd chosen a particular career path that required higher education and a relatively extended period as a journeywoman did a job purely for the money.

Extrinsic drivers

I realize many people have to take what work they can in order make ends meet. We often have external drivers, which means enjoying our work comes second to the pressures of being the provider for a family or repaying a mortgage or both. Sometimes we compensate by offsetting our lack of fulfillment at work with a trip we have planned or a new toy we intend to purchase.

Salary, bonuses, health care—especially for those that don't live in countries that have public healthcare—company cars, and other rewards help us satisfy our extrinsic drivers, whether providing for our families and us or otherwise.

However, many of us spend at least 40 hours a week at work, a significant portion of our waking lives. If we're not doing something we enjoy, are the things it enables us to do outside work enough to allow us to feel compensated? In my experience as a knowledge worker, probably not. Given the smart, well educated, technology savvy people that we are, once we have those things we will start to look for a more profound sense of satisfaction. When we start talking about what motivates us, this is when our intrinsic drivers begin to come into play.

Intrinsic drivers

Our intrinsic drivers are the things that naturally motivate us. Our choice of hobby often reflects what intrinsically drives us. When work is combined with this inner drive, our sense of job satisfaction increases. If we are lucky enough to work in our chosen field, intrinsic drivers are what get us out of bed in the morning.

Dan Pink in his Tedtalk (`https://www.youtube.com/watch?v=u6XAPnuFjJc`) nails much of it—once we take the question of money off the table, the typical things that many people seek at work are mastery, autonomy, and purpose.

Mastery

Early on, something in this industry peaked our interest and this is what started us on this journey, probably initially as a hobby; it laid down a challenge. We then spent long hours of study and modern apprenticeship in pursuit of mastering this craft—a craft that is evolving at such a rapid pace that it will provide us with a lifetime of learning and challenge.

Autonomy

Independence in the way we carry out our work is important because knowledge work is creative and creativity is unique from person to person.

Purpose

Our deep-down need is to do something in this life that makes a difference, something that either sets us apart from the crowd or gives us a sense of belonging.

Activity – moving motivators

To help us find out what makes us tick, *Jurgen Appello* created a game called Moving Motivators (`https://management30.com/product/moving-motivators/`). It takes the work of various people, including *Dan Pink*, *Steven Reiss*, and *Edward Deci*, and gives us a card deck that contains 10 motivators: curiosity, honor, acceptance, mastery, power, freedom, relatedness, order, goal, and status.

Best played with others so you can compare and discuss results, this is a great game to play as a team or in pairs.

It also allows us to play out different scenarios and see how our motivators change accordingly.

Why are intrinsic drivers important?

The main disadvantage of extrinsic rewards is that their effects are only temporary. However, if our intrinsic drivers align with our role, we attain job satisfaction with less need for extrinsic reward. We feel understood as individuals and our work is something that we truly care about. As a result, we are more motivated toward obtaining good outcomes at work and likely to do a much better job.

As employers, we are more likely to get better results if our people are happy in their work, feel trusted, and are able to do the best job they can. The additional benefit is that satisfied employees are less likely to be on an insatiable quest for rewards. Therefore, they are less inclined to seek increasing compensation for being in an unsatisfactory role or, worse still, go elsewhere.

As an industry, we're starting to tap into mastery and autonomy reasonably well, providing professional development and environments that encourage individual thinking and contribution. However, if we were able to align an individual's purpose with an organization's purpose, there'd be a collaboration of like-minded people at every level of your business. That's a powerful thing indeed.

In Chapter 9, *Seeking Value – How to Deliver Better Software Sooner*, we looked at how setting objectives to match our organizational purpose would help our team carry out its mission.

One of the things that I learned early on in my career was that the more we can align our purpose with that of the organization we work for, the more likely we are to feel fulfilled.

Ask any group of knowledge workers why they do what they do and you'll get a wide range of general answers. Anything from "I'm in it for the money" to "I love solving problems" and "It makes me happy when I build something that other people find useful."

But dig a little deeper and some of us might be surprised to find out why we do this work. For me, it was because I saw opportunities for technology to be used for social good. Not surprisingly, I chose to work for organizations that shared my values and purpose.

The deeper why is what makes us tick when everything else (money, food, shelter, and love) is off the table.

We'll discover this through the application/problem domain; for example, if you're a software developer passionate about music, you'll find work in the music industry. If money is your thing, you'll work in financial services.

Or for you it might be through the solution domain, the technologies that you use to solve the problems of the application domain, and your real why is in taking these solutions to the next level.

Or it may be because of the company culture, and how you align with it. For example, a company such as Zappos, an online shoe retail company, values teamwork and focuses on how its teams work well together.

Hopefully, you find work in an organization where you can align with all three.

Finding *your why* is an important first step, and the subject of two books written by author *Simon Sinek*—**Starting With Why** and **Finding Your Why**.

He describes it as akin to finding our piece in the jigsaw puzzle. The more our piece fits, the more of ourselves we give to our company, its products, or its problems, and the more likely we are to find something that excites us at work. We do spend half of our waking lives at work; isn't it only right that we're passionate about what we do?

The entrepreneurial developer

The one thing that unifies all software developers is at some point in our lives is when we created some software that did something cool, a light went on, and we got hooked. However, building software for ourselves is very different from building software for someone else. We have to be motivated to work collaboratively to set up the right environment and make the magic happen.

No matter what type of software product we're building, there is always an element of uncertainty in what the final shape of that outcome will be. And so, when we work with our customer to bring their idea to life, we work on the premise that the concept itself is likely to have holes in it and we will have to work to fill in the gaps.

We know as we begin to build out potential solutions that we will discover much new information and we will need to learn at a rapid rate. As we discussed back in `Chapter 11`, *Improving Our Team Dynamics to Increase Our Agility*, there has been a distinct shift in where the knowledge resides in an organization and as knowledge workers we operate at the intersection of three streams of information:

1. **The application/problem domain**—the business
2. **The solution domain**—technology
3. How we deliver, sometimes referred to as the **process domain**

At this confluence, we act as trusted advisors to guide our customer to get a good result. In my experience, this creates two opportunities:

1. We can create a direct bridge between our customer's world (the application/problem domain) and our world (the technology/solution domain) which helps us both begin to understand how we might build something truly useful.
2. We can set up an environment for discovery, where we need to learn rapidly and are prepared to take a degree of risk. Here we have to make a working agreement with our customer that we will work with them to uncover what we need to know.

So, we won't start with all our requirements nailed down. As we discussed earlier in this book in `Chapter 1`, *The Software Industry and the Agile Manifesto*, it's often not plausible to do so. The more novel the idea, either regarding its application or its solution, the higher the uncertainty will be. Especially if our customer is trying to create a point of difference—something that differentiates them from their competitors in the market.

Fortunately, if we use adaptive planning in quick cycles to build increments of working software, we will quickly discover what will and won't work. This will also work to reduce the risk rapidly for both us and our customer. Plus, using an adaptive strategy means our customer should experience a higher degree of control in the direction we take, creating a win-win.

This, in my mind, is what leads us to take a more entrepreneurial mindset to our work. We accept that we can't know everything up front, so we will have to work with a degree of uncertainty and risk. To get comfortable working with risk, our methods need to seek it and constantly try to reduce it.

An entrepreneurial culture is important because, for the adaptive approach to software development to work, we need to set up the environment in such a way that we can learn rapidly. Creating feedback loops is what tells us whether our idea is working or not.

It's only usually after experiencing this approach that our customer will understand and trust it. For them to enter our world, they will need to take a leap of faith. They are used to a world that tells them how much something is going to cost up front. Hopefully, we will be able to show them that adaptive approaches to building software products are more likely to result in something that they will find useful and may well delight them.

And while we might not be taking the financial risk ourselves, we should work with our customer responsibly, as if their money was our money. Therefore, we need to work closely with our customer for two reasons:

- So that they can learn about our world as much as we learn about theirs.
- Closer working will achieve a much better outcome.

What we learn pretty fast is that we need to be pragmatic and focused, getting the balance right between learning enough about the domain so that we can solve the problem with just the right technology, and then delivering it in a way that is going to get feedback early and often so that we can adjust our approach if necessary.

So, being entrepreneurial isn't necessarily about starting a new business, it's about the mindset that we need to have if we're continually investing energy into new ideas. This is something that we're very familiar with in the tech industry. The mindset requires people who are curious, collaborative, have humility, are adaptable, and can spot new opportunities.

The team player

As technology advances and our use of it becomes more prevalent, the type and size of problems we are asked to solve have become larger and more complex.

It's unusual for a single person to have all the necessary skills to complete the work, or have the time to do so. We, therefore, have to work in teams to get the job done.

When hiring, we often pay attention to the technical abilities of the candidates because we usually need a particular skill set, but we pay little attention to how an individual might work within a team. And hiring someone based on the words such as "is a good team player" in their CV or cover letter is not enough in this age of communication and close collaboration.

With an increasing emphasis on needing skills other than just technical abilities, we need to be able to recognize the characteristics of a good team player so that we can:

- Recognize them in others that are looking to join our team
- Treat them as skills that we need to cultivate

Google recently published the results coming out of its long-running Project Aristotle, research that they had been carrying out to study the phenomenon of what makes a group of individuals more likely to succeed at being a great team.

Their not-so-surprising results show the best teams at Google exhibit a range of soft skills, which include the following:

- Having a sense of equality and generosity
- Showing curiosity toward the ideas of teammates
- Having empathy and emotional intelligence
- Perhaps the most important, psychological safety

We first looked at the results of Project Aristotle and discussed how to create Psychological Safety back in `Chapter 11`, *Improving Our Team Dynamics to Increase Our Agility*, when looking at how time improves our team dynamics to increase our agility.

Just to recap, Psychological Safety is a term first coined by *Amy Edmondson* at Harvard University in her paper *Psychological Safety and Learning Behavior in Work Teams* (*Psychological Safety and Learning Behavior in Work Teams*, Amy Edmondson, Administrative Science Quarterly, Vol 44, Issue 2, pp. 350 - 383, First Published June 1, 1999, `https://doi.org/10.2307/2666999`).

In essence, if a team has a feeling of psychological safety, then individuals:

- Are confident about speaking up
- Believe their ideas are being listened to
- Feel that the team environment is a safe place to try new ideas

While some of this might seem like essential hygiene factors for teams, it's surprising how anything less than this can cause feelings of fear and of being bullied. Bullying doesn't need to be blatant either; it can be as simple as just ignoring an idea, or dismissing it without justification.

The problem with "rockstars"

Sometimes individuals can cause a toxic atmosphere within a team by "rockstar-ing" certain aspects of the development work. For example, I once worked in a team where one person decided we weren't going to successfully meet a deadline without a significant rewrite of the code.

Instead of working with the team and sharing their vision, they decided that we didn't have time for explanations, and we were unlikely to understand anyway. So, the first thing they did was withdraw their support for the team. Next, they took all the software that we had written so far and rewrote it in another repository, one that we didn't have access to.

Without this person's support, we were unable to complete the work we'd already started; few of us felt like continuing with it afterward, anyway. Yes, our former teammate worked so hard that they met the deadline and yes that person got to demonstrate some software, but for the rest of us it removed all feelings of team ownership.

It was the most demoralizing demonstration I've ever been a part of. The more we listened to the particular individual sell our software, the more dis-empowered and disenfranchised the rest of the team felt. None of us wanted to be on a team with that individual again because technically it wouldn't have been *working with*, it would have been *working under* anyway.

The biggest problem with "rockstar-ing" is that it cultivates a culture of fear; this is how the rockstar holds on to their status, by undermining everyone else. The second biggest problem it causes is a single point of failure within the group where everyone else in the team is just in support of the main act. It ends up where we literally can't perform without the rockstar.

Not many level-headed, resourceful, and capable individuals would want to be in a supporting role to a narcissist. So rockstars create a self-perpetuating culture of fear, by either deliberately keeping the people around them downtrodden or by surrounding themselves with people who aren't quite good enough to challenge their rockstar status.

Either way, in a team like that, nobody grows; the team is stunted by the fixed mindset of the rockstar.

We'll talk about the fixed mindset versus the growth mindset in the next section and how growth is essential if we're going to operate well in an environment requiring the ability to learn rapidly.

The growth mindset

Carol Dweck, author of the book *Mindset: The New Psychology of Success* and a researcher from Stanford University, has devoted her time to researching why some people seem to thrive when solving complex problems.

She discovered that people with a growth mindset "believe that their most basic abilities can be developed through dedication and hard work; brains and talent are just a starting point."

When we develop a growth mindset, instead of trying to control our environment to suit our abilities, we're more likely to explore it and try to overcome the challenges it presents.

In the following section, we'll take a look at the key differences between a growth mindset and fixed mindset. We'll also take a look at how to cultivate a growth mindset in our team.

Growth mindset versus fixed mindset

Each mindset has the following traits:

- **Fixed mindset**: We believe that we're born with our ability and it is fixed; we're the product of nature not nurture. This makes us scared to try radically new things for fear of failure.
- **Growth mindset**: We believe that ability can be learned and can be grown; we're the product of nurture not nature. We're willing to try new things knowing full well that sometimes we won't succeed. We view challenges we encounter along the way as learning opportunities.

An example of a fixed mindset behavior versus a growth mindset behavior

Back in Chapter 1, *The Software Industry and the Agile Manifesto*, we discussed the Agile Mindset and looked at the particular example of a late change being introduced just before a release.

When someone with a fixed mindset runs into this kind of problem, they will likely be grumpy that something was missed; it disconcerts them that not everything was thought of. This isn't how they usually do things and as a result, they're now being pushed out of their comfort zone.

If the problem or the solution has a degree of uncertainty around it, they will seek to reduce the uncertainty as much as possible before applying a fix.

If they can't resolve all of the uncertainty, they will likely seek to set up some form of verbal contract, usually with the caveat that the person who created or presented the problem accepts responsibility for its outcome. In other words, they will seek to attribute the blame so that, if and when things don't go exactly to plan, they are in the clear.

When someone with a growth mindset runs into a problem like this, they will see it as an opportunity to learn and grow. Their first instinct will be to accept the problem as their own, regardless of who or what caused it. They won't be interested in playing the blame game; they see it as collective responsibility. If anything, they will likely see the problem as being caused by the system, rather than somebody.

They'll implement changes to fix the problem as robustly and quickly as they can. They'll then perform some root cause analysis, most likely with other team members, to see if they can fix the cause of the problem and prevent it from happening again.

How can we embrace a growth mindset?

We need to create the right boundaries to allow all of us to make regular and small investments of effort to continuously learn and grow. We need to focus on the following points:

- We need time and support to create the habit of continuously growing
- We need to align growth with our organization's needs
- We need to add this approach as part of our culture

Watch a video on forming a habit to make you a badass software product maker (https://www.youtube.com/watch?v=FKTxC9p1-WM).

A growth mindset culture rewards the use of effort, strategy, and progress, even if *you're not there*. The key concept to understand is that *you're not there... yet*.

Fostering a learning habit

Software team members will often talk about learning on the job, for instance, when we're being asked to implement a new technology or new version of an existing technology. This is probably the main part of how we learn. There is also social learning aspect, where we learn from groups, sometimes within our organization, sometimes by joining external meet-ups.

Finding time to learn can be difficult, especially when we have our minds set on solving one particular problem. Putting that problem down so we can pick up something else is mentally taxing; context switching is shown to have a 20-30% impact on our time. This, in turn, has an impact on our already drained cognitive resources. So it's not surprising that, when team members are asked to put aside time for personal development, we often choose to take the easier path and continue working on the problem at hand.

We need to make space for own personal development, and finding enough time requires team members to have a few tricks up their sleeves to make space away from their regular teamwork.

Some examples of how we could do this:

- Allocate a fixed time for personal development. For example, an hour at the beginning of the day before teamwork begins. This can be either social or individual learning.
- Have core team hours. The team could have a core of 5 hours a day where they work together specifically on team tasks. The remainder they could use for professional development, administration of tasks, lunch, and breaks.
- Learning as a team. Just like the teams at Hunter Industries, the company that started Mob Programming, block out the first hour of the day and dedicate it to group learning. This can be reasonably free-form in nature and can range from learning a specific tool or technology to reviewing how a particular problem was solved by the team yesterday and what they could do to improve their solution.
- Allocate a fixed time where the group puts down tools. For example, some companies I've worked for set aside every Friday afternoon, which is equivalent to 4 hours every week or 10% of our time. A similar alternative is to take the whole Friday every other week.

The common theme with all of the preceding approaches is to ensure that we have the space to take the time we need.

Summary

In a profession where we've already spent significant time and money on our education if we want to make good on our investment we should understand what makes us passionate about why we come to work every day.

Understanding our *why* is key in understanding where we're going regarding our career, but also helps us be the best we can be for our team. We can be that person who turns up to work every day, fully motivated, volume dialed up to 10!

We've looked at some of the characteristics that have the makings of a great Agile team member. The purpose was to look at how we can each contribute as an individual to create a team that excels.

And having an entrepreneurial mindset doesn't mean we start a business, or take financial risks within our organization, but rather that we adopt the mindset of an entrepreneur. We seek to validate our ideas as soon as we can, proving whether our hypothesis is valid or not.

Finally, in the spirit of our continuous improvement, we discussed the importance of giving ourselves a learning habit. Making time to learn and, more importantly, learning how to learn within an environment that is fast-paced are important for both our own career development and our organization as well.

In the next chapter, we look a bit further into the learning mindset and discuss the importance of this from the team as well as the organizational perspective. As a team of knowledge workers, our job is to gather information around what people want and turn it into something that they need. In particular, we will look at how we scale this across our teams and the impact this will have on our organization.

14
Moving Beyond Isolated Agile Teams

Several things happen when your team starts to perform. Firstly, people will notice. Then their implicit trust in your team will increase significantly. As their confidence grows, they will start to change their management style. Through working with you closely, they will start to recognize that command and control approaches with long chains of command only slow things down. They will look to shorten decision-making time by delegating responsibility to your team for certain business decisions.

As time goes on, they will delegate more and more responsibility, and so the leadership model begins to switch from a management role to a more supportive role. Leaders will start to get out of the way so their teams can get things done, and subsequently the chain of command in the form of the organizational hierarchy will begin to flatten.

This chapter looks at modern leadership and different approaches to organizational structure which allow for a more democratic workplace. These systems of organization aim to empower our teams. We employ smart people; treat them as such, and they will do great things.

It may be that the organization you work for isn't quite there yet, but through real-world examples, this chapter will help you recognize the signs that an organizational transformation is taking place. The aim is to give you a taste of what is possible so that you can start to tweak things according to your situation to take advantages of this transformative approach to working.

How an Agile approach will organically flatten an organizational structure

How we embrace our technology teams will depend a lot on the organization.

If we're a tech company, such as Microsoft or Apple, who make software products for retail, or a company such as Spotify, which makes an online product, we're likely to have embraced the digital economy. We'll be aware of and geared up for the speed things move in the technology industry.

There won't be a technology division. Instead, the organizational structure for these companies will likely revolve around their product lines.

In a traditional corporate structure or government agency, if our organization isn't overtly a technology company, we will likely see IT as a service and a cost center (in accounting terms).

If we're an IT consultancy and build software for our clients, then we're likely to be whatever our client wants us to be and will integrate however they want us to.

Of course, with almost the entire world going online, and the associated rapid acceleration of technology, technology isn't something that can be ignored; it is now firmly in the spotlight. Even in those companies that saw it a service, there has been a rapid scramble to embrace technology across the board. Technology is the great leveler, with the potential to reduce cost through automation, and it can significantly lower the barrier to entry for young start-up companies and disrupt the market of established incumbents.

An example of a hierarchical organization looks something like this:

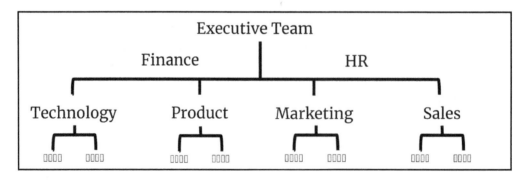

In a hierarchy, work is orchestrated from above, and communication tends to follow the same pathways up and down the line. The main issue with any hierarchical structure is that it tends to cause silos which stifle collaboration, maybe not intentionally, but just through a lack of knowledge of who to talk to, or even just being aware that there is someone in that role in the first place.

A feisty Agile team, such as the one shown as follows, often just wants to *get shit done;* it's their mode of operation:

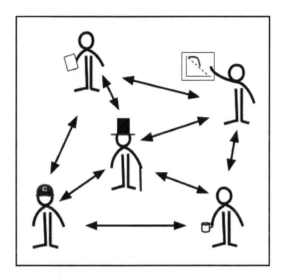

In their thirst for cross-functional knowledge and collaboration, they will naturally seek out the collaborators they need, pushing through the informational and operational congestion that happens when the organizational structure is divisional and uses a silo-based structure.

For instance, if the **Technology** and **Product** teams are separate in our hierarchy, these two will likely work closely together, albeit perhaps in a more service-oriented way to start with, that is, with **Technology** acting like a vendor.

As the following diagram shows, the **Product** team act as Product Owners to the technology teams and still tend to do all of the networking:

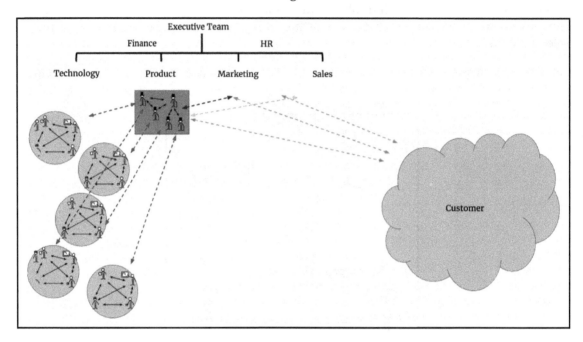

Over time, with the Product Owners acting as the bridge between different parts of the organization, the technology teams will start to form more direct contact with different parts of this network. As a result of this close collaboration, the **Product**, and **Technology** divisions merge, and now work as one group:

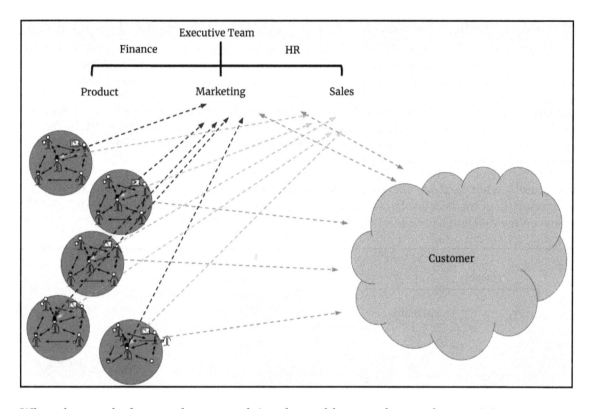

When the people that are closest to solving the problem are the people organizing themselves around how best to solve it, they will find the path of least resistance to the source of the information that they need. If we set up the right environment for them, by helping them make connections within the network, and demonstrate how they can start to collaborate, they will begin to learn at a rapid rate

Agile teams will become good at seeking out information; it's their job and it is all part of them closing down feedback loops as they aim to build the right thing. I've seen a few companies try to stifle this collaboration, which just ends up in confusion for the team and the customer. As leaders we should foster this and channel it, guiding our teams in how to become better at gathering information, not discouraging it. As leaders, this level of communication is something that we do day in day out; it's our bread and butter, and we can quickly teach our team how to own this.

This is the beginning of the flattening of the hierarchy—it's not that it isn't there, it's that our team just stopped using it. Gradually, the teams take on more of the responsibility and form relationships with their clients. This is particularly necessary because their approach requires fast feedback.

The team will also take on more responsibility for their governance; they, after all, are closest to the coalface, or as my wife calls it, the "pixel-face"—the place where the product gets built. This means they will also start to make decisions at a local level on how they carry out their work.

Eventually, what we'll see is a network of teams starting to form. As we can see in the following diagram, because the team network has developed, information flows directly between the divisions, instead of via the hierarchy:

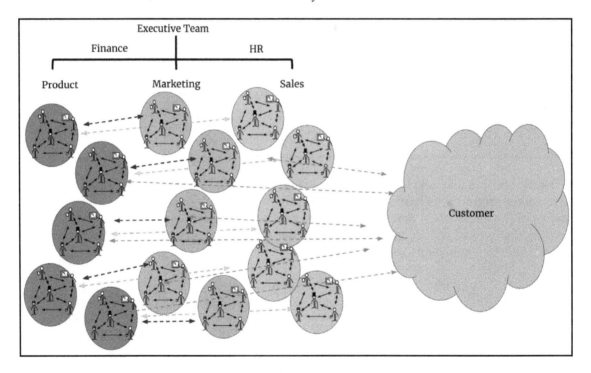

Divisions were originally set up to create efficiencies. They may have succeeded in doing this, but what we know now is that it creates silos—a literal division. Lean thinking also asks us to consider the system as a whole and argues that from an organizational perspective, we should optimize getting the job done, not the efficiency of each step.

From a hierarchical organization to collaborative governance

When Agile teams become successful, they instinctively gravitate toward the resources and information they need to get the job done. As your number of teams grows, a metamorphosis happens within the organizational structure; on paper, it looks like a hierarchy, but what's really in place is a network.

Even in organizations that have made the shift to a network of teams, a degree of hierarchy still exists, at the top level at least. The network allows the full potential of the organization to be unlocked, enabling the organization to work as a whole to seek value for the customer.

It's likely that executive teams will adopt some Agile practices as well, including transparent prioritization of initiatives and continuous planning. Transparency helps communicate relevance and ensures we're always working on the most critical objectives for the organization.

People often talk about executives talking a different language, instead frame it as them having a different view—the "50,000 ft view" or the "higher-level" view. Executives don't talk a different language, they just happen to be holding the biggest "big picture" of them all.

The last piece of the puzzle for the network to become genuinely productive is for the organization to remove divisional ("silo-ed") success measurement practices and replace them with measurements that cross-cut the entire group.

Remember, no-one likes surprises. If we create a view that makes sense to our executive team, it will give them an idea of what is happening. This needs to be a visible information radiator much like the big board in a war room. It's described in the next section.

The Big Agile board

The Big Agile board is used by upper management to track the execution of their vision. Making it visible increases the level of transparency, which is probably the most crucial aspect of this. At the very least, make sure there are no surprises along the lines of: "How's that very important thing I asked you to work on coming along?" and "Erm, yes, been meaning to tell you about that."

This is the nature of a planning-driven culture. What we've learned is not to sweep things under the carpet. All news is just news; there will be good and bad. Sometimes the bad is more important than the good; don't delay presenting it. Better still, make it visible so that you can actively do something about it and prevent it becoming much worse.

How we set the board up will differ from context to context. It may be that you have your teams and the executive team in one location, in which case this could be as simple as making each of the roadmaps visible: a war room style wall, which incorporates updates from the teams as they progress.

The key to any Agile/Lean endeavor is to expose the system to itself so that people within the system can identify problem areas and make continuous improvements. Without first making the problems visible—especially if we keep seeing information piecemeal—it's impossible to actually spot what is happening and how to unpick it.

A network of teams

Back in the previous section, *How an Agile approach will organically flatten an organizational structure*, we looked at one way that Agile teams will impact on an organization with a hierarchy.

Just to recap, because we're a self-organizing group of *just do it* people, when an impediment, such as our organizational structure, gets in the way, we tend to push on through. By recruiting our wider stakeholder group to this cause, they will connect us with the people who can help us.

That's the way we work; if we need the knowledge of a specialist in the marketing department to get our job done, we'll collaborate with them—we just need to find out who they are first.

Over time, we'll start to experience an informal shift in our organizational structure, so even though we might still look like a hierarchy on paper, functionally we operate more like a network.

Eventually, our organization may catch up with us and we'll formally restructure to take into account the way the orgnization works. That structure may look a little like the following, where the network has formalized around key products:

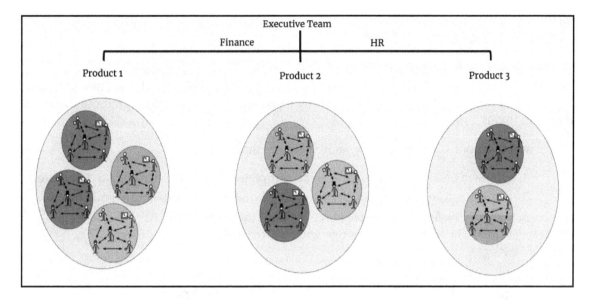

Here we see teams which were in the divisions called **Product**, **Marketing**, and **Sales**, now working in cross-functional collaboration in three different groups. The teams within each product group will be co-located at this point.

It's likely that this structure will continue to follow the same communication pattern; as you can see with **Product 3**, the **Sales** and **Marketing** teams have already merged. Over time, as the teams continue to hone their collaboration and communication network, they are likely to merge further.

If we do little else other than encourage it, the informal communication/collaboration structure will happen organically. If we want to influence the outcome, then we probably need to do some thinking about how our products are built, and more to the point, how we want them to be built.

The following are a few possible patterns:

- Completely separate (no interaction)
- Separate but of the same family, for example, interacting via an API
- The same product but different platforms, for example, split by device—web or mobile
- Different parts of the same product, for example, the search strategy across all devices, the membership strategy across all devices

Either way, we're likely to see the team's communications with each other follow the architectural patterns that we lay down.

The key takeaway from this is that if we let the people who are part of the system self-organize, they will find the path of least resistance to getting their jobs done. They're smart, capable, and resourceful people who want to be successful. If we set the right boundaries, they will find the right way.

When we talk about scaling our approach, there are three aspects:

1. How we break down the work to be completed by multiple teams (architecture).
2. Co-ordination, communication, and collaboration (team structure and culture).
3. Closing the feedback loops: Have we built the right thing? Are we building it right? (The instigator of change and improvement in our approach).

Self-selection to create a true-self organization

There will undoubtedly be some challenges in an Agile transformation, regardless of size. One of those is how to reorganize the teams around the work that we have to do while fitting into the template of small, cross-functional units that can operate both independently and interdependently.

As teams grow in size, and we have multiple teams working on various inter-related products or parts of a product, it gets harder for leadership to work out who goes where and be best placed to solve the challenges we have.

Many people will be affected by the decisions that leaders make as to how the company is going be organized from here on out. There is a degree of powerlessness that everyone at the team level will feel as they try to come to terms with their new roles and team reorganization. If we make them an active part of the process, in my experience it will go much more smoothly.

And just as we've shown in this book, when faced with solving a complex product problem, if we take the problem to a bunch of smart, capable people (the members of our teams) and set the right boundaries (purpose, vision, mission, objectives), they will work with us to help solve it.

This is just what we did with our teams in 2015 when faced with the reorganization of new team objectives. The following is a reflection on our experiment by my colleague Jaume Durany:

Our mission at that moment was to rewire the current teams in order to face new business goals in the best possible way while empowering self-organization. Instead of trying to manage team formations, processes, and workflows up front, we decided to start by applying the team self-selection experiment *shared by* Sandy Mamoli *and* David Mole *to kick off our new teams. In less than one hour we had our new teams defined and balanced by the same people forming them.*

The team self-selection activity was a really good example of how to promote self-organization by setting up the right boundaries. Our effort was focused on defining, structuring, and presenting the boundaries of the process so that everybody was aligned to face every decision in the best possible way.

The boundaries defined were business goals that the Product Owners pitched for their teams. Then the self-selection process was introduced and kept on the board so that the choice was based on three simple questions in priority order: "What is best for the company?", "Where would I be more valuable?", and "What do I want to learn?"

Our next step was to follow the same approach to come up with all the agreements needed to start working as a team. We decided to make use of visuals to define the boundaries of every discussion and facilitate the emergence of a team consensus around the minimum set of artifacts and ceremonies needed: the board, the Agile methodology, the alignment of communications with remote team members, and the working agreements.

The result of this experiment was truly exciting. We only spent 5 hours and 30 minutes, divided into five sessions during one week, to completely redefine our teams and, more importantly, every single step came from the teams. They'd self-organized since the very beginning to define their initial setup. We kept asking for feedback during the whole experiment and it was really helpful for us to keep adapting the visuals and the boundaries to their needs.

Since then, our main goal has been to keep the same principle in mind, keeping our focus on managing the boundaries and the environment to make sure that what emerges from the teams' self-organization has value to them and to the organization. Focus on managing boundaries and people will manage themselves.

I see self-selection, or at its base level, self-determination, as the catalyst that triggers self-organization. The reason self-selection is such a good exercise to go through is because it triggers the thought process of doing the right thing by the company, by your team, and then by you. You have to put the business and the team first. This is the core of the Agile movement to my mind—a responsible "service"-orientated culture.

As our hierarchy flattens, and with it the resulting network of teams, it probably follows that we need to have more fluidity with team membership to take advantage of the close collaboration of areas of our business.

Sometimes, this is because we have specialist skills that need to be shared around; sometimes it is because the team mission changes direction and people find themselves no longer making a full contribution. Sometimes it is because people feel they have a passion for another team's mission and can make a fuller contribution there.

Whatever your reason, there is a case to be made for setting up a "player transfer" system in your organization. As long as we set the appropriate boundaries, for example remembering that team stability becomes affected if membership changes significantly, then we should be able to easily accommodate a degree of movement between teams.

The easiest way to provide insight for our teams on how this might work is by walking them through some real-world examples. If we teach the team how to think about a reteaming event, they will be able to incorporate it as part of their toolkit.

For instance, imagine we are being asked to build a new product. Our reteaming strategy will likely be influenced by how the new product integrates with our existing product line.

If the new product is completely separate, no connection, we could form a new team and hire all new members. We'd have to onboard the team and instill our company culture, but this team would be able to operate independently of the others.

If the product is linked somehow to our existing product line, we will likely look to seed the team with existing team members. There are two strategies for this based on how tight the coupling is:

- If it's loosely coupled, we can seed the new team with one or two existing team members and hire the rest. We want the team to have enough information about the existing product to get started.
- If the product is closely coupled, we would look to split an existing team, and add new team members to each. An in-depth knowledge of both the existing and new products will be required by each team. At the inception of the new product, both teams will likely work closely together.

The preceding example is for forming a team around a new product. Sometimes we just want to form a team temporarily, for example, so we can build a shared service. We could do this by asking each team with an interest in the new service to supply the temporary team with 1 or 2 members. They would operate as a new team until the shared service has been implemented. The team members would then return to their original teams to share the knowledge of the new service.

The final example is where we have specialists who join teams temporarily to coach certain skills. The specialists would operate like an agency, going where they were needed the most. They will often temporarily join a team as a fully fledged member and work with them in the team's preferred style, either pair or mob programming so as to transfer knowledge.

The preceding are just a few examples of reteaming strategies. Once teams become familiar with the different approaches and understand the boundaries, it paves the way for them to become more fluid in their team membership.

In her book *Dynamic Reteaming*, Heidi Shetzer Helfand shares further examples.

When we combine self-organization with the need for team membership to change, "reteaming", we create a powerful thing indeed.

Further reading

- *Creating Great Teams: How Self-Selection Lets People Excel*, Sandy Mamoli and David Mole, `https://pragprog.com/book/mmteams/creating-great-teams`
- *Dynamic Reteaming: The Art and Wisdom of Changing Teams*, Heidi Shetzer Helfand, `https://leanpub.com/dynamicreteaming`

Modern leadership

For those of us who currently manage development teams and the work they carry out, sometimes it feels like we're one of those plate spinners you see on a variety show or busking on the street:

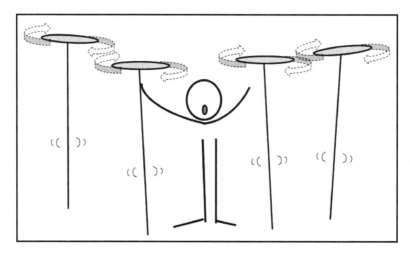

We're trying to keep many plates spinning at once. We have the team objectives (their missions), we're managing the ability to deliver on the objective (clarifying requirements, removing impediments), we ensure the teams have the right people with the right skills, we're hiring, and we look after our team members' professional development and individual performance. On top of this, we're trying to create high-performing teams that are getting into our customer's real needs and moving from just delivering software to making an impact and delighting our customer.

"We could reduce the number of plates that we're trying to spin," said no organization that I've ever worked for, ever. So, the only viable alternative that we have is to make some of the plates self-spinning:

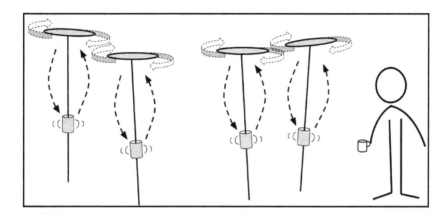

Leading a self-organizing team can be somewhat like watching your first child take their first steps without you; you really want to be there for them and support them in case they fall over, but if you're too hands-on, you know that you're going to hinder their development.

Situations will vary; some of us will have existing organizational structures in place, and some of us will be much freer in terms of our choices and how we set things up. In part, this is the reason start-up companies have been so successful in adopting Agile practices; they've started with a clean slate.

The one thing that I have learned, while tipping my hat to R Buckminster Fuller for the general sentiment, is that *we can't always change the existing system, but we can make a new one that makes more sense.*

Changing to a fly-by-wire system

Modern aircraft design has resulted in pilots trading direct control of the aircraft for an increase in aerodynamic ability. The computer systems that act as the intermediary between the pilot and the plane to make this possible are known as *fly-by-wire* control systems.

As a result, modern airliners are more fuel-efficient because of wing designs that have exchanged less stability for reduced drag. Increased instability isn't an issue because computer systems can compensate, so smooth flight is still achieved. It's this same computer control that modern military fighter jets take advantage of to give them both their speed and maneuverability in the air.

Similarly, in software development, when we have the intention of making more software than we currently have the capacity for, we either scale up our activity or improve our speed to market, or both. The more complex our system becomes, the more subtle our system of control needs to be. We can no longer take direct control of such a complex system; instead, we have to let the system do most of the work for us.

If we combine Agile and Lean thinking, we can set up a system that gives more responsibility to the people within the system. We may feel this relinquishes more control than we'd probably like, but if we set up a system with the right control surfaces and the proper feedback, we will find that we have more maneuverability or greater speed in terms of our business objectives.

Also, now that we're no longer focused on the minutiae of making things happen, we can focus on the things that matter—seeking out business value, setting our purpose, identifying the mission, and giving our teams the support they need to complete their mission.

Once we get comfortable with flying our aircraft in this way, we will find that it allows us to do more than we were capable of before. It will open up new possibilities and give us control in a more meaningful, more responsive way. It will certainly allow us to push the envelope of our system with less likelihood of breaking it.

Implementing a fly-by-wire approach

As we discussed back in `Chapter 11`, *Improving Our Team Dynamics to Increase Our Agility*, knowledge work has created a shift in where the knowledge within our organization resides. Our teams become the intersection for many different streams of information as they work out what their customer needs.

As leaders, our knowledge of how to perform those tasks becomes more redundant over time, especially as our teams continually improve their process. In fact, one tongue-in-cheek definition of the term **knowledge worker** is anyone who knows more about the work they perform than their managers.

We first have to accept that we were never had direct control in the first place. The sense of control that we felt we had was mostly about risk management and containment. Rather than seeking to manage risk, seek to reduce risk as quickly as possible via incremental delivery; that's the Agile way.

The management of knowledge workers has to become more supportive in style, and that support needs to revolve around the central theme of *how can we set this up for success?* A leader needs to consider both the organization's perspective and our people's perspective to create the necessary alignment.

Much of the leadership role now becomes about setting up the right environment and then getting out of the way. This transforms the role of manager to that of a leader who ensures that our specialists understand their objectives and are provided with the environment and support they need to carry out their tasks. Managers no longer need to define and distribute work, at least not at the task level.

Our sense of the leadership role is inverted to one where the leader exists to serve the needs of his/her people and gives rise to the term **Servant Leadership**.

Leaders serving their people and organization is not an entirely new concept. Literature refers to it as far back as ancient China. This is from the philosopher Lao Tzu, author of the *Tao Te Ching*: *"A leader is best when people barely know he exists; when his work is done, his aim fulfilled, they will say: we did it ourselves."*

In the modern era, we view the late Robert K. Greenleaf as the champion of Servant Leaders through his essay, *Essentials of Servant Leadership*, and through his work in setting up the Greenleaf Center for Servant Leadership.

The leader's role now becomes the following:

- Setting the challenge
- Cultivating culture
- Ensuring team engagement

Setting the challenge

Most of the great leaders of our time have rallied others by inspiring them to believe that theirs is a worthy cause. If people feel that they can contribute and make a real difference, they will be willing to bring the best of their abilities to make such things happen.

In Chapter 9, *Seeking Value – How to Deliver Better Software Sooner*, we looked at a few ways of giving our team their purpose. Setting high expectations makes it a challenge. The aim is to nudge people out of their comfort zones, but in a way that they connect and engage with.

This aspect of a leader's job is perhaps the most valuable. A clear problem statement for our team sparks motivation and engagement—it inspires them to do great things.

Cultivating culture

Simply put, our culture is *how we do things around here* and it's important that leaders own, drive, and demonstrate this. We should set the tone for our teams. This will particularly help in terms of team interaction and practice alignment.

We should take the opportunity to share our values and principles as often as possible, and not just by posting them in a location in which our people are likely to see them every day, but actually by referring to them and discussing how they affect our decision making.

Just as with purpose, it's likely that there will be company-wide values and principles that will trickle down. Our job is to highlight how they fit with our group's culture, maybe adjusting them to fit our context/put them in our own voice, and using them as a foundation to add our own, group-specific rules of conduct.

These are simple statements, easy to remember, and not so many that we can't remember all of them. One format is to set value and principle statements that follow the two headlines "Who we are" and "How we work":

Who we are:

- Trust and respect each other
- Honest and authentic
- Learn and improve
- Easy to deal with

How we work:

- Build user-focussed products
- Collaborate with everyone
- Try things and fail fast
- Consider the long-term value
- Have fun

Discuss these with your team at regular intervals and revise them if necessary. Simple things like making our values and principles part of our job descriptions create the expectation that our people need to work on the cultural aspects of their role as much as any other.

Ensuring team engagement

Engagement is *how we feel about how we do things around here*. The success of our culture is measured by how engaged with it our people are.

In essence, people like to be successful, and the more successful they feel, then the more they will contribute to our organization.

To feel successful, our people need to know why they are doing something; this is the deeper why. Not because I told you, not because someone else told me, this is the rock-solid what *connects our mission with the organization's purpose.*

Successful engagement will require leaders who:

- Connect our people with their purpose regularly, not through a poster on the wall but in an ongoing dialog
- Recognize and nurture individual team members, and identify how they can best contribute
- Act with authenticity and transparency, and don't hide or spin
- Make space for their people to grow and actively participate in their development
- Inspire people to do their best by respecting their time and their talent
- Don't subscribe to stupid rules or bureaucracy
- Thank people for their contribution and celebrate their successes

Why do we do this? Patrick Lencioni, in his book *The Three Signs of a Miserable Job: A Fable for Managers (And Their Employees)*, highlights that the three factors that are likely to make people feel unengaged at work are *anonymity*, *irrelevance*, and *immeasurement*:

- **Anonymity**: No-one, particularly those in charge, knows who we are. We feel like a cog in the machine—"My name isn't Cheryl, it's Shirley!"
- **Irrelevance**: Day after day, we turn up to work, but without a connection to the people who benefit from what we're doing, we have no way of telling if our work is valuable or even useful to them. Hopefully, we're making a difference, but who knows?
- **Immeasurement**: Without any constructive feedback, we're unable to grow, and we're not sure what our career path is or if we're moving in the right direction. We certainly have no way of gauging if anything we do to "change up" is making a difference. A sense of apathy is sweeping across us. Maybe it's time to start looking elsewhere for work.

Feeling recognized

A little bit of care for our team goes a long way and knowing our people is the first step. If we understand their background, their skills, and where they want to head with their career, we can help them optimize their contribution and their feeling of success. A win-win for both parties.

This could be as simple as:

1. Welcoming people when they start, announcing their arrival. Introduce them to the broader group individually or perhaps hold a morning tea or some other informal gathering. Share some background about them with the group and explain what their role will be.
2. Meeting regularly with our people to hear their views and find out if they have any problems.
3. Making ourselves available to talk with people, walk the floor, or sit with them in their team area—show an interest in what they're doing.

There is a mix of the formal and the informal needed to make people feel comfortable. For our people to share how they feel with us we need to build trust and act authentically, that is, care. For instance, explain to our people why we meet regularly *one-on-one* with them: "It's to understand how you're doing and how we can support and help you grow as an individual."

Feeling relevant

Creating relevance is as simple as asking for feedback from the people we work for. Making a connection with our customer is as simple as asking for feedback from our customer.

To an extent, this happens at the Sprint Review with our stakeholders, but it has to extend beyond that to the people who actually use our product. We need feedback from them that we're adding value to their lives. Then and only then will we find some fulfillment in the work we do.

In Chapter 13, *The Ultimate Software Team Member*, we suggested connecting our teams with their customers using **Team 360s**.

Feeling successful

Most of us crave meaningful feedback on how we can improve. Under the right circumstances, getting direct, constructive feedback from our peers, team, and other members of our network can be game-changing.

In Chapter 11, *Improving Our Team Dynamics to Increase Our Agility*, we discussed individual 360 reviews.

In Chapter 6, *Metrics that will Help your Software Team Deliver*, we looked at how to define success and we converted that into a simple team happiness survey.

Creating engagement

Here are some methods we can use to foster engagement amongst our teams:

1. **Give our people the opportunity to contribute, every single day**:
   - Give people a problem to solve rather than a solution to implement.
   - Keep reconnecting them to their purpose and mission.
   - Admit we don't have all the answers, and we don't expect anyone else in the team to have them all either. Together we can discover what we need to learn.
   - Empower our team to find the answers by asking a lot of questions. This both models the right behavior—they need to be curious—and also gives them the mandate.
   - Don't waste their time.

2. **Celebrate success**:
   - **Awards ceremony**: Hold an annual awards ceremony.
   - **WOW Wall**: Put together a survey that we can send out to our customers/stakeholders to get feedback for each team, then make it visible on a feedback wall. Kristen Hadeed, CEO of Student Maid, in her book *Permission to Screw Up*, calls this a WOW Wall; they put it in a location that everyone walks past every day.
   - **Shout outs**: Publicly recognize and thank our colleagues for their contribution.

3. **Monitor team sentiment**: Survey the team, particularly their ability to find the information they need to create solutions. Are we empowering them or impeding them? Monitor this for each team and track trends over time. Take action when action is needed.

4. **Give our teams the opportunity to grow**: Create a safe-to-fail environment and challenge them in their day to day work. Institute a professional development program—provide them with space to learn.

Example – Changing up the performance review

Performance reviews can provide an important feedback mechanism that gives us a measure of our success. We want to celebrate our successes and feel like we're contributing, and we want also to be challenged to improve and become better humans.

Traditionally, performance reviews have revolved around individual KPIs set up collaboratively with our managers the year before. Unfortunately, they often have varying results, mainly because little time is invested in them and they often end up, for one reason or another, as a *box-ticking exercise*. This is where a standard performance review can fall a little flat. Some feedback is better than none, but having a *praise culture* without constructive feedback stunts our personal growth, giving a somewhat hollow ring to the praise we do receive.

In most cases, if the organization doesn't care, why would our people?

So, the first improvement we could make is to consider our performance through three lenses: the organization, the team, and our colleagues. Favoring shared commitments over individual performance will increase our collaboration techniques.

Next, we often rely on our manager (who leads our people) to set the system up for us, but we don't need to. We are able to easily set this up ourselves. Also, we can ask for feedback at any time we'd like to; all we need to do is to convene a feedback session with the appropriate people.

We should consider an approach that is less taxing on individuals, timely, and more meaningful to those involved. Here are a couple of ideas as to how we can do that.

Performance review 360 – Intermediate level

Use an online 360 tool to gather direct feedback from a selection of colleagues and members of our network that can contribute to the three lenses. The People Manager/Lead then facilitates a session, taking us through the feedback we've gained, offering some insight, and discussing how we can improve.

Constructive Feedback Rating: 3.5/5. This approach provides many useful gems of constructive feedback; it would be even better if feedback was given face to face.

Performance Review 360 – Advanced level

Each individual uses an in-person 360 or survey tool to gather feedback directly from the people that they've elected. We should ensure that we get a broad spectrum of the people we interact with. Don't invite just the people who will only give praise as constructive feedback is what helps us improve. In `Chapter 11`, *Improving Our Team Dynamics to Increase Our Agility*, we looked at how to set up the **360 Hotseat Review**.

Constructive Feedback Rating: 4 to 5/5. Feedback is direct and provides a veritable goldmine of useful and constructive information. This not only gives each individual explicit items for them to work on but also gives them a clear picture of how they are perceived within their team. This builds trust and respect amongst the team and gives them tacit operational information about how the team can improve overall.

The art of Agile leadership

A few years ago I was working with a team new to Agile; we were coming to the end of our first Sprint and about to have our first Sprint Retrospective. I booked a meeting to catch up with them prior to the Retrospective because I wanted to explain the thought processes behind continuous improvement. Some of them had never been in a Retrospective before and I wanted them prepared and in the right mindset.

After explaining the basics, in particular, the philosophy of small continuous improvement (Kaizen), I asked them to reflect on our recent weeks together. We'd been through a lot in a short period of time: some Agile training, a team liftoff, their first Sprint. I asked them what they thought would be a good analogy for what we'd done so far.

We brainstormed, silently at first. I had asked them each to draw a picture of their analogy on paper. We then went, round-robin, around the table and everyone presented their drawings. One of our team had drawn a detailed picture of a delicious-looking cake. When it was her turn, she said, "It's like making a cake." She went on to explain, "Scrum, the Agile values and principles, our own professional disciplines, the problem that we're currently solving—they're all of the ingredients. How we put them together is the method."

This was the one idea that really resonated with everybody: "Like making a cake." So I asked them to expand on the idea a bit further; if those were all of our ingredients, and how we put them together was the method, then what was the Sprint Retrospective? Almost immediately, they agreed it would be us looking at how we could improve our recipe.

I suggested we start with the simplest recipe we could think of and go from there. Here's a picture of us making those "simple" cakes—microwave mug cakes:

We all have to start somewhere; the key thing is we'd made a cake, and although it might not have been perfect, within 5 to 10 minutes of starting the process, we got to taste it and work out how we could improve it.

By starting simply, we were able to start closing feedback loops, information that we could then use to make our recipe better. And because we started simply, our cake would be easy to improve. In the photo above, our team member on the left is already licking the spoon, a common cake mix test, while she's waiting for the microwave to do its job. From the look on her face, it must be pretty good, right?

The aim of this book has been to build up a set of practices that we need to help get our teams off the ground. These are all things that you can include in your recipe. Some of them you can't leave out, just like when you're making a cake. However, you can and should start to tweak the recipe, and that's when we need to teach our team the power of experimentation.

Experiments allow us to relentlessly pursue small, continuous improvements. This will enable us to add tools to our toolbox. For example, we can introduce pair programming, test-driven development, mob programming, behavior-driven development, and so on.

We talk about experiments because we want our learning to be scientific. For example, the microwave cake won't scale to more then one person, but if our reason for doing it is to start testing out flavor ideas, or to see how a gluten-free flourless recipe might work, then we will have succeeded in learning.

Never accept the status quo; always assume that you can do better. The key to getting our team on the journey of continual self-improvement is to cultivate a learning/growth mindset.

To facilitate this, we have to reward the effort that our people put into growing and remind them that they won't always get it right, but just like a scientist, if they set up their experiments in the right way, they should be able to harvest substantial learning regardless of whether their hypothesis turns out to be entirely correct.

When a team is at the beginning of an Agile journey, we need to keep the practices simple to start with and gradually build our team's understanding. Once we foster a continuous improvement/change mindset, our Agile practices will start to grow.

To do this, we need to:

1. Lay the foundations and set the challenge.
2. Teach the team how to improve. Demonstrate this as a leadership team—be authentic in this, that is, do it and mean it.
3. Provide them with the support they need.

It's my humble opinion that a framework like Scrum presents a set of training wheels just like those on a child's bike. A Scrum Master's key role is to support the team in understanding the mechanics of riding the bike, demonstrate why we use training wheels to start with, and then challenge the team to remove the wheels as soon as they can.

We achieve this by:

1. Demonstrating the mechanics, showing them how it works.
2. Transferring ownership to the team, creating more in-depth understanding—let them try and let them fail.
3. Gradually decreasing the support until they're able to go it alone.

At each step, we are using a different leadership stance. In step 1, we model/teach it. In step 2, we facilitate them doing it. In step 3, we coach until our team becomes self-sufficient in that particular practice.

If we're to foster a healthy network of teams, we need to teach specific skills to draw out the true meaning of the Agile values and principles.

Of course, it depends on your context, and where you and your teams are at in their journey, but to my mind these are the most important when beginning to conduct experiments:

- Collaboration and communication
- Continuous, unrelenting improvement and learning
- Self-organization/self-determination

Experiment – Creating informal networks as a nervous system

Encourage individuals and teams to create a network to connect them with others outside of their usual group. They can ask for introductions to those who they want to form a working relationship with, or they may be just interested to find out more about what that person or team does.

Premise: Helping our team to form a network will not only give them the context of the wider organization, it will give them contacts who will help them find the information they need.

Model: Foster a network that connects people with others from both inside and outside their team. The simplest format for individuals to meet each other is through one-on-ones. If it's team to team, organize a team meet and greet.

Teach: There are several formats; if in the same location, go for a coffee. If it's a nice day, go for a walking meeting (walking meetings work well in my experience; the sense of moving forward is both literal and metaphorical). If in different locations, use a virtual format—each person/team grabs a coffee and shares a video call in a meeting room or from a computer.

Support: As people leads, we're more likely to have wide-ranging connections, so we can help them discover who to talk to as they start to form their network.

For example, as an Agile coach in my current organization, I have fortnightly one-on-ones with my people lead, each of my fellow coaches, our head of UX, three of our product managers, three team members that I coach, and the eight people that I provide people leadership for.

Experiment – Communities

Set up communities to foster a support network and create a learning culture/environment for our teams.

Premise: If we want teams to deliver in a collaborative style as a network of teams, what better place to start than through a learning network? Communities allow us to form a support network around specific practices and technologies.

It's essential that our teams share their learning with each other.

These are split broadly along two lines:

1. A community of practice: A group of people who practice the same discipline or role, and who want to share ideas about how to improve, for example, testers.
2. A community of interest: A group with broad backgrounds who are interested in learning about a particular subject, such as a technology or a specific way of doing something, for example, JavaScript frameworks, behavior-driven development, DevOps.

Teach: **A community of practice** consists of a group of people from across different teams who all have the same specialization, for example, Product Owner. They meet regularly to discuss the ins and outs of product ownership, to learn from each other, and to work as a group to generally improve the practice of product ownership across the organization:

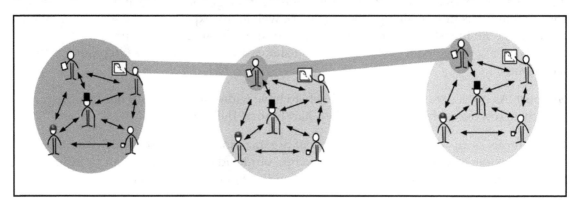

A **community of interest** consists of people with different specializations who all have a shared interest in a particular practice, for example, test-driven development or a set of related practices such as DevOps.

People with different backgrounds and roles will be interested in this type of community, as the following diagram shows:

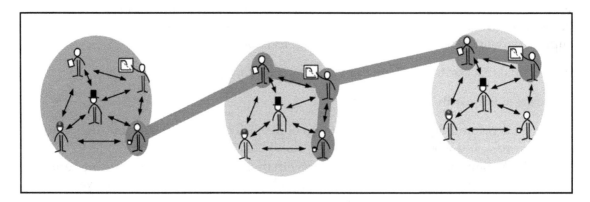

To set up a community, we should first demonstrate how to do it and model the correct behavior.

Model: Set up initial communities of practice and interest; be present to coach the team. Set the topics for the first few by polling team members for ideas. You can run/facilitate this at first to set the tone. Have a Retrospective session with the group afterwards; ask them whether there was a good **return on time invested (ROTI)**.

Coach: Seek volunteers to run a session. Coach the preparation of the session beforehand, run through their ideas, help them create a structure, and so on. Co-facilitate with them to run the session.

Support: Help the group become freestanding and cede ownership by handing over the role to members of the community. To do, this create a group of community co-organizers. Stop facilitating. Feel free to attend when the group offers something of interest to you.

Organizational styles for flatter structures

In this final section, we'll look at where an Agile transformation might lead in the organization you work for; it might lead to a very different way of working compared to where you currently are. Of course, you might not be there yet in terms of your Agile journey, and so this section is merely food for thought.

You'll know when you are ready for organizational transformation because thoughts of going down this road will seem entirely sensible and will not trouble you.

We've seen that by delegating some of the decision making and responsibility to cross-functional teams, we increase the chances of building a useful and successful product.

This results in two things happening within our organization:

- Those that have direct contact with Agile teams become *infected* with their ideas. They recognize that some aspects of what our software teams are doing will work for them and create better opportunities for success. As software becomes an ever more pervasive part of what we do, this rubbing of shoulders and spreading of ideas will only increase. This is a grassroots, team-level upwards and sideways implementation of Agile.
- Eventually, the success of the software teams hits a ceiling. Once the teams have achieved local success, it's likely that the impediments to further success are actually in the organizational structure itself.

Divisional organization structures have a tendency to create hierarchy, and hierarchies aren't responsive; they were designed for a time where we treated the people and teams in our organization like cogs in a machine. The work was directed and people were told what to do and when to do it. This worked well up to the point where the problems we were trying to solve became too complex to divide up in this way.

And while Agile teams are specifically designed to tackle complex problems, they will instigate change in organizational structure, which tends to follow the information flow. This then raises a question: If that's the case, do we need to rethink our organizational structure to capitalize on the benefits of cross-functional thinking?

For some newly established companies who know that a traditional organizational structure won't serve them, it has made complete sense to take a look at their organizational operating system. Take Valve Corporation, the makers of the Steam online gaming platform, for instance. They've opted for an approach that optimizes their creativity.

Founded by former Microsoft employees, they set out to create an organizational structure where their employees could go on "a fearless adventure in knowing what to do when no one's there telling you what to do." This unique philosophy has created an organization with higher profitability per employee than most big corporations, with a reported revenue of just under $3.5 billion, and approximately 360 employees in 2016.

The founder of Valve's aim was to hire the best people, and rather than stifling their creativity by telling them what to do, give them an environment in which they can unleash their creative talents.

As they put it in their handbook, they take an idea like Google's 20% time allocated to self-projects and turn it into 100% self-directed work. Their employee handbook is published online and makes for some inspiring reading.

Their principal aim is to make a direct connection between their customer and their creatives, so that their teams can create an experience that their customers want and need.

It isn't just tech companies who are taking a self-managing approach. Another example is Dutch healthcare provider Buurtzorg, founded by healthcare professional Jos de Block in 2006 after he became disillusioned with the community healthcare system. Buurtzorg translates to "neighborhood care."

The main issues with the healthcare system in the Netherlands at the time were:

1. *Economies of scale* thinking had created a healthcare system that was numbers-driven, not people-driven. Each caregiver was given a detailed plan the night before their daily rounds which included timing down to the minute.
2. It was seen as inefficient that there should be a one-to-one relationship between patient and healthcare professional. This led to patients being seen by multiple (up to 40) different nurses. No relationships were formed and there was a distinct lack of continuity between treatments.
3. A tiered healthcare system meant that the providers on the ground had to make decisions about what treatments were and weren't available. This led to professionals not always being able to give the care they thought was required.

Buurtzorg aimed to create a system which addressed all three of the issues by:

- Focusing on the outcome for the client, instead of providing healthcare by numbers
- Developing consistency and continuity in the relationship with the client, as well as a spirit of community within the local area
- Providing the healthcare a client needed rather than the healthcare they could only afford

Buurtzorg achieved this by creating small autonomous teams of qualified nurses and carers. Each team looked after a specific geographic area and set out to create a network within their neighborhood of other healthcare professionals: doctors, physiotherapists, pharmacists, and so on.

The teams were responsible for finding new clients, managing their workload, caregiving, and hiring into their team. The teams linked with each other when they needed to and shared information and ideas via the Buurtzorg intranet, a computer system designed and built specifically for the company.

The shift in thinking that Buurtzorg made was to stop thinking of healthcare as an exercise in efficiency and instead as an opportunity to focus on client outcomes, returning people to long-term health and improving their quality of life.

Implementing these changes had a direct impact on just that, with less likelihood of a reccurrence of the health issue for the client. Also, a single-tier healthcare system meant that there was little to no need to police the system, which previously would have taken qualified carers from the frontline and put them in positions of management. Thus, this created significant savings in terms of overhead and gave qualified carers more time to attend to clients.

Buurtzorg's growth has been phenomenal, from 4 to 14,000 in 10 years, with only 50 back-office administrators, 18 coaches, and zero managers in support.

The small centralized administration group is responsible for handling the company accounts, including billing their clients. The coaches support the teams and help improve their dynamic or resolve issues.

It has spawned an approach that is spreading internationally, with nurses and care workers once again passionate about their work and spending more time doing what they genuinely care about—looking after people.

Neither Valve nor Buurtzorg deliberately set out to create the specific organizational structures that they grew into. Instead, they both laid the foundation for how they wanted to work. In particular, they focussed on the outcomes they wanted to achieve based on their company purpose.

Their similarity is that they both wanted to connect with their customer at a much more profoundly human level than they'd previously done. As a result, both companies have organically grown into different organizations.

That's the thing to understand with the network of teams approach: organizational systems are highly complex. Trying to superimpose the template of another company such as Valve, Buurtzorg, Spotify, or Netflix just won't work.

As we discussed in `Chapter 1`, *The Software Industry and the Agile Manifesto*, it's not something that we can merely transplant into our organization; it first has to be built with solid foundations.

Ask any of the CEOs of companies who have taken this path how they did it and they'll either avoid answering the question or more than likely point out that you'll need to work it out for yourself.

Without a doubt, patterns will emerge that we can capitalize on, and there are experiments that we can use to encourage a network of teams to form.

Purpose is the driver that tips an organization into this state. When an organization shifts its focus from just making profits and starts to focus on outcomes for a higher cause, like Tesla and it's mission *to accelerate the world's transition to sustainable energy*, then it starts to develop a noble purpose. When Tesla released their patents for electric vehicles so as not to stifle innovation in the sector, Elon Musk made it clear he was truly committed to the cause. He realized that his company alone couldn't replace the 1.2 billion gasoline-powered vehicles currently on the roads without a little help from others.

Frederic Laloux, in his book *Reinventing Organisations*, discusses a concept which takes this one step further: **evolutionary purpose**. He describes it as a purpose that goes beyond noble, a purpose an organization *listens* to and *dances* with. At this point, when an organization reaches this state, Laloux says it has made it to the highest level of self-management.

The concept is similar to the planning-driven approach of an Agile team, except now it's our purpose that is no longer set in stone. It's constantly being redefined as we listen to our customers and shape it to match their needs.

As Laloux points out, it's only when we let go and give up thoughts that we were ever in control in the first place that we can truly start to dance with our customer.

Further reading

This is a link to Valve's employee handbook from 2012, available to read in full online; read the "Your first day" section if nothing else:

- Valve Employee Handbook: `http://www.valvesoftware.com/company/Valve_Handbook_LowRes.pdf`

Two books that look at the evolution of purpose-driven, liberated workplaces are:

- *Reinventing Organizations: A Guide to Creating Organizations Inspired by the Next Stage of Human Consciousness*, Frederic Laloux
- *Freedom, Inc.: Free Your Employees and Let Them Lead Your Business to Higher Productivity, Profits, and Growth*, by Brian M. Carney and Isaac Getz

While there is no way to transplant the mindset, there are frameworks that may help with this shift in thinking. Sociocracy and Holacracy are two similar ideas:

- *We the People: Consenting to a Deeper Democracy*, by John Buck and Sharon Villines
- *Holacracy: The New Management System for a Rapidly Changing World*, by Brian J. Robertson

Worldblu is an example of an organization that advocates more democratic workplaces: `https://www.worldblu.com/`.

Summary

In this chapter, we started by looking at modern leadership and the case for managing systems, as complex problem solving requires a more subtle form of control than we have perhaps considered in the past.

To make this subtle system of control work, we need to set up meaningful feedback loops at various levels which provide information to help tune and tweak our approach to make sure we're all heading in the desired direction. The simplest and most powerful way to do this is to empower the individuals and teams operating within the system to create a living, breathing, learning ecosystem that evolves as it needs to.

We looked at how can set up our system so that it becomes self-governing as we shift to a more dynamic organizational structure that relies on clear objectives and a network of teams who carry out tasks they've been assigned. Devolving command and control structures will enable the teams in the network to get to the source of the information that they need faster, enabling more informed decision making at the point where it's most relevant.

It's not that the hierarchy goes away, it just becomes less and less traversed in order for the teams to obtain information. People will start to feel redundant; the nature of their work will change significantly.

When you're trying to create a system that makes more sense, you have to be sensitive to the impact this will have on people's working lives. The nature of their work is going to change, and some will see this as an opportunity for growth. Others will see it as a threat and will react with resistance. Both are legitimate responses and we have to be able to guide both groups of people, as well as those in between.

Start with *why*. Communicate *why* over and over. When you feel you've said why enough, say *why* some more. If our people understand why, it will empower them to be part of the solution.

In the final section, we looked at alternative approaches to organizational operating systems. One thing is clear, there is no one-size-fits-all approach. We certainly shouldn't try to blueprint the organizational structure of another company and superimpose it on ours.

Organizations are too complex for that; we'll need to discover what works for us and what doesn't. So while it's fine to take ideas from other companies and try them out for ourselves, anything we do try should be set up as an experiment so that we can measure whether it will take us in the direction we want to go.

The aim of this book was to take you on a journey and give you a feel for the types of Agile practice we need to adopt and practice in order to become Agile. Every team's journey is different, as is every individual's. Agile is not something we can transplant, it's something we need to study and experiment with daily.

Other Books You May Enjoy

If you enjoyed this book, you may be interested in these other books by Packt:

Practical DevOps

Joakim Verona

ISBN: 978-1-78728-020-5

- Appreciate the merits of DevOps and continuous delivery and see how DevOps supports the agile process
- Understand how all the systems fit together to form a larger whole
- Set up and familiarize yourself with all the tools you need to be efficient with DevOps
- Design an application that is suitable for continuous deployment systems with Devops in mind
- Store and manage your code effectively using different options such as Git, Gerrit, and Gitlab
- Configure a job to build a sample CRUD application
- Test the code using automated regression testing with Jenkins Selenium
- Deploy your code using tools such as Puppet, Ansible, Palletops, Chef, and Vagrant
- Monitor the health of your code with Nagios, Munin, and Graphite
- Explore the workings of Trac—a tool used for issue tracking

JIRA 7 Essentials - Fourth Edition
Patrick Li

ISBN: 978-1-78646-251-0

- Understand JIRA's data hierarchy and how to design and work with projects in JIRA
- Plan and set up a new JIRA 7 instance from scratch for production use
- Using JIRA for agile software projects, business process management, customer service support, and more
- Understand issues and work with them
- Design both system and custom fields to behave differently under different contexts
- Create and design your own screens and apply them to different project and issue types
- Gain an understanding of the workflow and its various components
- Set up both incoming and outgoing mail servers to work with e-mails

Leave a review - let other readers know what you think

Please share your thoughts on this book with others by leaving a review on the site that you bought it from. If you purchased the book from Amazon, please leave us an honest review on this book's Amazon page. This is vital so that other potential readers can see and use your unbiased opinion to make purchasing decisions, we can understand what our customers think about our products, and our authors can see your feedback on the title that they have worked with Packt to create. It will only take a few minutes of your time, but is valuable to other potential customers, our authors, and Packt. Thank you!

Index

Y

www.ingramcontent.com/pod-product-compliance
Lightning Source LLC
Chambersburg PA
CBHW080609060326
40690CB00021B/4633